Top 100
Power Verbs

Top 100 Power Verbs

THE MOST POWERFUL VERBS AND PHRASES YOU CAN USE TO WIN IN ANY SITUATION

MICHAEL FAULKNER
WITH MICHELLE FAULKNER-LUNSFORD

Vice President, Publisher: Tim Moore
Associate Publisher and Director of Marketing: Amy Neidlinger
Executive Editor: Jeanne Glasser
Operations Specialist: Jodi Kemper
Marketing Manager: Megan Graue
Cover Designer: Chuti Prasertsith
Managing Editor: Kristy Hart
Project Editor: Elaine Wiley
Copy Editor: Deadline Driven Publishing
Proofreader: Anne Goebel
Senior Indexer: Cheryl Lenser
Senior Compositor: Gloria Schurick
Manufacturing Buyer: Dan Uhrig

FT Press offers excellent discounts on this book when ordered in quantity for bulk purchases or special sales. For more information, please contact U.S. Corporate and Government Sales, 1-800-382-3419, corpsales@pearsontechgroup.com. For sales outside the U.S., please contact International Sales at international@pearsoned.com.

Company and product names mentioned herein are the trademarks or registered trademarks of their respective owners.

Pearson Education LTD.
Pearson Education Australia PTY, Limited.
Pearson Education Singapore, Pte. Ltd.
Pearson Education Asia, Ltd.
Pearson Education Canada, Ltd.
Pearson Educación de Mexico, S.A. de C.V.
Pearson Education—Japan
Pearson Education Malaysia, Pte. Ltd.

Library of Congress Control Number: 2013937280

To our families:
Without them, we are nothing.
With them, anything is possible.

Contents

Foreword

I have enjoyed a friendship with Michael Faulkner (Dr. Faulkner) over many years, starting when he was a student of mine during the Vietnam War era. I am certain Michael has enjoyed and appreciated the collaboration of his daughter Michelle Faulkner-Lunsford in this *Power Verbs* series. His writing a series of books on verbs is not a surprise to me, to some extent because he was a Marine. His military background complements the skills of a man who has led as a student, businessman, and educator. I will not forget hiking with him in the mid-1970s on the Berryman Trail in the Missouri Ozarks. The plan was to hike the trail in two days. With Mike as our point man, we finished it in one. So if I had to choose a part of speech to describe Michael, you know what it would be.

When taking into account Michael's energy and creativity with this book's subject matter, I recall architect Buckminster Fuller's book, *I Seem to Be a Verb*. Fuller describes himself, "I know that I am not a category. I am not a thing, a noun…I seem to be a verb, an evolutionary process." Fuller's quote describes the author of *The Top 100 Power Verbs*. To get to this culminating publication on power verbs for "all occasions," he has steadily moved from power verbs for (1) job seekers, (2) presenters, (3) leaders, managers, and supervisors, and (4) career consultants, coaches, and mentors. In all of these, he spotlights verbs as the "spark of the sentence," selecting them for rhetorical purposes and basing this last one on Professor Barry Posner's practices of exemplary leadership.

Grammarians, editors, and teachers of composition often argue what should be the heart of the matter for a writer. All agree that the writer needs to know his audience before putting pen to paper. Faulkner addresses this issue early when he cites political consultant Dr. Frank Luntz: "The key to successful communication is to take the imaginative leap of stuffing yourself right into your listeners' shoes to know what they are thinking and feeling in the deepest recesses of their minds and hearts." It's clear that Faulkner selected verbs with Luntz's belief in mind, "Eighty percent of our life is emotion, and only 20 percent is intellect." So the reader should not be surprised to see verbs like "gin up, grapple, hang tough, hunker down, and kick start." Getting into your listeners' shoes and emotions is a gentler way of saying that the writer must become a sharpshooter, spotting his audience from a distance like a bulls-eye on a target.

Faulkner soon turns his focus to choosing and employing the power of the verb. This book is a verb thesaurus comprising a collection of verbs that challenge, encourage, lead, and inspire. Indeed, in some verbs, the author's military background shines through. We don't find "ten hut, check fire, carry on, march, and fall out"; however, we do find verbs with tails, such as "cross the Rubicon, catch fire, call the shot, deep six, draw lines in the sand, and did-a-one-eighty." Faulkner cautions about using clichéd expressions, but some remain valuable for appropriate audiences and occasions. Other verbs—"dither, jawbone, jockey, marshal, nettle"—might be most appropriate for challenging a process or modeling a way. Others, such as "delegate, deliberate, innovate, and perpetuate," might be more appropriate, enabling others to act.

Readers will soon tap into the energy and drive of this author. His words capture the confident tone he holds in *The Top 100 Power Verbs*: "It is a book that can help you choose the most powerful verbs—the spark of sentences—powerful verbs that will resonate deeply with people."

My son is a cardiologist. He tells his students with tongue-in-cheek, "Do you know the heart is the most important organ in the body? People don't say, 'I love you with all my brains or my kidneys or my colon.' They say, 'I love you with all my *heart*.'" Dr. Michael Faulkner maintains that the verb is not just the heart of the sentence, but it is fire itself, the "flame" that ignites the writer's purpose and kindles the audience into action.

I am pleased to see his passion and commitment to successful communication. As one of Dr. Faulkner's teachers many years ago, I knew him as the recently returned Vietnam veteran looking to put his life together. Since our walk on the Berryman Trail, he has traveled a much longer trail in his successful professional career. And in this publication and series, he has provided writers with a proper tool for accomplishing their purpose. For these reasons, I am most pleased to recommend this book for your communication needs.

—*Ken Boyer*
English Professor (Retired)
St. Louis Community College/FV

Acknowledgments

I would like to acknowledge and thank all of the members of the FT Press Publishing team. Every single person with whom I had the privilege to work, from the editors to the proofreaders, copy, and style specialists, to the layout and production people, and all the others who did work for my books, were the best. They were professional, patient, and dedicated to turning out a superior product.

About the Author

Dr. Michael Lawrence Faulkner is the author of six books. He is a professor at the Keller Graduate School of Management at DeVry University. He is a former U.S. Marine who spent 30 years in a variety of leadership and executive management positions with Fortune 500 firms and major nonprofit trade associations. He also helped his family run the family business before beginning his second career in academics. Michael is a member of MENSA, a Rotary International Fellow, and a Keller Master Teacher Award recipient. He holds a Silver Certification by the Toastmaster's International. In addition to his Ph.D., Michael has earned two Master's degrees: one from NYU and an MBA from NYIT.

Michelle Faulkner-Lunsford is a 2001 graduate of Middle Tennessee State University where she majored in English and minored in Writing. Mrs. Lunsford spent 10+ years in the world of advertising and marketing as an Account Manager and Director of Marketing and New Business Development, managing multimillion dollar accounts from male-enhancement medications to beer ads. In 2011, Michelle left the corporate world for the opportunity to raise her daughter.

Introduction

There is little doubt that communication is one of man's most important tools. We use the tool (speaking, listening, graphic expression, and writing) to help us make sense of our world, to interact with other people, to network, and to express our feelings, moods, and intent. Communication, particularly with our words, affects who and what we are as a species, and it is one of the key things that differentiate us from other species. In fact, our species (*Homo sapiens*) managed to overpower and eliminate two earlier human species (*Neanderthal* and *Homo erectus*) who had far less communication skills than *Homo sapiens*.

There is a quote attributed to Plutarch—although there are no sources that can trace it to him— which says, "When Cicero spoke, people said, 'How well Cicero speaks!' But, when Demosthenes spoke, they said, 'Let us march against Phillip.'" The point here is that when leaders speak, it is usually, but not always, to persuade. Sometimes the purpose is to inform, but as Rudyard Kipling said, "Words are the most powerful drug used by mankind," so whenever we speak, we use a powerful human tool. Thomas Fuller may have said it best, "When the heart is afire, some sparks will fly out of the mouth." This book gives you some sparks.

This book is not intended to teach specific public speaking skills, oration, rhetoric, or how to deliver a good presentation. You do not learn detailed skills of visualization or in-depth channeling of your message. You do not learn details of tone, cadence, pitch, or resonance. You do not learn the details of nonverbal body language such as hand and arm gestures. This book introduces these concepts (and hopefully, you will explore them further on your own).

It is a book that can help make you more successful in whatever you do by helping you become a more powerful and more effective communicator. It can do this because it helps you choose the most powerful verbs—the spark of sentences—powerful verbs that resonate deeply with people, powerful verbs that people react to and remember.

I am referring to the power verbs that are the flame that make phrases and sentences that ignite peoples' passions, the power verbs that kindle, illuminate purpose, and make people want to take action… to march on Phillip.

—Michael Faulkner

1

The Connection Between Communications and Success

"Volatility of words is carelessness in actions; words are the wings of actions."
—*Lavater*

There are two factors for which there are mountains of empirical evidence that overwhelmingly account for the success of individuals in any field. These variables are the verbal and networking skills of the successful people.

Common sense and simple observation can be your laboratory. Just look at the people you have worked for and most of the people you know. Furthermore, look at the people who run or own the organizations and firms where people work. Think about the people who own and run the vendor firms and organizations that service and supply the firms and organizations for which you, or people you know, have owned or worked. What is it that most of these people have in common?

The vast majority of these people have big vocabularies and extensive networks. Consequently, these are probably primary reasons why many are successful and why they are the managers, leaders, and owners of businesses and organizations as well as civic and social leaders. The common denominator of the most successful people is a cross-section of fields; it isn't education, family money, race, or gender. It's what they know and who they know!

It has long been known that successful people in every field do not have large, useful vocabularies merely because of their positions. That would be an incorrect correlation and not a proper explanation of cause and effect. In fact, it is the opposite that is true. Successful people in all fields are successful because they are helped tremendously by their skills in vocabulary and networking (Funk and Lewis, 1942, p. 3).

Success is not something achieved by birthright or tenure but rather something that is gained by hard, smart work and the help of an active network. This is a consequence of the successful person's behavior, actions, work, effort, results, intentions, plans, worldview, responses, and practices, and it is mostly what they do and say in every moment of every opportunity.

2

It has been said before that it isn't what one says that matters but how a person says it that counts. Dr. Frank Luntz takes it a step further and claims that it isn't what you say that counts; it's what people hear. The issue is you have to choose your words! In addition, you have to time the right words and give the right words the necessary emphasis with the correct supporting body language, so the receiver fully grasps what is said and does not pause or hesitate to understand your meaning.

Verbs are the catalysts of sentences. Power verbs bring sentences to life. More to the point, the right power verbs bring conversations, meetings, speeches, directives, resumés, memos, presentations, networking contacts, sales plans, marketing plans, and business and branding plans to life. Frankly, the right power verbs can put a pop into all interpersonal communications.

The definitive source for the English Language—*The Oxford English Dictionary*—states it this way: "It is a simple truth that in most sentences, you should express action through verbs just as you do when you speak. Yet, in so many sentences, the verbs are smothered; all their vitality is trapped beneath heavy noun phrases based on the verbs themselves" (AskOxford.com, 2008).

A successful person uses the power of human communication to give expressive life to their strategies, operational plans, directives, proposals, ideas, and positions. Human communication is, of course, a combination of nonverbal cues (body language) and the actual words spoken. Even the words that are chosen to be spoken by successful people are frequently invigorated and fortified with linguistic enhancements, such as metaphors, similes, figures of speech, and other vigorous uses of imagery, including hyperbole.

Sometimes the words are combined in rhythmic and symbolic phrasing called alliteration, repetition, antithesis, and parallelism. Successful leaders, managers, and supervisors are generally considered good communicators, or at least it is recognized that communication skills are necessary for them to succeed. These people can enhance their positions with their staff, direct reports, stakeholders, upper level management, vendors, students, media, and others with greater communication skills through the use of stories, citing references, using quotations, and figures of speech. However, there are two very important caveats. Whatever is used has to be fresh and it has to be *apropos*. Tired metaphors, idioms, similes, figures of speech, old stories, and lame references are worse than none at all. More importantly, using an inappropriate phrase, figure of speech, metaphor, simile, or a poor analogy can hamper communication.

Some readers may be old enough to remember when live radio entertainment included speakers who had to sell listeners on the plot or story by painting verbal pictures with words. Today, we still have the need to create vivid imagery in our daily communication with what we say and how we say it. Furthermore, we have one more issue and that is, we are dealing with a more attention-conflicted audience. So we add a third need and that is, we have to be aware of the fact that it is not always what we say that matters, or even how we say it, but now we have to deal with what it is people hear.

There are so many filtering biases, prejudices, attention sappers, and diversions that many people simply do not hear what has been said; instead they hear only what they want or need to hear. We cannot always control this phenomenon, nor do we want to, but we need to be aware of this dynamic.

Table 1.1 lists examples of tired metaphors, idioms, and clichés and their more contemporary versions.

Table 1.1 *Tired Metaphors, Idioms, and Clichés and Contemporary Replacements*

Time is money.	Time is profit.
Information is power.	Knowledge is power.
Business is a game.	Business is the game.
Hit the ball out of the park.	Hit for the show.
Take the hill.	Go around the opposition.
Take no prisoners.	Do whatever it takes.
Beat the bushes.	Scope out options.
Beat a dead horse.	Been down that road.
Been to hell and back.	Go the distance or went the distance.
Behind the eight ball.	Pinned down.

People respond to language that is highly certain, highly optimistic, highly realistic, and highly active.

Dull and uninteresting verbs make communications of any type dull, uninteresting, boring, and lifeless. On the other hand, the properly chosen power-packed verbs can electrify your communications. Your listeners and readers will be drawn to your topic and point of view like electromagnets.

Power verbs can be used in many ways; however, this book focuses on helping you understand how to use power verbs more effectively where they truly count, such as:

- In your everyday communications (discussions with peers, family members, friends, clients, customers, stakeholders, vendors, suppliers, and investors)
- In business documents (memos, reports, plans, and other documents)
- In toasts and impromptu comments
- In your networking communications
- In speeches, presentations, and executive briefings
- In resumés, cover letters, and interviews

We live, work, and communicate in a Mixed Martial Arts world, and our communication needs to be fresh and crisp, yet it does not need to reflect street lingo or be overwhelmingly "hip." Some power verbs are meant to assist you in putting life into your communications, giving them a special impact.

The power verbs are shown in the present tense. However, as the examples throughout show, the tense in which you use them depends on the circumstances.

VERB FORMS

In English, main verbs also known as "lexical verbs" (except the verb "be") have between four and six forms. Because this is not a text or style book, we are not going to get into the minutiae of what constitutes regular or irregular verbs or the thrilling discourse on the verb "to be," which has nine forms. We are more concerned with power verbs that you will be using in everyday communications and that you can use without a style book or cue card.

We will assume you can figure out the base verb from the progressive form we use. For example, if we use the present progressive form "accomplishing," we'll assume you will know the base form of the verb is "accomplish." Or if we use the past progressive form "was accomplished," we'll assume you know the base form of the verb is still "accomplish."

Progressive Forms

The progressive form is a verb tense used to show an ongoing action in progress at some point in time. It shows an action still in progress. Verbs can appear in any one of three progressive tenses: present progressive, past progressive, and future progressive.

The Present Progressive Tense—Verbs Showing ONGOING ACTION

The present progressive tense is one form that describes an action that is ongoing and one that happens at the same moment for which the action is being spoken about or written about.

To form this tense, use **am/is/are** with the verb form ending in **ing**.

Examples:

I **am meeting** with the others tomorrow. [present progressive ongoing action—using am + ing]

The project management team **is examining** the stakeholder's proposal. [present progressive ongoing action—using is + ing]

The team members **are researching** ideation options. [present progressive ongoing action— using are + ing]

She **is feeling** happy. [present progressive ongoing action—using are + ing]

Use the present tense to describe something that is true regardless of time.

Past Progressive Tense—Verbs Showing SIMULTANIOUS ACTION

The past progressive tense is one that describes an action that happened when another action occurred. To form this tense, use **was/were** with the verb form ending in **ing.**

Examples:

The new project team **was presenting** its recent findings when the power went out. [past progressive on simultaneous action—using was + ing]

Four team members **were meeting** with the sponsor when the news broke about the award. [past progressive on simultaneous action—using were + ing]

Future Progressive Tense—Verbs Showing FUTURE ACTION

The future progressive tense is one that describes an action that is ongoing or continuous and one that takes place in the future. This tense is formed by using the verbs **will be** or **shall be** with the verb form ending in **ing**.

Examples:

Only one team member **will be presenting** during the annual meeting in June. [future progressive on future action—using will be + ing]

The clock **is** ticking. [future progressive on future action—using is + ing]

The band **is** playing. [future progressive on future action—using is + ing]

When the progressive form is not used for continuing events, a dramatic style effect can be produced.

The clock **ticks**.

The band **plays**.

Present Perfect Progressive—Verbs Showing PAST ACTION, CONTINUOUS ACTION, and POSSIBLY ONGOING ACTION

The present perfect progressive tense is one that describes an action that began in the past, continues in the present, and may continue into the future. To form this tense, use **has/have been** and the present participle of the verb (the verb form ending in **ing**).

Example: The project sponsor **has been considering** an increase in the budget.

Past Perfect Progressive—Verbs Showing PAST ACTION and ONGOING ACTION COMPLETED BFORE SOME OTHER PAST ACTION

The past perfect progressive tense describes a past ongoing action that was completed before some other past action. This tense is formed by using **had been** and the present perfect of the verb (the verb form ending in **ing**).

Example: Before the budget increase, the project team **had been participating** in many sponsor meetings.

Future Perfect Progressive—Verbs Showing ONGOING ACTION OCCURING BEFORE SOME SPECIFIED TIME

The future perfect progressive tense describes a future, ongoing action that will occur before some specified future time. This tense is formed by using **will have been** and the present participle of the verb (the verb form ending in **ing**).

Example: By the next fiscal year, the new product development project team **will have been researching** and **proposing** more than 60 new product categories.

Finally, we need to mention transitive and intransitive verbs.

Transitive Verbs

A *transitive verb* takes a *direct object;* that is, the verb transmits action to an object:

She **sent** the **text** (*text* = direct object of *sent*)
She **gave** the **lecture.** (*lecture* = direct object of *gave*)

In these sentences, something is being done to an object.

Intransitive Verbs

An *intransitive verb* does not take an object:

He **works** too hard.
He **complains** frequently.

In these sentences, nothing receives the action of the verbs *works* and *complains*.

Typical for English, there are many rules and exceptions to the rules for transitive and intransitive verbs, including some power verbs that can be either transitive or intransitive.

Recognize an intransitive verb when you see one

An intransitive verb has two characteristics. First, it is an <u>action verb</u>, expressing a doable activity such as **arrive, go, lie, sneeze, sit, die**, and so on. Second, unlike a <u>transitive verb</u>, it does not have a <u>direct object</u> receiving the action.

Here are some examples of intransitive verbs:

Huffing and puffing, we **arrived** at the church with only seconds to spare. **[arrived** = intransitive verb]

Jorge **went** to the campus cafe for a bowl of hot chicken noodle soup. **[went** = intransitive verb]

To escape the midday heat, the dogs **lie** in the shade under our trees. **[lie** = intransitive verb]

Around fresh ground pepper, Sheryl **sneezes** with violence. **[sneezes** = intransitive verb]

In the early morning, Mom **sits** on the front porch to admire her beautiful flowers. **[sits** = intransitive verb]

Sorry, Ms. Finney (my seventh grade English teacher), I know you would want me to talk about lexical and auxiliary verbs, compound verbs, copulas, prepositional phrases, gerunds, participles, adverbs, tense, aspect, mood, model and nonmodel verbs, subjects, objects, complements, modifiers, and so on, but I promised this would not be a style manual.

2

How to Use This Book

If you have a presentation or a speech to give, there are BASIC rules of the road for every presentation. The following are the fundamental rules for any presentation in addition to including power verbs. You can find different rules in other sources about how to use verbs in your sentences. These rules are a summary of 35 years of personal experience and research:

- Know to whom you are speaking. You have to know who is listening to you. Who are the people and what are their education levels, work histories, social statuses, and cultural backgrounds?
- Prepare, prepare, and prepare. What you say and how you say it are both important elements. As a coach, mentor, leader, manager, or executive, your position gives you power, prestige, and elevated authority. People look up to you.
- People read body language and especially nonverbal cues before they hear your words. They begin to interpret the meaning of what you are saying before you are finished, so your nonverbal clues and language should connect with the thoughts and ideas you want to get expressed.
- Select a tone, style, pitch, rate, and time that are appropriate.
- From the following chapters, carefully select powerful verbs that add punch to your sentences.

Power verbs are arranged alphabetically. You have to put the rest of your sentences together using good grammar, style, syntax, and tense but the power, the muscle, the clout, the sway of your sentences and phrases come from your power verbs.

The more than 600 power verbs in this book are listed in chapters showing the top 100 power verbs in 6 different and useful categories for everyday life and they include:

3. Business, brokering, banking, bargaining, and occasionally betting the farm
4. Challenging situations, difficult moments, calumny, comebacks, or when you just want to get in the last word

5. Mind games, mental panache, mastermind monkey business, meeting MENSAs, or just showing off

6. Presenters, professors, preachers, poets, playwrights, and pundits searing for savior faire

7. Schooling, sagacity, shrewdness, and other times to be sharp and serious

8. Schmoozing, socializing, shindigs, getting sentimental, or using your networking to work the room

In each category, the power verbs are listed in straight alphabetical order and in most cases, the power verbs have examples of the specific word in actual use. These examples include the power verb used in sentences, famous speeches, quotations, and in newspaper and magazine articles. Some power verbs have a list of words that collocate or have a tendency to be grouped or chunked with those power verbs.

Additional Support for You

To give you additional support, following is a selection of some of Dr. Frank Luntz's list of the *Twenty-Eight Words that Work for the Twenty-First Century*:

- **Consequences**: n. The phenomenon that follows and is caused by some previous phenomenon.
- **Impact**: n. A forceful consequence causes listeners to assume they will see and feel a measurable difference. No longer good enough to speak about potential solutions or best effort, people want results.
- **Impact**: v. To have an effect upon; causes listeners to assume they will see and feel a measurable difference. No longer good enough to speak about potential solutions, or best effort, people want results.
- **Diplomacy**: n. Subtle, skillful, peaceful, nondramatic solution to problems. People are tired of drama, anxiety, and tension; they want leadership in diplomacy.
- **Dialogue**: n. Dialogue is the discussion of diplomatic issues.
- **Reliability**: n. The quality of being dependable in a way that is expected or better.
- **Mission**: n. An authentic and genuine purpose.
- **Commitment**: n. Dedication to what one promised.

In addition to these aids, where possible and appropriate, examples of using the power verb in more vivid language phrasing and form are included. These include:

- **Alliteration:** The repetition of the consonant sound of close or adjoining words. An example of alliteration is:

"Step forward, Tin Man. You dare to come to me for a heart, do you? You ςlinking, ςlanking, ςlattering ςollection of ςaliginous junk... And you, Scarecrow, have the effrontery to ask for a brain! You billowing bale of bovine fodder!"

—Delivered by Frank "Wizard of Oz" Morgan (from the movie *The Wizard of Oz*)

• **Antithesis:** The juxtaposition of contrasting ideas frequently in parallel structure. Examples include:

"Ask not what your country can do for you; ask what you can do for your country."

—John Kennedy

"All men dream, but not equally. Those who dream by night in the dusty recesses of their minds, wake in the day to find that it was vanity: But the dreamers of the day are dangerous men, for they may act on their dreams with open eyes, to make them possible."

—T. E. Lawrence

• **Metaphor:** An implicit comparison between things that are essentially different, yet have something in common. It is different from the simile because the metaphor does not contain words such as "like" or "as." Examples of metaphors include:

The same sun warms rich and poor.

Great managers manage by chess; good managers manage by checkers.

Life is a journey; travel it well.

Life is a zoo in a jungle.

• **Parallelism:** A pair or series of related words, phrases, or sentences. An example of parallelism is:

*"We **defeated** communism. We **defeated** fascism. We **defeated** them on the field of battle, and we **defeated** them on the field of ideas."*

—Colin Powell

• **Repetition:** Repeating the same word or set of words at the beginning or end of successive sentences, phrases, or clauses. Repetition usually results in parallelism and builds a strong cadence in the speaker's delivery. Examples of repetition are:

"We will not tire, we will not falter, and we will not fail."

—George W. Bush

"The ever important murmur, dramatize it, dramatize it!"

—Henry James, American expatriate writer 1843–1916.

- **Similes:** An explicit comparison between things that are essentially different yet have something in common and always includes word such as "like" or "as." Examples of similes include

  Busy as a bee

  Hungry as a tiger

  Light as a feather

  It is important to note that overuse of similes creates clichés and diminishes the vivid impression you are trying to create.

Following are some power verb examples from the book.

Benchmark

(1) assessment of something so it can be compared; make a measurement that becomes a standard; to make a comparison of performance or effectiveness.

*"My parents" generation's **benchmark** was simple: Fat equals bad."*

—Arabella Weir, British comedian, actress, and writer (1957–)

*"A Chinese animation studio is already using an early commercial version of the software to increase the quality of its television productions, and Zhou is collaborating with the Frankfurtbased gaming studio Crytek, maker of the popular Crysis series of games, which are often used to **benchmark** the graphics performance of PCs to improve the realism of its products."*

—Anonymous. "The Next Generation of Technology: 35 Innovators Under 35," *Technology Review*, September and October, 2011.

*"This **benchmarking** process realigns the job positions with the most-up-to-date strategic business initiatives."*

—Hayashi, Shawn Kent. *Conversations for Creating Star Performers*, McGraw Hill: NY, 2012: p. 19.

*"After brainstorming and formalizing our instincts, we commissioned a consulting firm to provide us with competitor **benchmarketing**. Our instincts confirmed, we clearly saw the way forward. We would reinforce our Burberry heritage, our Britishness, by emphasizing and growing our core luxury products, innovating them, and keeping them at the heart of everything we do."*

—Angele Ahrendts. "Turning an Aging British Icon into a Global Luxury Brand: How I Did It," *Harvard Business Review*, January and February, 2013: p. 41.

Debauch

(1) corrupt; debase; degrade; deprave; lead astray morally; lower in character; ruin

*(1) "The best way to destroy the capitalist system is to **debauch** the currency."*

—Vladimir Lenin, Russian communist revolutionary, politician, and political theorist (1870–1924)

Absquatulate

(1) abscond; bolt; decamp; depart in a hurry; escape; flee; hurry off; leave; make off; run off; take flight

*(1) In the early days of fire insurance, the insurance companies also ran fire houses and would sometimes show up at a fire, and if the burning home wasn't a policy holder, the fire brigade would try to sell a policy. If the policy couldn't be sold, in many instances, the fire brigade would **absquatulate**, leaving the building to burn.*

The lists of power verbs in the following chapters are displayed in alphabetical order. The list includes the power verbs, several synonyms, abbreviated definitions, examples of the power verbs used in sentences and quotes, and for many power verbs, words that the verbs collocates with.

In the list of power verbs, the verbs are listed in the present tense.

Now, go search for the power verbs that will pump up your verbal communications!

3

100 Top Action Verbs for Business, Brokering, Banking, Bargaining, and Occasionally Betting the Farm

Abandon

(1) abdicate; abjure; break off; cast aside; cede; cop out; desert; discard; drop; eliminate; forfeit; forgo; forsake; give over; give up; halt in progress; jettison; leave; not continue; quit; relinquish; renounce; surrender; throw over; yield; waive; walk out

(2) ease; lightheartedness; natural spontaneity; unrestraint; cast aside

(3) give in to emotion

Word Used in Sentence(s)

*(1) "Once you start a working on something, don't be afraid of failure and don't **abandon** it. People who work sincerely are the happiest."*

—Chanakya, Indian politician, strategist, and writer (350 BC–275 BC)

*(1) "Hope never abandons you; you **abandon** it."*

—George Weinberg, American psychologist, writer, and activist

*(1) "When you have faults, do not fear to **abandon** them."*

—Confucius, philosopher, and political theorist (551–479 BC)

Abolish

(1) abrogate; annihilate; annul; eradicate; invalidate; negate; nullify; renounce; repeal; rescind

(2) bring an end to; cancel; close down; do away with; put an end to; stop

Word Used in Sentence(s)

(1) "This year, the Colorado House Judiciary Committee voted to __abolish__ the death penalty, replacing it with a sentence of life without parole, and to use the money currently spent on capital punishment to help solve some 1,200 cold-case homicides."

—Goodman, Brenda. "Georgia Murder Case's Cost Saps Public Defense System," *New York Times*, Section A, Column 5, National Desk, March 22, 2007: pg. 16.

Collocates to: coalition, death, department, education, federal, penalty, slavery, tax, voted, wants

Abridge

(1) abbreviate; condense; shorten; truncate; reduce the length of

Word Used in Sentence(s)

(1) A thoughtful editor __abridged__ the textbook by eliminating redundant graphics and boring cases.

(1) "__Abridge__ provided that congress shall make no law abridging the freedom of speech or of the press."

—U.S. Constitution, 1st Amendment

(1) "The use of the head __abridges__ the labor of the hands."

—Henry Ward Beecher, liberal U.S. congregational minister (1813–1887)

Collocates to: immunities, law, privileges, rights

Accede

(1) agree; allow; approach; ascend; attain; come to; comply; conform; consent; enter upon; give assent; grant; succeed to; take over

(2) enter upon an office

Word Used in Sentence(s)

(1) By __acceding__ to the minority stockholder demands, the board has established a dangerous policy.

(1) The union leaders eventually __acceded__ to the demands of management committee.

*(1) "I am not willing to be drawn further into the toils. I cannot **accede** to the acceptance of gifts upon terms which take the education policy of the university out of the hands of the Trustees and Faculty and permit it to be determined by those who give money."*

—Woodrow Wilson, 28th U.S. President (1826–1924)

Collocates to: demands, requests, treaty, refused, wishes

Accelerate

(1) gather speed; go faster; hasten; hurry; increase speed; move increasingly quicker; pick up speed; pick up the pace; step up

(2) happen or develop faster; progress faster

Word Used in Sentence(s)

*(1) "The rush shows the extent to which wrangling in Washington over deficit reduction already is affecting the way taxpayers are spending their money. In addition to rethinking their charitable giving, some tax-payers are **accelerating** large medical expenses, selling appreciated stock, and even prepaying mortgages."*

—Saunders, Laura and Hanna Karp. "Fiscal Talks Spur Charitable Giving," *Wall Street Journal*, December 7, 2012: p. A1.

*(1) "The concept of teaming helps individuals acquire knowledge, skills, and networks. And it lets companies **accelerate** the delivery of current products of services while responding to new opportunities."*

—Edmondson, Amy C. "Teamwork on the Fly," *Harvard Business Review*, April 2012: p. 74.

Accomplish

(1) achieve; attain; bring about; carry out; cause to happen; complete; do; gain; get done; finish; fulfill; make happen; make possible; produce; pull off; reach; realize; undertake

Word Used in Sentence(s)

*(1) "Success is not measured by what you **accomplish**, but by the opposi-tion you have encountered, and the courage with which you have main-tained the struggle against overwhelming odds."*

—Orison Swett Marden, American spiritual author (1850–1924)

*(1) "Chance can allow you to **accomplish** a goal every once in a while, but consistent achievement happens only if you love what you are doing."*

—Bart Conner, American Olympic gymnast (1958–)

Collocates to: goals, job, mission, objectives strategy, tactics, task, work

Achieve

(1) accomplish; attain; complete; conclude; do; finish; get; perform; pull off; reach; realize

(2) succeed in doing something

Word Used in Sentence(s)

*(1) "The results you **achieve** will be in direct proportion to the effort you apply."*

—Denis Waitley, American motivational speaker and author (1933–)

*(1) "When we think of failure, failure will be ours. If we remain undecided, nothing will ever change. All we need to do is want to **achieve** something great and then simply to do it. Never think of failure for what we think will come about."*

—Maharishi Mahesh, Yogi

*(1) "First, have a definite, clear practical ideal; a goal, an objective. Second, have the necessary means to **achieve** your ends—wisdom, money, materials, and methods. Third, adjust all your means to that end."*

—Aristotle, ancient Greek philosopher, scientist, and physician (384 BC–322 BC)

*(1) "Organizations do well when the people in them work hard to **achieve** high performance as individuals and as members of teams."*

—Schermerhorn, John and Richard Osborn, Mary UHL-Bien, and James Hunt. *Organizational Behavior*, 12th Ed. NY: John Wiley & Sons, Inc., 2012.

Collocates to: able, goals, help, objectives, results, necessary, order, success

Acquire

(1) attain; buy; come to possess; earn; gain; get; hold; obtain; purchase; receive

Word Used in Sentence(s)

(1) "A true friend is the greatest of all blessings, and that which we take the least care of all to __acquire__."

—Francois de La Rochefoucauld, French author (1630–1680)

(1) "Men __acquire__ a particular quality by constantly acting in a particular way."

—Aristotle, ancient Greek philosopher and polymath (384 BC–322 BC)

(1) "The drive to __acquire__ is most easily satisfied by an organization's reward system—how effectively it discriminates between good and poor performances, ties rewards to performance, and gives the best people opportunities for advancement."

—Nohria, Nitin, Boris Groysberg. and Linda-Eling Lee. "Employee Motivation: A Powerful New Tool, Honing Your Competitive Edge," *Harvard Business Review*, July August 2008, p. 81.

(1) "The more I read, the more I meditate; and the more I __acquire__, the more I am enabled to affirm that I know nothing."

—Voltaire, French philosopher and writer (1694–1778)

(1) "Nobody can __acquire__ honor by doing what is wrong."

—Thomas Jefferson, American founding father, 3rd U.S. President (1743–1826)

Collocates to: ability, able, information, land, knowledge, necessary, students, skills

Actuate

(1)   activate; arouse to action; motivate; put into motion; start; trigger

Word Used in Sentence(s)

(1) Great leaders can begin __actuating__ a new movement just with his or her vision.

(1) Toni's speech __actuated__ the Congress to finally act on the bill.

Adjust

(1)   accommodate; alter; amend; attune; bend; change; correct; fine-tune; fix;
modify; pacify; regulate; resolve; rectify; settle; tune up; tweak

Word Used in Sentence(s)

*(1) "There are things I can't force. I must **adjust**. There are times when
the greatest change needed is a change of my viewpoint."*

—Denis Diderot, French man of letters and philosopher (1713–1784)

*(1) "When it is obvious that the goals cannot be reached, don't **adjust**
the goals; adjust the action steps."*

—Confucius, China's most famous teacher, philosopher, and political
theorist (551–479 BC)

*(1) "First, have a definite, clear practical ideal; a goal, an objective.
Second, have the necessary means to achieve your ends—wisdom,
money, materials, and methods. Third, **adjust** all your means to that
end."*

—Aristotle, ancient Greek philosopher, scientist, and physician (384
BC–322 BC)

Collocates to: compensate, ideas, models, standards, themes, work

Administer

(1)   control; deal out; direct; dispense; furnish a benefit; give out; govern;
hand out; manage; mete out; order; oversee a process; run; supervise

Word Used in Sentence(s)

*(1) "A pure democracy is a society consisting of a small number of citi-
zens who assemble and **administer** the government in person."*

—James Madison, 4th U.S. President (1751–1836)

*(1) "It is as useless to argue with those who have renounced the use of
reason as to **administer** medication to the dead."*

—Thomas Jefferson, American founding father, 3rd U.S. President
(1743–1826)

Collocates to: contracts, exams, plans, polices, programs, projects, tests

Advise

(1) counsel; direct; give advice; give opinion; inform; let know; make aware; notify; offer a personal opinion to somebody; recommend; opine; seek advice or information; tell someone what has happened; warn

Word Used in Sentence(s)

*(1) A career counselor can **advise**, but the client has to act.*

*(1) It is better not to decide on a career until somebody can **advise** you.*

*(1) "In every society, some men are born to rule, and some to **advise**."*

—Ralph Waldo Emerson, American poet, lecturer, and essayist (1803–1882)

Align

(1) adjust; be or come into adjustment; bring into proper or desirable coordination; correlate

(2) arrange something in reference with something else; place in line so as to arrange in a particular order

Word Used in Sentence(s)

*(1) As I consider this position, I want to be sure I am **aligned** with the values and culture of the organization.*

*(1) The firm's objectives and goals must be **aligned**.*

*(1) "Intuitional logic should be **aligned** with economic logic but need not be subordinate to it. For example, all companies require capital to carry out business activities and sustain themselves. However, at great companies profit is not the sole end; rather, it is a way of ensuring that returns will continue."*

— Kanter, Rosabeth. "How Great Companies Think Differently," *Harvard Business Review*, November, 2011, pg. 68.

*(1) "When you examine the lives of the most influential people who have ever walked among us, you discover one thread that winds through them all. They have been **aligned** first with their spiritual nature and only then with their physical selves."*

—Albert Einstein, American physicist (1879–1955)

(1) "Parallels between ancient leaders and modern executives will never
align *perfectly, but there is definite value in making the comparisons.*
Ancient leaders obviously operated under different conditions and lacked
many advantages that modern day CEOs take for granted, but they ran
their empires by utilizing similar styles of leadership."

—Forbes, Steve and John Prevas. *Power, Ambition, Glory*, NY: Crown
Business Press, 2009: pg.10.

Allocate

(1)   allot; designate; devote; distribute

(2)   divide a sum of money or amount of resources

Word Used in Sentence(s)

*(1) We will be **allocating** reserve funds for the project.*

*(1) I will **allocate** an annual budget toward the direct costs of the group's*
work.

(1) "'Ironically, managing a law firm's own resources is one of the
biggest challenges for lawyers in managing a client's work. It was so
*hard for firms to realize that they had to **allocate** money among different*
practice departments,' Roster says. For example, due to a shift in antici-
*pated workload, 'They had to decide how to **allocate** more money one*
year to their labor department than their tax department... That is some-
thing clients have to do all the time.'"

—Chanen, Jill Schachner. "Constructing Team Spirit," *ABA Journal*,
Volume 83, Issue 8, August 1997: pg. 58, 4p, 3c.

Collocates to: available, budgets, capital, cash, energy, limited, money,
resources

Allow

(1)   admit; allot; appropriate; countenance; give up; grant; let; permit; provide for; make provision for; set aside; take into account; tolerate

Word Used in Sentence(s)

*(1) "Chance can **allow** you to accomplish a goal every once in a while,*
but consistent achievement happens only if you love what you are doing."

—Bart Conner, American gold-medal gymnast (1988–)

*(1) "Sometimes being a friend means mastering the art of timing. There is a time for silence. A time to let go and **allow** people to hurl themselves into their own destiny. And a time to prepare to pick up the pieces when it's all over."*

—Gloria Naylor, African-American novelist and educator (1950–)

*(1) "You will achieve grand dreams, a day at a time, so set goals for each day / not long and difficult projects, but chores that will take you, step by step, toward your rainbow. Write them down, if you must, but limit your list so that you won't have to drag today's undone matters into tomorrow. Remember that you cannot build your pyramid in twenty-four hours. Be patient. Never **allow** your day to become so cluttered that you neglect your most important goal / to do the best you can, enjoy this day, and rest satisfied with what you have accomplished."*

—Og Mandino, American essayist and psychologist (1923–1996)

Analyze

(1)   consider; dissect; evaluate; examine; explore; interpret; investigate; probe; question; scrutinize; study

Word Used in Sentence(s)

*(1) Randi **analyzed** the situation from all positions before making her decision.*

*(1) Rick will be given the responsibility of **analyzing** the impact of the new quotas on the sales department's budget.*

*(1) "You are a product of your environment. So choose the environment that will best develop you toward your objective. **Analyze** your life in terms of its environment. Are the things around you helping you toward success— or are they holding you back?"*

—W. Clement Stone, American author (1902–2002)

*(1) "There is nothing to fear except the persistent refusal to find out the truth, the persistent refusal to **analyze** the causes of happenings."*

—Dorothy Thompson, American writer (1893–1961)

*(1) "The method of nature: who could ever **analyze** it?"*

—Ralph Waldo Emerson, American poet, lecturer, and essayist (1803–1882)

Collocates to: ability, collect, data, evaluate, identify, information, results, sample, situation, used

Anticipate

(1) await; be hopeful for; expect; discussion or treatment; give advance thought; look forward to; think likely; to foresee and deal with in advance; wait for

Word Used in Sentence(s)

*(1) We need to **anticipate** our customers' concerns and be prepared with the proper response.*

*(1) If we **anticipate** the potential risk factors, we can build into the budget a more defensible contingency.*

*(1) "Research shows that morning people get better grades in school, which get them into better colleges, which then lead to better job opportunities. Morning people also **anticipate** problems and try to minimize them."*

—Randler, Christopher. "The Early Bird Really Does Get the Worm: Defend Your Research," *Harvard Business Review*, July–August 2012: p. 30.

Arrange

(1) array; authorize; catalogue; classify; fix; order; organize; position; set up; sort; stage
(2) make plans for something to be done

Word Used in Sentence(s)

*(1) "A shrewd man has to **arrange** his interests in order of importance and deal with them one by one; but often our greed upsets this order and makes us run after so many things at once that through over-anxiety to obtain the trivial, we miss the most important."*

—François de la Rochefoucauld, French classical author (1613–1680)

Collocates to: alphabetically, ascending, carefully, chronologically, descending, haphazardly, hierarchically, symmetrically

Assimilate

(1) absorb; accommodate; incorporate; standardize

Word Used in Sentence(s)

> *(1) "True ideas are those that we can **assimilate**, validate, corroborate, and verify. False ideas are those that we cannot."*

—William James, American philosopher and psychologist (1842–1910)

> *(1) "Nothing is more revolting than the majority; for it consists of few vigorous predecessors, of knaves who accommodate themselves, of weak people who **assimilate** themselves, and the mass that toddles after them without knowing in the least what it wants."*

—Johann Wolfgang von Goethe, German playwright, poet, novelist, and dramatist (1749–1832)

> *(1) "It's important for companies to gather insights from former outsiders who have **assimilated** successfully; managers who have grown up in an organization often don't realize they even have a culture."*

—Watkins, Michael. "Help Newly Hired Executives Adapt Quickly," *Corporate Culture Harvard Business Review*, June 2007: pg. 26.

Attain

(1)   accomplish; achieve; acquire; arrive at; conquer; gain; make; manage; obtain; procure; reach; realize

Word Used in Sentence(s)

> *(1) "Desire is the key to motivation, but it's determination and commitment to an unrelenting pursuit of your goal—a commitment to excellence—that will enable you to **attain** the success you seek."*

—Mario Andretti, American race car driver (1940–)

> *(1) "The highest activity a human being can **attain** is learning for understanding, because to understand is to be free."*

—Baruch Spinoza, Dutch philosopher (1632–1677)

> *(1) "While progress has been made in many firms, more work clearly needs to be done. Even among the best and brightest managers, gender equality has yet to be **attained**."*

—Carter, Nancy and Christine Silva. "Women in Management: Delusions of Progress," *Harvard Business Review*, March 2010: pg. 21.

Augment

(1)   add to; boost; bump up; enlarge; expand; increase; make bigger;
supplement

Word Used in Sentence(s)

*(1) Today, a person can digitally **augment** his music collection by
hundreds of songs in a matter of minutes.*

*(1) We plan to **augment** the company security with an outside vendor.*

*(1) "The traditional product life cycle has created a kind of tunnel vision
for marketers. Typically, they layer new product benefits on top of old
ones in an endless struggle to differentiate... Over time the **augmented**
product becomes the expected product."*

—Moon, Youngme. "Break Free from the Product Life Cycle," *Harvard
Business Review*, May 2005: pg. 88.

*(1) "There are two ways of being happy: We must either diminish our
wants or **augment** our means—either may do—the result is the same and
it is for each man to decide for himself and to do that which happens to
be easier."*

—Benjamin Franklin, American statesman, scientist, philosopher,
printer, writer, and inventor (1706–1790)

Collocates to: ability, current, data, design, income, replace

Authorize

(1)   accredit; commission; empower; enable; entitle; grant; license; qualify

Word Used in Sentence(s)

*(1) "So great moreover is the regard of the law for private property, that
it will not **authorize** the least violation of it; no, not even for the general
good of the whole community."*

—William Blackstone, English jurist (1723–1780)

*(1) Only a vice president can **authorize** an expenditure that has not been
budgeted.*

Balance

(1) assess; calculate; collate; compare; consider; equalize; evaluate; even out; keep upright; offset; settle; square; stabilize; stay poised; steady; tally; total; weigh; weight up

Word Used in Sentence(s)

(1) Managing a global enterprise requires a CEO who is adept at **_balancing_** *many interests.*

(1) Managers need to use a **_balanced_** *approach in handling worker disputes.*

Ballpark

(1) approximate; be imprecise, inexact, or vague; estimate; guess; roughly estimate; use a range

Word Used in Sentence(s)

(1) The product development team **_ballparked_** *its costs rather than use net present value.*

(1) The project management team **_ballparked_** *the costs at 20 percent of sales.*

Ballyhoo

(1) advertise; commotion; create a to-do; hullabaloo; kerfuffle; make known; make a racket, ruckus, or uproar; promote

Word Used in Sentence(s)

(1) "For all the **_ballyhoo_** *about the West's rugged individualism, such alterations required state intervention on an unprecedented scale. The costs of damming and moving water grew prohibitive even for the largest ranchers and growers, particularly as the natural flow of artesian wells ceased."*

—Dawson, Robert and Grey Brechin. "How Paradise Lost," *Mother Jones*, Volume 21, Issue 6, November/December 1996: pg. 38.

Bandy

(1) exchange; give and receive

(2) spread something in an unfavorable context

(3) toss or hit something back and forth

Word Used in Sentence(s)

*(1) "The wise speak only of what they know, Grima son of Galmod. A witless worm have you become. Therefore be silent, and keep your forked tongue behind your teeth. I have not passed through fire and death to **bandy** crooked words with a serving-man till then."*

—J.R.R. Tolkien, English writer (1892–1973)

*(1) "To judge by the life choices we make, then, there are dozens of reasons for women to be pro-abortion. Yet not since the heady early days of the abortion rights movement in the late 1960s have we heard its leadership **bandy** around the phrase that summarizes the right we want and have come to expect: 'abortion on demand.'"*

—Hax, Carolyn. "No Birth, No Pangs," *Washington Post*, March 21, 1993.

Battle test

(1) test something under the most difficult of conditions

Word Used in Sentence(s)

*(1) New product development teams are **battle tested** by the unknown risks they will face.*

*(1) An uncertain economic period may be the ideal condition for **battle testing** your inexperienced marketing team.*

Be Argus-eyed

(1) In Greek mythology, Argus was a giant with one hundred eyes each looking in a different direction. Argus was employed by the goddess Hera as a watchman to guard the nymph Io. Zeus had Argus killed by Hermes so he could pursue his passionate love, Io.

(2) having keen eyes; keenly watchful for danger; sleepless; vigilant; watchful; wary; wide awake

Word Used in Sentence(s)

> *(1) Corporate espionage costs firms billions of dollars so it is imperative that all employees **be Argus-eyed** and report any suspicious activity.*

Belabor

(1) to go over and over again; ply diligently; repeat; to work carefully upon

Word Used in Sentence(s)

> *(1) "I wish more people would **belabor** the obvious, and more often."*

—Ibn Warraq, *Why I Am Not a Muslim*. Amherst, NY: Prometheus Books, 1995.

> *(1) I feel like we are wasting time if we **belabor** the same points already covered in previous negations.*

> *(1) Because we **belabored** so long on detailed points of the budget, none of the other agenda items were covered.*

<u>**Collocates to:**</u> need, not, obvious, point, want

Benchmark

(1) assessment of something so it can be compared; make a measurement that becomes a standard; to make a comparison of performance or effectiveness

Word Used in Sentence(s)

> *(1) "My parents' generation's **benchmark** was simple: Fat equals bad."*

—Arabella Weir, British comedian, actress, and writer (1957–)

> *(1) "A Chinese animation studio is already using an early commercial version of the software to increase the quality of its television productions, and Zhou is collaborating with the Frankfurtbased gaming studio Crytek, maker of the popular Crysis series of games, which are often used to **benchmark** the graphics performance of PCs to improve the realism of its products."*

—Anonymous. "The Next Generation of Technology: 35 Innovators Under 35," *Technology Review*, September and October 2011.

*(1) "This **benchmarking** process realigns the job positions with the most-up-to-date strategic business initiatives."*

—Hayashi, Shawn Kent. *Conversations for Creating Star Performers.* NY: McGraw Hill, 2012.

*(1) "After brainstorming and formalizing our instincts, we commissioned a consulting firm to provide us with competitor **benchmarketing**. Our instincts confirmed, we clearly saw the way forward. We would reinforce our Burberry heritage, our Brutishness, by emphasizing and growing our core luxury products, innovating them, and keeping them at the heart of everything we do."*

—Ahrendts, Angele. "Turning an Aging British Icon into a Global Luxury Brand: How I Did It," *Harvard Business Review*, January and February, 2013: pg. 41.

Bootstrap

(1)   initiative; manage without assistance; succeed with few resources

Word Used in Sentence(s)

*(1) Many entrepreneurs **bootstrap** the startup of their new businesses rather than seeking venture capital.*

Build

(1)   assemble; construct; erect; fabricate; join together; make; manufacture; put together; put up

(2)   encourage; foster; grow

Word Used in Sentence(s)

*(1) "The TAD covering Atlantic Station has poured nearly $330 million in bonds to transform a former steel mill into one of the city's biggest retail attractions. The money helped **build** office towers, retail developments, housing units, and the posh Twelve Hotel, as well as the roads and infrastructure that help link the complex to the rest of Atlanta."*

—Bluestein, Greg. "Uneven Results for Tax Districts," *Atlanta Journal Constitution*, June 13, 2012: pg. 1A.

*(1) "Law firms seeking to become international behemoths are chasing cross-border mergers to **build** brands with thousands of lawyers from Boston to Beijing and beyond."*

—Smith, Jennifer. "With CROSS-Border Mergers, Law Firms Enter Arms Race, Marketplace," *Wall Street Journal*, December 10, 2012: pg. B1.

*(1) "To **build** may have to be the slow and laborious task of years. To destroy can be the thoughtless act of a single day."*

—Winston Churchill, British orator, author, and prime minister (1874–1965)

*(1) "I don't **build** in order to have clients. I have clients in order to **build**."*

—Ayn Rand, American writer and novelist (1905–1982)

Burn one's boats

(1) burn one's bridges; choose a killing ground; commit to a course of action; cut oneself off from all means or hope of retreat; go for broke; irreversible course of action; nail one's colors to the mast; to put oneself in a position from which there is no going back

Word Used in Sentence(s)

*(1) In 310 BC, Agathocles of Syracuse sailed his army to Carthage and **burned his boats** so his soldiers knew that the price of failure would be their death.*

Campaign

(1) battle; canvass; engage; fight; hold an operation; participate; push; struggle; to crusade;

Word Used in Sentence(s)

*(1) "I have tried to talk about the issues in this **campaign**... and this has sometimes been a lonely road, because I never meet anybody coming the other way."*

—Adlai E. Stevenson, American politician (1900–1965)

(1) "To campaign against colonialism is like barking up a tree that has already been cut down."

—Andrew Cohen, American philosopher and visionary (1955–)

Capitalize

(1) benefit; finance; profit from; supply funds for profit; take advantage of

Word Used in Sentence(s)

(1) "Expect the best. Prepare for the worst. __Capitalize__ on what comes."

—Zig Ziglar, American author, salesman, and motivational speaker (1906–2012)

(1) "What you have, what you are—your looks, your personality, your way of thinking—is unique. No one in the world is like you. So __capitalize__ on it."

—Jack Lord, American television, film, and Broadway actor (1920–1998)

(1) "We're looking to have the ability to come in and be able to __capitalize__ on the marketing in order to grow the top-line. We basically leverage what has worked with our other successful acquisitions—investment in marketing, retention, and student services."

—John Larson, American, U.S. Representative (1948–)

(1) "He poured resources in R&D and __capitalized__ on two of the company's exceptional capabilities—rapid innovation using deep customer insights and flexible manufacturing."

—Hirsh, Evan and Kasturi Rangan. "The Grass Isn't Greener: Idea Watch," *Harvard Business Review*, January–February 2013: pg. 23.

Capitulate

(1) acquiesce; cede; give in; give up; give way; relent; submit; surrender; yield

Word Used in Sentence(s)

(1) When the company brought in non-union workers, the union __capitulated__ and went back to work without a new contract.

*(1) The union bargaining team was forced to **capitulate** on the pension issue.*

*(1) "I will be conquered; I will not **capitulate**."*

—Samuel Johnson, English poet, critic, and writer (1709–1784)

*(1) Today, successful selling should produce a win-win outcome, not one in which the buyer feels like they had to **capitulate**.*

Catapult

(1)   fling; hurl; hurtle; project; propel; shoot; sling; sling shot; throw; throw with great force; thrust suddenly; toss

Word Used in Sentence(s)

*(1) "Mr. Petrosian—whose father names him Tigran after a former chess champion with the same surname—is one of a legion of top chess players that have **catapulted** the poor nation of three million into world beaters on the 64-square board."*

—Parkinson, Joe. "Winning Move: Chess Reigns as Kingly Pursuit in Armenia," *WSJ*, December 4, 2012: pg. A1.

*(1) "Some authors have what amounts to a metaphysical approach. They admit to inspiration. Sudden and unaccountable urgencies to write **catapults** them out of sleep and bed. For myself, I have never awakened to jot down an idea that was acceptable the following morning."*

—Fannie Hurst, American novelist (1889–1968)

*(1) "The initiative, known as a middle college high school, is patterned after similar programs in California, Texas, and New York. It is the first of its kind in Maryland. 'The idea behind the program is to **catapult** a young person forward, providing them not just with access but with skills on how to be successful,' said Cecilia Cunningham, the executive director of the New York-based Middle College National Consortium."*

—Wiggins, Ovetta. "Doubling Up on Education," *Chicago Sun Times*, Metro June 14, 2012: pg. B01.

(1) "By positioning—or repositioning—their products in unexpected ways, companies can change how customers mentally categorize them. As a result, companies can rescue products foundering in the maturity stage of the product life cycle and return them to the growth phase. And

*they can **catapult** new products forward into the growth phase, leapfrogging obstacles that could slow consumers' acceptance."*

—Moon, Youngme. "Break Free from the Product Life Cycle," *Harvard Business Review*, May 2005: pg. 88.

Catch fire

(1) to become remarkably successful

(2) ignite; to burn;

Word Used in Sentence(s)

*(1) "**Catch on fire** with enthusiasm and people will come for miles to watch you burn."*

—John Wesley, English evangelist (1703–1791)

*(1) "For it is your business, when the wall next door **catches fire**."*

—Horace, Ancient Roman poet (65 BC–8 BC)

Catch the wave

(1) take advantage of a trend to seize an opportunity

Word Used in Sentence(s)

*(1) Many businesses will try to **catch the wave** with social media.*

*(1) A business strategy is a well thought-out plan, not "let's **catch the wave**" of the next hot industry cycle.*

Catenate

(1) connect in a series of ties or links; to chain

Champion

(1) advocate; back; campaign for; crusade for; excel; fight for; stand up for; support; to be a winner uphold

Word Used in Sentence(s)

*(1) Sharon was the **champion** for the new compensation plan.*

*(1) "We cannot be both the world's leading **champion** of peace and the world's leading supplier of the weapons of war."*

—Jimmy Carter, 39th U.S. President (1924–)

*(1) "**Champion** the right to be yourself; dare to be different and to set your own pattern; live your own life and follow your own star."*

—Wilfred Peterson, American author (1900–1995)

Channel

(1) concentrate; conduit; control; convey; course; direct; feed; focus; path; route

Word Used in Sentence(s)

*(1) "A strong man and a waterfall always **channel** their own path."*

—Unknown

*(1) "Goals help you **channel** your energy into action."*

—Les Brown, American author, entrepreneur, and motivational speaker (1912–2001)

*(1) "You know how often the turning down this street or that, the accepting or rejecting of an invitation, may deflect the whole current of our lives into some other **channel**. Are we mere leaves, fluttered hither and thither by the wind, or are we rather, with every conviction that we are free agents, carried steadily along to a definite and pre-determined end?"*

—Arthur Conan Doyle, Sr., Scottish writer (1859–1930)

*(1) "Marketing and finance have a famously fractious relationship, with each accusing the other of failing to understand how to create value. That tension may seem to be dysfunctional, but when **channeled** right, it can actually be productive."*

—Reprint F0706D, Harvard Business Review, June 2007: pg. 25.

Classify

(1) arrange; assort; catalog; categorize; class; distribute into groups; grade; group; list by some order or sequence; organize; sort

Word Used in Sentence(s)

*(1) "The small part of ignorance that we arrange and **classify**, we give the name of knowledge."*

—Ambrose Bierce, American writer, journalist, and editor (1842–1914)

Collaborate

(1) act as a team; assist; cooperate; join forces; pool resources; team up; work with others to achieve common goals; work together

Word Used in Sentence(s)

*(1) A professional career counselor will **collaborate** with a client rather than see him or her as a customer.*

*(1) "The way to create job benchmarks is by inviting the key stakeholders and the team of subject matter experts to **collaborate** on defining the position."*

—Hayashi, Shawn Kent. *Conversations for Creating Star Performers*, NY: McGraw Hill, 2012.

*(1) "EMCF's ability to **collaborate** with industry peers created substantial benefits for society and set an example for others—notably the Obama administration, which found the pilot and inspiration for its Social Innovation Fund…"*

—Tierney, Thomas. "Collaborating for the Common Good," *Harvard Business Review*, July–August 2011: pg. 38.

*(1) "A traditional project management approach would not work for the proposed project. Success depended on bridging dramatically different national, organizational, and occupational cultures to **collaborate** in fluid groupings that emerged and dissolved in response to needs that were identified as the work progressed."*

—Edmondson, Amy C. "Teamwork on the Fly: Spotlight," *Harvard Business Review*, April 2012: pg. 74.

*(1) In today's global economy, many businesses must practice co-opitition which is **collaboration** with not only intra-departmental groups but also vendors, suppliers, stakeholders, NGOs, and, in some cases, competitors.*

Communicate

(1)   be in touch; be in verbal contact; call; connect; converse; convey; correspond; e-mail; impart; interconnect; join; publish; reveal; share; speak;
talk; text; transmit information, thoughts, or feelings; wire; write

Word Used in Sentence(s)

*(1) "Great companies have three sets of stakeholders: customers,
employees, and shareholders—in order of importance...the board should
communicate that formula to the shareholders so they understand the
greater good that the company represents."*

—Horst, Gary. Business Advisor, "CEOs Need a NEW Set of Beliefs,"
HBR Blog, September 21, 2012: pg. 22.

*(1) "Ninety percent of leadership is the ability to **communicate** something people want."*

—Dianne Feinstein, American Senator (1933–)

*(1) "Start with good people, lay out the rules, **communicate** with your
employees, motivate them, and reward them. If you do all those things
effectively, you can't miss."*

—Lee Iacocca, American business executive (1924–)

*(1) "Mayor Bill Akers of Seaside Heights, NJ now removed from the
whirlwind of Hurricane Sandy's ferocity, and with the benefit of hindsight, the major says he has his regrets. He could, he says, have stopped
by one of the shelters to speak to residents personally. He would have
communicated information sooner."*

—Goldberg, Dan. "Responses to Sandy: From Great to Galling, In
Perspective, Middlesex Edition," *Star Ledger*, November 11, 2012: pg. 1.

Collocates to: ability, able, effectively, information, language, ways

Conduct

(1)   carry on; control; direct; guide; head; lead; manage; operate; steer;
supervise

Word Used in Sentence(s)

*(1) The tests were **conducted** last week.*

*(1) Hank will manage the team **conducting** the pre-launch tests.*

Conform

(1) comply; follow actions of others; go along with

Word Used in Sentence(s)

*(1) "This is the very devilish thing about foreign affairs: They are foreign and will not always **conform** to our whim."*

—James Reston, Scottish journalist (1909–1995)

*(1) "A man's faults all **conform** to his type of mind. Observe his faults and you may know his virtues."*

—Chinese Proverb

Conserve

(1) avoid waste; be careful with; go easy on; husband; keep something from damage, harm, or loss; maintain; preserve; protect; safeguard; save; support; use sparingly so not to exhaust

(2) bottle; can; put up; store

Word Used in Sentence(s)

*(1) The firm's new energy policy will **conserve** more than 50 thousand megawatts of electrical power per month.*

*(1) "The U.S. Department of Defense took an unprecedented step on May 15, 2007, blocking troop access to MySpace, YouTube, and other popular websites. The official reason was to **conserve** bandwidth."*

—Fritzon, Art, Lloyd Howell, and Dov Zakheim. "Military of Millennials," *Strategy +Business*, Issue 9, Winter 2000: pg. 18.

*(1) "In the end, we will **conserve** only what we love. We will love only what we understand. We will understand only what we are taught."*

—Baba Dioum, Senegalese environmentalist and poet (1937–)

Collocates to: biodiversity, cash, effort, electricity, energy, fuel, heat, help, power, resources, species, water

Consider

(1) bear in mind; believe; care about; chew over; cogitate; contemplate; deliberate; deem; judge; ponder; regard as; reflect or mull over; ruminate; study; take into account; think; weigh

Word Used in Sentence(s)

*(1) "You must **consider** the bottom line, but make it integrity before profits."*

—Denis Waitley, American motivational speaker and author (1933–)

*(1) "The greatest difficulty is that men do not think enough of themselves, do not **consider** what it is that they are sacrificing when they follow in a herd, or when they cater for their establishment."*

—Ralph Waldo Emerson, American poet, lecturer, and essayist (1803–1882)

Constitute

(1) build; compose; comprise; consist of; enact; establish; form; found; habit; habits; make; make up; physique; set up

Word Used in Sentence(s)

*(1) "Bad planning on your part does not **constitute** an emergency on my part."*

—Unknown

*(1) "Force does not **constitute** right...obedience is due only to legitimate powers."*

—Jean-Jacques Rousseau, French philosopher and writer (1712–1778)

*(1) "Books **constitute** capital. A library book lasts as long as a house, for hundreds of years. It is not, then, an article of mere consumption but fairly of capital, and often in the case of professional men, setting out in life, it is their only capital."*

—Thomas Jefferson, American founding father, 3rd U.S. President (1743–1826)

Coordinate

(1) bring together; combine; direct; harmonize; manage; match up; organize; synchronize; work together

Word Used in Sentence(s)

*(1) I want to see that marketing and sales have **coordinated** their efforts much better.*

(1) "Of all the things I have done, the most vital is __coordinating__ the talents of those who work for us and pointing them towards a certain goal."

—Walt Disney, American film producer, director, screenwriter, voice actor, animator, entrepreneur, entertainer, and international icon (1901-1965)

(1) "My experience in government is that when things are non-controversial and beautifully __coordinated__, there is not much going on."

—John F. Kennedy, 35th U.S. President (1917–1963)

Create

(1)   bring about; build; cause to come into being; compose; design; give rise to; produce

Word Used in Sentence(s)

(1) "Effective leaders __create__ a relationship through conversations that engage their followers. The quality of the relationship we have with our employees and teams is based on the intentional developmental conversations we __create__ with them over time."

—Hayashi, Shawn Kent. *Conversations for Creating Star Performers*, NY: McGraw Hill, 2012.

(1) "__Creating__ success requires respect for everyone's needs, talents, and aspirations, as well as an understanding of the dynamics of human behavior in organizational systems."

—Schermerhorn, John, Richard Osborn, Mary UHL-Bien, and James Hunt. *Organizational Behavior*, 12th Ed. NY: John Wiley & Sons, Inc., 2012.

(1) "In the sky, there is no distinction of east and west; people __create__ distinctions out of their own minds and then believe them to be true."

—Buddha, India, spiritual teacher from the Indian subcontinent, on whose teachings Buddhism was founded (circa 556 BC–456 BC)

(1) "If you don't __create__ change, change will __create__ you."

—Unknown

Cross the Rubicon

(1)   decision that cannot be reversed; die is cast; no turning back; pass a point of no return; take the plunge

Word Used in Sentence(s)

*(1) "A great statesman **crosses the Rubicon** without considering the depth of the river. Once he or she declares to cross it, they must face any challenges and risks during the journey. Fretting on the shore won't make the dangers go away."*

—Chang Dal-Joong, *Korea JoongAng Daily*

Curtail

(1)   abridge; cut short; make less; scale back; shorten

Word Used in Sentence(s)

*(1) Many school districts have had to **curtail** the non-core classes and add that time to science and math courses.*

*(1) We were forced to **curtail** the grand opening celebration due to power failure.*

*(1) "The budget should be balanced. Public debt should be reduced. The arrogance of officialdom should be tempered, and assistance to foreign lands should be **curtailed**, lest Rome become bankrupt."*

—Marcus Tullius Cicero, ancient Roman lawyer, writer, scholar, orator, and statesman (106 BC–43 BC)

Decide

(1)   adopt; agree; conclude; elect; fix on; go for; make a choice or come to a conclusion; make up your mind; opt; pick; resolve; select; settle on; take

Word Used in Sentence(s)

*(1) "Whatever you do, you need courage. Whatever course you **decide** upon, there is always someone to tell you that you are wrong. There are always difficulties arising that tempt you to believe your critics are right."*

—Ralph Waldo Emerson, American poet, lecturer, and essayist (1803–1882)

*(1) "The possibilities are numerous once we **decide** to act and not react."*

—George Bernard Shaw, Irish literary critic, playwright, and essayist
(1856–1950)

Defer

(1) adjourn; bow; delay; give ground; hold off; lay over; postpone; put off;
remit; shelve; stay; submit; suspend; stay; table; yield; wait; waive

Word Used in Sentence(s)

*(1) ""Morgan Stanley Chairman and Chief Executive James Gorman
has been a strong proponent of **deferred** pay, an approach favored by
regulators and risk management experts. Traders are less likely to
engage in risky behavior if they know the firm owes them millions of dollars in **deferred** compensation, according to his argument."*

—Lucchetti, Aaron and Brett Phibin. "Bankers Get IOUs Instead of
Bonus Cash," *Wall Street Journal*, January 16, 2013: pg. A1.

Delegate

(1) appoint; assign; person assigned to represent others; transfer power

Word Used in Sentence(s)

*(1) "Based upon studies on the practices of 20 leading multinational cor-
porations, we conclude that a heavy reliance on first tier suppliers is
dangerous and the **delegation** has gone too far."*

—Choi, Thomas and Tom Linton. "Don't Let Your Supply Chain Control
Your Business," *Harvard Business Review*, December 2011: pg. 113.

*(1) "Best practice companies such as Apple, Dell, HP, Honda, IBM,
LGE, and Toyota do what we just advised: They have approved vendor
lists but never completely relinquish decisions about a product's components and material to top-tier suppliers. They carefully determine which
items they should directly source themselves and which they should
totally **delegate**."*

—Choi, Thomas and Tom Linton. "Don't Let Your Supply Chain Control
Your Business," *Harvard Business Review*, December 2011: pg. 113.

Deliberate

(1)   confer; consider; consult; debate; meditate; mull over; plan; ponder; reflect; think carefully; weigh carefully

Word Used in Sentence(s)

*(1) "Take time to **deliberate**, but when the time for action has arrived, stop thinking and go in."*

—Napoleon Bonaparte, French military and political leader (1769–1821)

*(1) "It is only after time has been given for a cool and **deliberate** reflection that the real voice of the people can be known."*

—George Washington, American, one of the founding fathers of the United States, serving as the commander-in-chief of the Continental Army during the American Revolutionary War, 1st U.S. President (1732–1799)

Collocates to: act, attempt, choice, decision, deliberate, effort, policy, slow, speed, strategy

Delineate

(1)   describe accurately; determine; draw an outline; identify or indicate by marking with precision; fix boundaries; represent something

Word Used in Sentence(s)

*(1) I plan to **delineate** my ideas regarding the new product in my presentation to the executive committee.*

*(1) "Do you want to know who you are? Don't ask. Act! Action will **delineate** and define you."*

—Thomas Jefferson, American founding father, 3rd U.S. President (1743–1826)

*(1) His responsibility was to **delineate** the scope of internal audits for the board finance committee.*

Collocates to: boundary, combinations, limit, sections, scope, used

Demand

(1)   ask; call for; claim; command; entail; exact; insist; mandate; necessitate; order; petition; require; requisition; stipulate; ultimatum; want

Word Used in Sentence(s)

*(1) "Coaching and mentoring **demand** a multilayered knowledge that managers don't need to call their own."*

—Nigro, Nicholas. *The Everything Coaching and Mentoring Book*, Avon, Ma.: Adams Media Corp., 2003.

*(1) "Power concedes nothing without a **demand**. It never did and it never will."*

—Frederick Douglass, American abolitionist, lecturer, author (1817–1895)

*(1) "Great organizations **demand** a high level of commitment by the people involved."*

—Bill Gates, American entrepreneur and founder of Microsoft Co. (1955–)

Depreciate

(1) belittle; derogate; disparage; lower the value of

Word Used in Sentence(s)

*(1) "Today people who hold cash equivalents feel comfortable. They shouldn't. They have opted for a terrible long-term asset, one that pays virtually nothing and is certain to **depreciate** in value."*

—Warren Buffet, American business magnate, investor, and philanthropist (1930–)

*(1) "Those who profess to favor freedom, and yet **depreciate** agitation, are men who want crops without plowing up the ground."*

—Frederick Douglass, American social reformer, orator, writer, and statesman (1818–1895)

Develop

(1) achieve; advance; build up; evolve; expand; exploit; expound; extend; gain; generate; grow; increase; mature; strengthen; unfold; widen

(2) make known gradually

Word Used in Sentence(s)

> *(1) Someone will have to **develop** the software for this project.*

> *(1) A manager's role includes **developing** his or her people to their fullest potential.*

> *(1) "Smaller scale financial models since have been **developed**, with more advanced techniques including models called Edo and Sigma."*

> —Hilenrath, Jon. "Fed's Computer Models Pose Problems," *Wall Street Journal*, December 31, 2012: pg. A3.

Collocates to: ability, help, plan, program, relationships, skills, strategies, students, understanding

Devise

(1)   conceive; concoct; contrive; create; design; develop; formulate; imagine or guess; invent; plan; plot; sot up; think up; work out or create something

Word Used in Sentence(s)

> *(1) The engineering team **devised** the solution to the problem.*

Differentiate

(1)   acquire a different and unique character; be a distinctive feature, attribute, or trait; become different or specialized by being modified; become distinct; mark as different; segregate; separate; set apart; tell apart

Word Used in Sentence(s)

> *(1) "Jack Trout updated his ideas on positioning consumer products with his book,* The New Positioning, *co-authored with Steve Rivikin. Trout also began talking about **differentiation**, in which the focus of the marketing effort is communicating how your product is unique compared to competitive products."*

> —Trout, Jack and Steve Rivikin. *Differentiate or Die,* Editor, Chris Murray. NY: Penguin Books, 2006.

Direct

(1) address; aim; calculate; command; conduct; engineer; guide; head; immediate; lead; maneuver; orchestrate; send; take aim; target

(2) control the course; guide; point the way; show the way; steer

Word Used in Sentence(s)

*(1) **Directing** is one of the four primary functions of management.*

*(1) "The results you achieve will be in **direct** proportion to the effort you apply."*

—Denis Waitley, American motivational speaker and author (1933–)

*(1) "In essence, if we want to **direct** our lives, we must take control of our consistent actions. It's not what we do once in a while that shapes our lives, but what we do consistently."*

—Anthony Robbins, American advisor to leaders (1960–)

*"Great ambition is the passion of a great character. Those endowed with it may perform very good or very bad acts. All depends on the principals which **direct** them."*

—Napoleon Bonaparte, French general, politician, and emperor (1769–1821)

Disburse

(1) distribute; expend; give out; hand out; lay out; pay out

Word Used in Sentence(s)

*(1) Our company **disburses** thousands of dollars in college scholarships every year.*

Do your homework

(1) be informed; be prepared; get ready

Word Used in Sentence(s)

*(1) Shana really **did her homework** in preparation for the job interview.*

Double down

(1) to engage in risky behavior, especially when one is already in a dangerous situation

*(1) "Voters go to the polls with an unusually clear choice in U.S. eco-
nomic policy: We can **double down** on the current approach in hopes
that bigger government will create jobs, or we can adopt growth policies
that are more market-oriented and less government-centered."*

—Malpass, David. "Romney, Obama, and the Economic Choice," *Wall
Street Journal*, November 6, 2012: PA17.

*(1) "Leading figures on both sides **doubled down** on their positions in
interviews that aired Sunday. They blamed each other for the current
standoff, reflecting the talks that House Speaker John Boehner (R, Ohio)
told Fox News Sunday have gone nowhere."*

—Paletta, Damiah. "Fiscal Cliff Talks at Stalemate," *Wall Street Journal*,
December 3, 2012: pA3.

Down scope

(1) downsizing a project; reevaluating whether a project should be done;
strategic divestiture undertaken to refocus the firm on its core businesses and back to a more optimal level of diversification

Word Used in Sentence(s)

*(1) Unlike **down scoping**, downsizing involves strategically laying-off
employees during times of economic stress. Such activity is clearly different from **down scoping**, which centers on refocusing to capture proper
strategic control of the firm.*

Draw lines in the sand

(1) a particular idea or activity will not be supported or accepted; to create
or declare an artificial boundary and imply that crossing it will cause
trouble

Word Used in Sentence(s)

*(1) "House Speaker John Boehner of Ohio in a conference call Wednesday told fellow Republicans to avoid **drawing lines in the sand**. 'We don't want to box the White House out.'"*

—Paletta, Damiam, Carol E. Lee, and Bendavid Naftali, "Pressure Rises on Financial Crisis," *WSJ*, November 9, 2012.

*"My **Line in the Sand**: No More Defense Cuts"*

—Headline of *Wall Street Journal* Article by Senator Joe Lieberman, November 26, 2012.

*(1) If you have been negotiating in good faith and have been truthful, yet the other side continues to hold on to untenable positions, you may have to **draw a line in the sand** and be prepared to walk away.*

Drive

(1) ambition; determination to make something occur; energy; force into a particular state or condition; get up and go; initiative; instinct; move or propel forcefully; passion to succeed; provide momentum; steer progress towards

Word Used in Sentence(s)

*(1) "We herd sheep, we **drive** cattle, we lead people. Lead me, follow me, or get out of my way."*

—General George S. Patton, American general in World Wars I and II (1885–1945)

*(1) "Enthusiasm releases the **drive** to carry you over obstacles and adds significance to all you do."*

—Norman Vincent Peale, American Protestant clergyman and writer (1898–1993)

*(1) "Good business leaders create a vision, articulate the vision, passionately own the vision, and relentlessly **drive** it to completion."*

—Jack Welch, American chemical engineer, business executive, and author (1935–)

Earmark

(1) allocate; allot; appropriate; assign; set aside; to set aside or reserve for special purpose

(2) to mark the ears of livestock for special identification

(3) to set a distinctive mark on

Word Used in Sentence(s)

*(1) "The **earmark** favor factory needs to be boarded up and demolished, not turned over to new management that may or may not have a better eye for **earmarks** with 'merit.'"*

—Tom Colburn, American, United States Senator, medical doctor (1948–)

Collocates to: ban, money, process reform, request, spending

Earn one's wings

(1) authorize; certify; check out; cut it; empower; enable; endow; entitle; equip; fill the bill; fit; make it; make ready; make the cut; measure up; pass; pass muster; prepared; prove competency or worth; sanction; score; qualify; to be reliable

Word Used in Sentence(s)

*(1) There are too many young people coming out of college today who don't want to **earn their wings** in the traditional manner as a generalist but rather by specializing in a highly individualized role.*

Effect

(1) accomplish; bring about; make happen; to go into operation

Word Used in Sentence(s)

*(1) The strategic plan is now in **effect**.*

*(1) "Words differently arranged have a different meaning, and meanings differently arranged have a different **effect**."*

—Blaise Pascal, French mathematician, philosopher, and physicist (1623–1662)

*(1) "Cause and **effect**, means and ends, seed and fruit cannot be severed; for the **effect** already blooms in the cause, the end preexists in the means, the fruit in the seed."*

—Ralph Waldo Emerson, American poet, lecturer, and essayist (1803–1882)

Embed

(1) implant; insert; place something or place something solidly; set in; set or fix firmly in a surrounding mass to set flowers in the earth

(2) fix in the mind or memory

(3) insert a code or virus, a routine for monitoring into a software program

(4) assign an observer to a group

Word Used in Sentence(s)

*(1) "Business leaders naturally want their company's strategy to be understood and accepted by employees or, as we call it, '**embedded**.'"*

—Calunic, Charles and Immanuel Hermerck. "How to Help Employees 'Get' Strategy," *Harvard Business Review*, 2012: pg. 24.

*(1) "What accounts for the overwhelming importance of top managers to **embeddedness**? We believe the explanation is two-fold. Senior leaders should have a unique understanding of their company's strategy; there may be no equal substitute when it comes to communicating and discussing it. And their position at the top is powerfully symbolic, giving them more credibility and authority than others have."*

—Calunic, Charles and Immanuel Hermerck. "How to Help Employees 'Get' Strategy," *Harvard Business Review*, 2012: pg. 24.

*(1) "**Embedded** in the five fundamental practices of exemplary leadership discussed above are behaviors that can serve as the basis for learning to lead. We call these the Ten Commandments of Leadership."*

—Kouzes, James and Barry Posner. *The Leadership Challenge.* San Francisco, CA: Jossey-Bass Publisher, 1999.

Empower

(1) allow; authorize; give authority or power to; sanction

(2) make one stronger and more confident, especially in controlling their life and claiming their rights

Word Used in Sentence(s)

(1) "I'm slowly becoming a convert to the principle that you can't moti-
vate people to do things, you can only demotivate them. The primary job
*of the manager is not to **empower** but to remove obstacles."*

—Scott Adams, American cartoonist (1957–)

(1) "As we look ahead into the next century, leaders will be those who
***empower** others."*

—Bill Gates, American business magnate, philanthropist, and former
chief executive and current chairman of Microsoft (1955–)

*(1) "Fear does not have any special power unless you **empower** it by*
submitting to it."

—Les Brown, American big band leader and composer (1912–2001)

*(1) "In most companies, cultural resistance to **empowering** employees to*
use technology is system wide."

—Bernoff, Jeff and Ted Schadler. "Empowered," *Harvard Business*
Review, July–August 2010: pg. 95.

Collocates to: America, individuals, people, students, women

Enable

(1)   aid; allow; assist; empower; facilitate; make possible; permit; render
capable or able for some task; qualify; support

Word Used in Sentence(s)

(1) "The 1648 settlement at Westphalia, though setbacks were many and
*vicious, **enabled** procedures fostering what eventually would be 'the*
international community,' a term that curled many a lip in the midst of
the twentieth-century world wars."

—Hill, Charles. "Notable & Quotable," *Wall Street Journal*, December
1, 2012: pg. A13.

*(1) "Still, creating a system that **enables** employees to achieve great*
things—as a group—often comes down to the work of a single leader."

—Hann, Christopher. "The Masters," *Entrepreneur*, March 2012:
pg. 58.

*(1) "Moral courage **enables** people to stand up for a principle rather than stand on the sidelines."*

—Kanter, Rosabeth. "Courage in the C-Suite," *Harvard Business Review*, December 2011: pg. 38.

*(1) "Employees are motivated by jobs that challenge and **enable** them to grow and learn, and they are demoralized by those that seem to be monotonous or lead to a dead end."*

—Nohria, Nitin, Boris Groysberg, and Linda-Eling Lee. "Employee Motivation: A Powerful New Tool, Honing Your Competitive Edge," *Harvard Business Review*, July–August 2008: pg. 81.

Encourage

(1)   advance; assist something to occur; boost; further; give hope, confidence, or courage; motivate to take a course of action

Word Used in Sentence(s)

*(1) "Our duty is to **encourage** everyone in his struggle to live up to his own highest idea, and strive at the same time to make the ideal as near as possible to the truth."*

—Swami Vivekananda, Indian spiritual leader of the Hindu religion (1863–1902)

*(1) "Leaders must **encourage** their organizations to dance to forms of music yet to be heard."*

—Warren G. Bennis, American scholar, organizational consultant, and author (1925–)

*(1) "Our analysis, to our knowledge, the first of its kind, found that firms that indiscriminately **encourage** all their customers to buy more by cross-selling are making a costly mistake: A significantly subset of cross-buyers are highly unprofitable."*

—Shah, Denish, and V. Kumar. "The Dark Side of Cross-Selling, Idea Watch," *Harvard Business Review*, December 2012: pg. 21.

*(1) "Big business can do more to support smaller enterprises in their supply and distribution chains. To **encourage** small and medium-size businesses on the basis of their productivity rather than their experience or size would help establish the idea that everyone has a stake in the capitalist system."*

—Forester de Rothschild, Lynn and Adam Posen. "How Capitalism Can Repair Its Bruised Image: Opinion," *Wall Street Journal*, January 2, 2013: pg. A17.

Collocates to: designed, development, efforts, growth, investment, polices, students, teachers

Encroach

Word Used in Sentence(s)

*(1) "Never give way to melancholy; resist it steadily, for the habit will **encroach**."*

—Sydney Smith, English clergyman and essayist (1771–1845)

Collocates to: land, on, upon, rights, territory

Energize

(1)   active; arouse; brace; excite; pump up; stimulate; to put fourth energy; vigorous

Word Used in Sentence(s)

*(1) "The world of the 1990s and beyond will not belong to 'managers' or those who can make the numbers dance. The world will belong to passionate, driven leaders—people who not only have enormous amounts of energy but who can **energize** those whom they lead."*

—Jack Welch, American chemical engineer, business executive, and author (1935–)

*(1) "We look at the dance to impart the sensation of living in an affirmation of life, to **energize** the spectator into keener awareness of the vigor, the mystery, the humor, the variety, and the wonder of life. This is the function of the American dance."*

—Martha Graham, American dancer, teacher, and choreographer (1894–1991)

Establish

(1) begin; bring about; create; form; found; inaugurate; launch; set up or start something

(2) ascertain; authenticate; confirm; corroborate; cause something to be recognized; determine; find out; prove; show; verify

Word Used in Sentence(s)

*(1) "Leaders **establish** the vision for the future and set the strategy for getting there; they cause change. They motivate and inspire others to go in the right direction and they, along with everyone else, sacrifice to get there."*

—John Kotter, American, former professor at the Harvard Business School, and acclaimed author (1947–)

*(1) "College football ad deals also give marketers the chance to **establish** a presence on college campuses, notes marketers such as GM'S Chevrolet brand."*

—Bachman, Rachel and Mathew Futterman. "College Football's Big-Money, Big-Risk Business Model," *Wall Street Journal*, December 10, 2012: pg. B1.

Exceed

(1) beat; go beyond; surpass what was expected or thought possible; outdo; overachieve; to be more or greater than

Word Used in Sentence(s)

*(1) "People expect a certain reaction from a business, and when you pleasantly **exceed** those expectations, you've somehow passed an important psychological threshold."*

—Richard Thalheimer, American business executive

*(1) "Rarely do the followers **exceed** the expectations of the leaders."*

—Unknown

Excel

(1) shine; stand out; surpass

(2) be better, greater, or superior to others in the same field, profession, endeavor

Word Used in Sentence(s)

*(1) "Allow yourself to be inspired. Allow yourself to succeed. Dare to **excel**."*

—Unknown

*(1) "Those who are blessed with the most talent don't necessarily out-perform everyone else. It's the people with follow-through who **excel**."*

—Mary Kay Ash, American businesswoman, founder of Mary Kay Cosmetics (1915–)

*(1) "I founded Wang Laboratories to show that Chinese could **excel** at things other than running laundries and restaurants."*

—An Wang, Chinese-born American computer engineer and inventor (1920–1990)

Expedite

(1) ease the progress of; hasten; speed up

Word Used in Sentence(s)

*(1) "The art of statesmanship is to foresee the inevitable and to **expedite** its occurrence."*

—Charles M. de Talleyrand, French statesman (1754–1838)

Expunge

(1) blot out; cancel; cut; delete; erase completely; wipe out

Word Used in Sentence(s)

*(1) "There is no man, however wise, who has not at some period of his youth said things, or lived in a way the consciousness of which is so unpleasant to him in later life that he would gladly, if he could, **expunge** it from his memory."*

—Marcel Proust, French novelist, critic, and essayist (1871–1922)

*(1) "Every burned book or house enlightens the world; every suppressed or **expunged** word reverberates through the earth from side to side."*

—Ralph Waldo Emerson, American poet, lecturer, and essayist (1803–1882)

Expurgate

(1) seize property from owner for public sale

(2) remove passages from works deemed obscene

(3) delete; expunge

Word Used in Sentence(s)

*(1) It was clear that the outside consultant did not understand our market because I had to **expurgate** nearly the entire marketing plan he submitted.*

Fight on death ground

(1) deliberately choose a strategy that leaves no options other than winning

Word Used in Sentence(s)

*(1) "When it comes to the carbon pricing agenda, PM Gillard and her Labor Government are **fighting on death ground**—the terrain that the military strategist Sun Tzu described more than 2,000 years ago in* The Art of War.*"*

—Ewbank, Leigh, "Carbon Price Fight on Death Ground," *ABCnews.net*, March 17, 2011.

First move

(1) first to market; initial action; quick action

Word Used in Sentence(s)

*(1) An experienced web developer's **first move** is to get the client's signature on a comprehensive website development contract before starting any project.*

(1) "The advantages to those who are __first movers__ are three: (1) Technological leadership, (2) Preemption of assets and capital, and (3) Increase in buyer switching costs."

—Lieberman, Marvin and David Montgomery. "First-Mover Advantages," *Research Paper 969*, Stanford Business School, October 1987.

Forge

(1)   come up with a concept, explanation, idea, theory, principle or theory; contrive; create

(2)   beat; make out of components

(3)   move ahead or act with sudden increase in motion or speed

Word Used in Sentence(s)

(1) "People are more inclined to be drawn in if their leader has a compelling vision. Great leaders help people get in touch with their own aspirations and then will help them __forge__ those aspirations into a personal vision."

—John Kotter, former professor at the Harvard Business School and acclaimed author (1947–)

(1) "The President's offer is very much in keeping with history of insisting that negotiation consists of the other side giving him everything he wants. That approach has given him the reputation as the modern president least able to __forge__ a consensus."

—Strassel, Kimberley. "This Unserious White House," *Wall Street Journal*, November 30, 2012: pg. A13.

(1) "We __forge__ the chains we wear in life."

—Charles Dickens, English writer and social critic (1812–1870)

(1) "Bad men cannot make good citizens. It is when a people forget God that tyrants __forge__ their chains. A vitiated state of morals, a corrupted public conscience, is incompatible with freedom. No free government, or the blessings of liberty, can be preserved to any people but by a firm adherence to justice, moderation, temperance, frugality, and virtue; and by a frequent recurrence to fundamental principles."

—Patrick Henry, American lawyer, patriot, and orator, symbol of the American struggle for liberty (1736–1799)

Formulate

(1) articulate; contrive; create; develop; devise; draft; elaborate; express; frame; invent; make; originate; plan; prepare; put into words or expressions; verbalize; voice

Word Used in Sentence(s)

(1) It is critical to __formulate__ a clear mission statement.

Foster

(1) advance; back; bring up; care for; cherish; encourage; favor; forward; help develop; maintain; promote the growth of; raise; rear; support

Word Used in Sentence(s)

(1) "William Smith founded Euclid Elements...His awareness of his own strengths and weaknesses led him to hire far more experienced managers and engineers... Their hiring, in turn, __fostered__ a culture at Euclid in which Smith does not hesitate to rely on those around him."

—Hann, Christopher. "The Masters," *Entrepreneur*, March 2012: pg. 58.

(1) "Volunteer activities can __foster__ enormous leadership skills. The non-professional volunteer world is a laboratory for self-realization."

—Mae West, American actress (1892–1980)

(1) "It is not my intention to do away with government. It is rather to make it work—work with us, not over us; stand by our side, not ride on our back. Government can and must provide opportunity, not smother it; __foster__ productivity, not stifle it."

—Ronald Reagan, 40th U.S. President (1911–2004)

(1) "Moreover, laudable and beguiling though professional standards and ethics may be, and however appealing professional status is, hanging the mantle 'professional' on business education __fosters__ inappropriate analysis and misguided prescriptions."

— Barker, Richard. "No, Management Is Not a Profession," *Harvard Business Review*, July–August 2012: pg. 54.

Fulfill

(1) accomplish; achieve expected desire; bear out; feel satisfied with accomplishment; justify; live out; realize ambition; satisfy

(2) carryout an order or request; bring to fruition; complete something started; execute; follow through; implement; make happen; obey; perform

Word Used in Sentence(s)

*(1) "Employment in the manufacturing sector contracted for the first time in three years...however production surged, but order backlogs fell, a sign that businesses are **fulfilling** old orders rather than receiving new ones."*

—Shah, Neil. "Slow Hiring, Spending Hit Factories," *Wall Street Journal*, December 4, 2012: pg. A2.

*(1) "We must make the choices that enable us to **fulfill** the deepest capacities of our real selves."*

—Thomas Merton, American and Trappist monk (1915–1968)

*(1) "Whenever I hear people talking about liberal ideas, I am always astounded that men should love to fool themselves with empty sounds. An idea should never be liberal; it must be vigorous, positive, and without loose ends so that it may **fulfill** its divine mission and be productive. The proper place for liberality is in the realm of the emotions."*

—Johann Wolfgang von Goethe, German playwright, poet, novelist, and dramatist (1749–1832)

*(1) Consumer products and services are purchased to **fulfill** certain basic human needs. Whether it is Maslow's hierarchy of needs or the more contemporary Lawrence and Nohria Four Drives that Underline Human Motivation, marketers have to discover the proper need and **fulfill** them or there will be no long-term customer relationship.*

Garner

(1) accumulate; acquire; amass; bring; collect; earn; gather; get; harvest; put away; reap; save; search out; store; to lay or place at rest

Word Used in Sentence(s)

(1) "Work and live to serve others, to leave the world a little better than you found it and __garner__ for yourself as much peace of mind as you can. This is happiness."

—David Sarnoff, Russian born American inventor (1891–1971)

(1) "__Garner__ up pleasant thoughts in your mind, for pleasant thoughts make pleasant lives."

—John Wilkins, English clergyman, natural philosopher, and author (1614–1672)

Galvanize

(1) activate; propel someone or something into sudden action; stimulate

Word Used in Sentence(s)

(1) "Fear has a lot of flavors and textures; there's a sharp, silver fear that runs like lightning through your arms and legs, __galvanizes__ you into action, power, motion."

—Jim Butcher, American author, *Grave Peril* (1971–)

Gambol

(1) caper; cavort; dance; frisk; prance; rollick; romp; run; skip or jump in a playful or joyous fashion

Word Used in Sentence(s)

(1) "We all have these places where shy humiliations __gambol__ on sunny afternoons."

—Unknown

Generate

(1) begat; breed; bring into being; cause; create; develop; engender; hatch; induce; make; produce; provoke; spawn; stir; touch off

Word Used in Sentence(s)

*(1) "Tasks outside the core should only be undertaken if they **generate** excess revenue that can support the core."*

—Romano, Richard. "Looking behind Community College Budgets for Future Policy Considerations," *Community College Review*, Volume 40, Issue 2, April 2012: pg. 165–189.

*(1) "Under the stewardship of Darwin Clark, Kimberly Clark **generated** cumulative stock returns 4.1 times the general market, beating its direct rival Scott Paper and Procter & Gamble and outperforming such venerable companies as Coca Cola, Hewlett-Packard, 3M, and General Electric."*

—Collins, Jim. *Good to Great*, NY: Harper Collins, 2001: pg.18.

Collocates to: ability, electricity, energy, ideas, income, interest, jobs, power, revenue

Get up to speed

(1) adapt and learn quickly

Word Used in Sentence(s)

*(1) "The stable project management teams we grew up with still work in many contexts...Situations that call for teaming are, by contrast, complex and uncertain, full of unexpected events that require rapid changes in course. No two teaming projects are alike, so people must **get up to speed** quickly on brand-need topics, again and again. Because solutions can come from anywhere, team members do, too."*

—Edmondson, Amy C. "Teamwork on the Fly," *Harvard Business Review*, April 2012: pg. 74.

Greenwash

(1) misrepresent one or an organization as being environmentally green

Word Used in Sentence(s)

*(1) "Things are so bad out there that the report's author, TerraChoice Environmental Marketing, had to add a seventh sin of **greenwashing** to the original six it developed for its first report, in 2007.'*

—Shapley, Dan. "Study: 98% of Products' Green Claims Are Misleading," *Goodhouskeeping.com*, April 16, 2009.

Gin up

(1) create; encourage; increase speed of an activity; produce something quicker; rev up or speed up an activity with a goal in mind

Word Used in Sentence(s)

*(1) Supply-side economics in theory should help in **ginning up** markets.*

Go down the line

(1) all in; all out; compete with dead earnest; do whatever is necessary; give or take no quarter; go balls out; go down swinging; go for broke; go for the fences; go for gold; go for all the marbles; go full bore; go great guns; go the distance; go the limit; go toe to toe; go to the wall; full steam; make the maximum effort; valiant try

Word Used in Sentence(s)

*(1) A manager's dream team would include members who would **go down the line**.*

Grapple

(1) clasp; come to grips with; fight; grab hold of someone; grip; struggle with someone or something; tackle; wrestle with

Word Used in Sentence(s)

*(1) "Tom Enders, CEO of EADS said, 'I have mixed feelings about innovation' as his company **grappled** with cracks inside the wings of the newest plane in the skies, the A380 superjumbo."*

—Michaels, Daniel. "Innovation Is Messy Business," *Wall Street Journal*, January 24, 2013: pg. B1.

Gravitate

(1) be inclined; move steadily toward; to have a natural inclination toward

Word Used in Sentence(s)

*(1) "Responsibilities **gravitate** to the man who can shoulder them and the power to him who knows how."*

—Elbert Hubbard, American editor, publisher, and writer (1856–1915)

*(1) "The excitement factor is a strong one with his top students, says Dr. Zurbuchen. The students tend to have an entrepreneurial spirit, he says, and **gravitate** toward the opportunities that may be risky in terms of job security, but give them the feeling that, 'hey, we're going to kick in some doors and have an impact,' he says."*

—Spotts, Pete. "SpaceX Launch: Private Industry Inspires New Generation of Rocketeers," *Christian Science Monitor*, May 22, 2011.

Impact

(1) fix firmly; forcefully; make contact, especially force tightly together; wedge

(2) affect

Word Used in Sentence(s)

*(1) "I like my job because it involves learning. I like being around smart people who are trying to figure out new things. I like the fact that if people really try they can figure out how to invent things that actually have an **impact**."*

—Bill Gates, American entrepreneur and founder of Microsoft Co. (1955–)

*(1) "A serious problem in America is the gap between academe and the mass media, which is our culture. Professors of humanities, with all their leftist fantasies, have little direct knowledge of American life and no **impact** whatever on public policy."*

—Camille Paglia, American author, teacher, and social critic (1947–)

Increase

(1) add to; amplify; augment; boost; enhance; enlarge; improve; multiply; raise; swell

(2) encourage; foster; fuel; intensify; redouble; strengthen

(3) escalate; expand; grow; mushroom; multiply; proliferate; rise; soar; spread; swell

Word Used in Sentence(s)

*(1) "Think of an investment portfolio; there are methods of managing risk and **increasing** efficiency, but you cannot get away from the fundamental fact that you need diversity for the overall portfolio to win."*

—Wang, Jennifer. "Radicals & Visionaries," *Entrepreneur*, March 2012: pg. 52.

*(1) "Difficulties **increase** the nearer we approach the goal."*

—Johann Wolfgang von Goethe, German playwright, poet, novelist, and dramatist (1749–1832)

Implement

(1) apply; carry out; enforce; execute; fulfill; instigate; put into action, effect, operation, service, or practice; realize

Word Used in Sentence(s)

*(1) Sometimes leaders are better at creating new ideas than **implementing** them.*

*(1) "It is not always what we know or analyze before we make a decision that makes it a great decision. It is what we do after we make the decision to **implement** and execute it that makes it a good decision."*

—William Pollard, American physicist and Episcopal priest (1911–1989)

*(1) "Palestinian President Mahmoud Abbas officially changed his government's name to the 'the State of Palestine' in an attempt to **implement**—even if only symbolically—a recent United Nations vote to granting it the status of non-observer state."*

—Mitnick, Joshua. "Palestinians Adopt Name to Show Off New 'State' Status," World News, *Wall Street Journal*, January 7, 2013: pg. A7.

Collocates to: changes, develop, measures, necessary, plan, policies, program, reform, strategies

Initiate

(1) begin; commence; create; inaugurate; induct; install; instate; instigate; introduce; invest; kick off; open; set off; start

(2) coach; instruct; mentor; teach; train; tutor

Word Used in Sentence(s)

> *(1) "Without change there is no innovation, creativity, or incentive for improvement. Those who **initiate** change will have a better opportunity to manage the change that is inevitable."*

—William Pollard, American physicist and Episcopal priest (1911–1989)

> *(1) "Advertising generally works to reinforce consumer trends rather than to **initiate** them."*

—Michael Schudson, American academic sociologist (1946–)

Collocates to: action, conversation, discussion, process, program, sex

Innerve

(1)   animate; call to action; invigorate; provoke; stimulate something; stir

Word Used in Sentence(s)

> *(1) A leader will **innerve** followers to accomplish amazing feats.*

Innovate

(1)   begin with something new; create; derive; devise; coin; commence; introduce something new; instigate; invent; make; modernize; originate; remodel; renew; renovate; revolutionize; transform; update

Word Used in Sentence(s)

> *(1) Because we were able to **innovate** the production process, our costs fell 20 places below our top competitors.*

> *(1) "To turn really interesting ideas and fledgling technologies into a company that can continue to **innovate** for years, it requires a lot of discipline."*

> *(1) "Sometimes when you **innovate**, you make mistakes. It is best to admit them quickly, and get on with improving your other innovations."*

—Steve Jobs, American entrepreneur, best known as the co-founder, chairman, and CEO of Apple Inc. (1955–2011)

Invest

(1) endow with a special quality; gift; infuse; initiate; spend resources

Word Used in Sentence(s)

(1) "__Investing__ in apprenticeships and other training programs means a more productive and engaged workforce and better aligns workers' motivations with the success of their employers."

—Forester de Rothschild, Lynn and Adam Posen. "How Capitalism Can Repair Its Bruised Image," *Wall Street Journal*, January 2, 2013: pg. A17.

(1) "Some firms are taking steps to expand the talent pool—for example, by __investing__ in apprenticeships and other training programs."

—Hancock, Bryan and Dianna Ellsworth. "Redesigning Knowledge Work," *Harvard Business Review*, January–February 2013: pg. 60.

(1) "If you __invest__ in improving your employees' view of your firm's corporate character, those positive attitudes will rub off and boost customers' opinions of the company. That will drive growth."

—Davis, Gary and Rosa Chun. "To Thine Own Staff Be Agreeable," *Harvard Business Review*, June 2007: pg. 30.

(1) "Professor Katz of Harvard said it would make sense to create a more progressive tax system when corporations and the top 1 percent are commanding more of the economic pie. He said those on top should agree to some redistribution and to __invest__ in the next generation."

—Greenhouse, Steve. "Our Economic Pickle," *New York Times*, January 13, 2013: pg. 5.

Invigorate

(1) animate; energize; enliven; galvanize; increase; liven; refresh; revitalize; strengthen; stimulate

Word Used in Sentence(s)

(1) "Four years ago we said we would __invigorate__ our economy by giving people greater freedom and incentives to take risks and letting them keep more of what they earned. We did what we promised, and a great industrial giant is reborn."

—Ronald Reagan, 40th U.S. President (1911–2004)

*(1) "In our drive to comprehend, we want very much a sense of the world around us and we are frustrated when things seem senseless, and we are **invigorated**, typically, by the challenge of working out answers."*

— Nohria, Nitin, Boris Groysberg, and Linda-Eling Lee. "Employee Motivation: A Powerful New Tool, Honing Your Competitive Edge," *Harvard Business Review*, July–August 2008: pg. 81.

Jettison

(1)   abandon; discard; throw away; toss aside

Word Used in Sentence(s)

*(1) "What seems to gall reformers most is the recent pattern of big companies using Chapter 11 of the bankruptcy code to **jettison** the debt of underfunded pension plans, then exit bankruptcy and survive."*

—Adams, Marilyn. "'Fundamentally broken' pension system in 'crying need' of a fix," *USA Today*, November 15, 2005.

Jump onboard

(1)   bustle; decide to join; energetically move on something; full of activity; hustle; join in enthusiastically; obey or decide quickly; rise suddenly or quickly

Word Used in Sentence(s)

*(1) "Aspiring entrepreneurs are increasingly **jumping onboard** with sites like Kickstarter, IndieGoGo, Peerbackers, and ChipIn."*

—Moran, Gwen, "Mob Money." *Entrepreneur*, March 2012: pg. 4.

*(1) Job seekers should give serious consideration to the move before **jumping onboard** startups if they have never been in that kind of business environment.*

Kick-start

(1)   advantage; get a jump; head start

Word Used in Sentence(s)

*(1) "Yes, investment flows have slowed in the green-tech sector, but the promise of new money in the stimulus package for solar, wind, electric cars, and smart grids engendered lively debates about which new technologies will help **kick-start** the economy and generate the most green-collar jobs."*

—Dumaine, Brian. "Getting the Economy Back on Track," *Fortune*, Volume 159, Issue 11, May 25, 2009: pg. 25.

<u>**Collocates to:**</u> economy, effort, fat, help metabolism

Kick the tires

(1) cursory check; do grassroots investigation on an investment; make a quick check or inspection of the fundamentals; superficial check

Word Used in Sentence(s)

*(1) Individual investors and fund managers both participate in **kicking the tires** before investing.*

Launch

(1) begin; commence; dispatch; embark; get underway; hurl; initial steps; introduce; launch; let loose something; release something; sendoff; shoot; start or kick off something

(2) inaugurate; introduce something; present; reveal; start marketing; unleash; unveil

Word Used in Sentence(s)

*(1) I plan to **launch** the new advertising plan during the Christmas season.*

*(1) "Many companies react to competitors' acquisition sprees reflexively, by **launching** bids of their own. Smart managers should consider other moves."*

—Keil, Thomas and Tomi Laamanen. "When Rivals Merge, Think Before You Follow Suit," *Harvard Business Review*, Idea Watch, December 2011: pg. 25.

*(1) "Yesterday, the Japanese government also **launched** an attack against Malaya.*

Last night, Japanese forces attacked Hong Kong.

Last night, Japanese forces attacked Guam.

Last night, Japanese forces attacked the Philippine Islands.

Last night, the Japanese attacked Wake Island.

And this morning, the Japanese attacked Midway Island."

—President Franklin Roosevelt, 32nd U.S. President, Pearl Harbor Address to the nation, Washington, D.C., December 8, 1941.

Lead

(1) captain; command; conduct; control; direct; direct the operations, activity, or performance; escort; go ahead; go in front; guide on a way especially by going in advance; head; manage; officer; pilot; show the way; to be first

Word Used in Sentence(s)

*(1) I will **lead** the task force looking into ways to cut costs.*

*(1) "A company at the forefront of this effort is Tyco. Instead of simply offering training to employees in emerging markets, Tyco has compliance personnel **lead** focus group-like sessions with its employees."*

—Currell, Dan and Tracy D. Bradley. "Greased Palms, Giant Headaches, Idea Watch," *Harvard Business Review*, September 2012: pg. 23.

*(1) "Many rising stars trip when they shift from **leading** a function to **leading** an enterprise and for the first time taking responsibility for P&L and oversight of executive decisions across corporate functions."*

—Watson, Michael. "How Managers Become Leaders," *Harvard Business Review*, June 2012: pg. 68.

*(1) "**Leading** is one of the four functions of management instilling enthusiasm by communicating with others, motivating them to work hard, and maintaining good interpersonal relations."*

—Schermerhorn, John, Richard Osborn, Mary UHL-Bien, and James Hunt. *Organizational Behavior*, 12th Ed. NY: John Wiley & Sons, Inc., 2012.

Liquidate

(1) convert assets into cash

(2) pay off debt; settle

(3) eliminate or kill the competition

Word Used in Sentence(s)

> *(1) "Hostess owners have decided to __liquidate__ rather than ride out a nationwide strike by one of the largest of its dozen unions, the Bakery, Confectionary, Tobacco Workers and Grain Millers International Union, the Texas-based company owned by the private-equity shop Ripplewood Holdings and other hedge funds essentially gave up."*

—WSJ Editors. *Wall Street Journal*, November 18, 2012: pg. A16.

> *(2) "Let me live onward; you shall find that, though slower, the progress of my character will __liquidate__ all these debts without injustice to higher claims. If a man should dedicate himself to the payment of notes, would not this be an injustice? Does he owe no debt but money? And are all claims on him to be postponed to a landlord's or a banker's?"*
> —Ralph Waldo Emerson, U.S. essayist, poet, and philosopher (1802–1883)

> *(1) "The death tax causes one-third of all family-owned small businesses to __liquidate__ after the death of the owner. It is also an unfair tax because the assets have already been taxed once at their income level."*
> —Ric Keller, American, member of U.S. House (1964–)

Manage

(1) administer; be in charge of; conduct or direct affairs; oversee; regulate; run; supervise

(2) do; fare; fend; get along; get by; make do; muddle through

(3) control the behavior of; handle; succeed in dealing with

(4) succeed despite difficulties

Word Used in Sentence(s)

> *(1) __Managing__ is a skill that involves allocating limited resources to accomplish specific objectives.*

*(1) "It's self-evident that an entrepreneur's ability to hire talented people is vital to a company's success. But how the entrepreneur **manages** those people helps define the company culture."*

—Hann, Christopher. "The Masters," *Entrepreneur*, March 2012: pg. 58.

*(1) "Business executives don't **manage** information as well as they manage talent, capital, and brand."*

—Shah, Shvetank, Andrew Horne, and Jamie Capella. "Good Data Won't Guarantee Good Decisions," *Harvard Business Review*, April 2012: pg. 24.

*(1) To effectively **manage**, it is generally recognized one should be skilled in four functions—planning, organizing, leading, and controlling.*

*(1) There are three types of skills necessary to **manage** skillfully— technical, human, and conceptual.*

Collocates to: ability, able, affairs, difficulty, effectively, how, resources, somehow, stress

Maneuver

(1) carefully manipulate in order to achieve an end; finagle; jockey; manipulate; navigate; pilot; specific tactic; steer

Word Used in Sentence(s)

*(1) "What makes the issue so difficult is trying to **maneuver** around controversial past U.S. actions at Guantanamo—harsh interrogations and alleged torture, bypassing the Geneva Conventions, use of coerced statements to justify further detention, military commissions with stripped-down due process protections."*

—Warren, Richey. "Sorting Out Guantanamo Detainees," *Christian Science Monitor,* January 22, 2009: pg. 1.

Market

(1) advertise; offer to sell; promote

Marshal

(1) arrange; assemble; gather all resources to achieve a goal; mobilize; organize

(2) put in delineated order

Word Used in Sentence(s)

*(1) Senator Smith **marshaled** his staff in preparation for his reelection bid.*

*(1) "Of Ernest Hemingway, for example, I feel that he was unable to **marshal** any adequate defense against the powerful events of his childhood, and this despite his famous toughness and the courage he could call upon in war, in hunting, in all the dangerous enterprises that seduced him."*

—Dianna Trilling, American literary critic and author (1905–1996)

Maximize

(1)   make as great or as large as possible; make best use of; raise to the highest possible degree

Word Used in Sentence(s)

*(1) "We must expect to fail...but fail in a learning posture, determined not to repeat the mistakes, and to **maximize** the benefits from what is learned in the process."*

—Ted W. Engstrom, American evangelical leader and author (1919–2006)

*"Superior business performance requires striking a healthy balance between customer value and cost structure. The goal is neither to **maximize** customer benefit—which would entail giving away your product—nor to minimize costs in isolation but rather to optimize the relationship between the two. Marketing and finance both have important insights to offer, so the goal is to manage the tension between them, not to eliminate it."*

—Reprint F0706D, *Harvard Business Review*, June 2007: pg. 24.

Measure

(1)   appraise; assess; calculate; compute; determine; evaluate; gauge; mete; rate; quantify

Word Used in Sentence(s)

> *(1) "Managing a nonprofit and working with people is a totally different __measure__ of success."*

—Stark Healy, Wendy. "Ten Years Later, the Wounds Remain Open," *USA Today*, September 2011.

> *(1) "Just how do constituents __measure__ a characteristic as subjective as honesty, though? In our discussions with survey respondents, we learned that the leader's behavior provided the evidence. In other words, regardless of what the leaders say about their own integrity, people wait to be shown—they observe behavior."*

—Kouzes, James and Barry Posner. *The Leadership Challenge.* San Francisco, CA: Jossey-Bass Publisher, 1999.

Collocates to: ballot, design, distance, items, pass, performance, progress, scale, success, tape

Mentor

(1)   provide advice or guidance; give assistance in career or business matters

Word Used in Sentence(s)

> *(1) There is one positive thing about growing older, and that is younger people are looking for someone your age to __mentor__ them.*

> *(1) __Mentoring__ someone is one of the most rewarding experiences one can have.*

Collocates to: assigned, became, coach, facility, former, friend, long time, mentee, relationship, served, spiritual, student, teacher, role

Open the kimono

(1)   to expose or reveal secrets or proprietary information

Word Used in Sentence(s)

> *(1) "Look, I will let you invest a million dollars in Apple if you will sort of __open the kimono__ at Xerox PARC."*

—Steve Jobs, American entrepreneur and best known as the co-founder, chairman, and CEO of Apple Inc. (1955–2011)

Oversee

(1)   administer; direct; keep an eye on; manage; mastermind; run; supervise; watch over

Word Used in Sentence(s)

*(1) "Harald's first challenge as head of the plastics resins unit was shifting from leading a single function to **overseeing** the full set of business functions."*

—Watson, Michael. "How Managers Become Leaders,"" *Harvard Business Review*, June 2012: pg. 68.

Partner

(1)   ally; common cause; confederate; join; team; work or perform together

Word Used in Sentence(s)

*(1) "Courage makes change possible...Verizon's leaders saw growth limits in traditional telecom, so they invested billions in fiber optics to speed up landlines and **partnered** with Google to deploy Android smartphones, requiring substantial changes in the firm's practices."*

—Kanter, Rosabeth. "Courage in the C-Suite," *Harvard Business Review*, December 2011: pg. 38.

Collocates to: business, firm, former, law, longtime, managing, partner, senior, sexual, trading

Persist

(1)   endure; prevail; refuse to give up or quit; remain; take and maintain a stand

Word Used in Sentence(s)

*(1) "That which we **persist** in doing becomes easier for us to do; not that the nature of the thing itself is changed, but that our power to do is increased."*

—Ralph Waldo Emerson, American poet, lecturer, and essayist (1803–1882)

*"The U.S. Department of Education said last year it will require states to use a common graduation rate formula that compares the number of students who enter schools as freshmen with the number who graduate four years later. But because that formula also factors out transfers, Georgia's problems are likely to **persist** if schools and the state don't clean up their data."*

—Vogell, Heather. "Student Rolls Don't Add Up," *Atlanta Journal Constitution*, June 7, 2009: pg. 1A.

Collocates to: allowed, despite, differences, likely, longer, problems, questions, rumors, symptoms

Plan

(1) arrange; design; have in mind a project or purpose; intend; prepare; purpose; set up

(2) arrangement of strategic ideas in diagrams, charts, sketches, graphs, tables, maps, and other documents

Word Used in Sentence(s)

*(1) The ability to **plan** and execute the **plan** is a sought after management skill.*

*(1) Having **planned** the sales meeting and organized all the activities demonstrates superb organization skills.*

*(1) "**Planning** will help you think in terms of laying down a foundation of the particular experiences you need to create a resume to move you into senior management."*

—Wellington, Sheila. *Be Your Own Mentor*, NY: Random House, 2001: pg. 33.

*(1) "One of the four functions of management is **planning**—setting specific performance objectives, and identifying the actions needed to achieve them."*

—Schermerhorn, John, Richard Osborn, Mary UHL-Bien, and James Hunt. *Organizational Behavior*, 12th Ed. NY: John Wiley & Sons, Inc., 2012.

*(1) "In order to **plan** your future wisely, it is necessary that you understand and appreciate your past."*

—Jo Coudert, American author (1923–)

Produce

(1)   accomplish; achieve; finish a task

(2)   bring forth; produce; yield

Word Used in Sentence(s)

*(1) "One obvious difference between coaches in business and licensed therapists is that coaches have to **produce** results. Managers who don't **produce** positive performance results will be out of a job in short order."*

—Nigro, Nicholas. *The Everything Coaching and Mentoring Book*, Avon, MA: Adams Media, 2008.

*(1) "My research also indicates that the process that **produces** great leaders are similar or perhaps even identical to those that **produce** awful ones, and this is true in domains ranging from politics to business to science. Unfiltered leaders can be domain experts—such expertise is rarely company specific. What they are not is evaluated by their new organizations, so, whatever their expertise, it is difficult to what they will do in power and impossible to be sure that one is the right person for the job."*

—Kader, Abdul, Regional Health and Wellness Director (NC) Walmart, U.S. "The Best Leaders Have Sort Resumes," *Harvard Business Review*, December 2012: pg. 18.

*(1) Creating and **producing** product-driven line extensions will add ten percent new revenue.*

Prototype

(1)   create models and replicas of what is to be produced

Word Used in Sentence(s)

*(1) "...**prototyping** not only speeds up the design of solutions but helps solicit valuable input and get buy-in from diverse constituents."*

—Vossoghi, Shorab. "Is the Social Sector Thinking Small Enough?" *Harvard Business Review*, December 2011: pg. 40.

Publicize

(1)   announce widely; give or draw public attention to; make public

Word Used in Sentence(s)

*(1) They will **publicize** the town hall meeting a month in advance.*

Pull the trigger

(1)   going ahead after thinking and planning; make the final decision to act or do something; no going back

Word Used in Sentence(s)

*(1) The board brought in Hank to make the tough decisions, so he is going to have to **pull the trigger** on this acquisition or his reputation is tarnished.*

Reinforce

(1)   confirm; expand; give added strength

(2)   increase the number or amount of

(3)   add or make stronger by construction techniques

Word Used in Sentence(s)

*(1) "After brainstorming and formalizing our instincts, we commissioned a consulting firm to provide us with competitor benchmarketing. Our instincts confirmed, we clearly saw the way forward; we would **reinforce** our Burberry heritage, our Britishness, by emphasizing and growing our core luxury products, innovating them and keeping them at the heart of everything we do."*

—Ahrendts, Angele. "Turning an Aging British Icon into a Global Luxury Brand: How I Did it," *Harvard Business Review*, January–February 2013: pg. 41.

Reintegrate

(1)   make whole again; reestablish; renew

Word Used in Sentence(s)

*(1) "If you don't want to have to kill or capture every bad guy in the country, you have to **reintegrate** those who are willing to be reconciled and become part of the solution instead of a continued part of the problem."*

—David Petraeus, retired American military officer and public official (1952–)

Schedule

(1) make arrangements or a plan for carrying out something

(2) plan events and activities for certain times

Word Used in Sentence(s)

*(1) "The key is not to prioritize what's on your schedule, but to **schedule** your priorities."*

—Steven Covey, American educator, author, and businessman (1932–2012)

Collocates to: ahead, behind, busy, daily, full, games, hectic, interview, regular, strength

Shape

(1) build; design; hone; model; plan

(2) arrange; devise; fashion; shape

(3) adapt; adjust; become suited; conform

Word Used in Sentence(s)

*(1) "We know, however, that leaders with no patience for history are missing a vital truth: A sophisticated understanding of the past is one of the most powerful tools we have for **shaping** the future."*

—Seaman, John T. and George David Smith. "Your Company's History as a Leadership Tool," *Harvard Business Review*, December 2012: pg. 46.

Solve

(1)   find a solution; provide or find a suitable answer to a problem; settle an
      issue

Word Used in Sentence(s)

*(1) "As she was (very bad handwriting apart) a more than indifferent
speller, and as Joe was a more than indifferent reader, extraordinary
complications arose between them, which I was always called in to
__solve__."*

—Charles Dickens, author of *Great Expectations* (1812–1870)

Spearhead

(1)   be in front of something; leader; point; take the lead

Word Used in Sentence(s)

(1) She __spearheaded__ the company-sponsored civic fund drive.

*(1) A leader will step forward and __spearhead__ the writing of the com-
pany's strategic mission statement.*

*(1) In the commercial real estate business, brokers __spearhead__ major
accounts. But they wouldn't have customers without the people who
oversee construction.*

Standardize

(1)   even out; homogenize; normalize; order; regiment; regulate; remove
      variations; stereotype; systematize

Word Used in Sentence(s)

*(1) "The framers of the constitution knew human nature as well as we
do. They too had lived in dangerous days; they too knew the suffocating
influence of orthodoxy and __standardized__ thought. They weighed the com-
pulsions for restrained speech and thought against the abuses of liberty.
They chose liberty."*

—William Orville Douglas, American, Associate Justice of the Supreme
Court of the United States (1898–1980)

*(1) "Thousands of manufacturing companies have achieved tremendous improvements in quality and efficiency by copying the Toyota Production System, which combines rigorous work **standardization** with approaches such as just-in-time delivery of components and the use of visual controls to highlight deviations."*

—Hall, Joseph and M. Eric Johnson. "When Should A Process Be An Art and Not A Science?" *Harvard Business Review*, March 2009: pg. 60.

Collocates to: across, data, efforts, equipment, order, procedures

Take Risks

(1) put oneself in danger or in hazard; take or run the chance of; venture upon

Word Used in Sentence(s)

*(1) A leader **takes risks** as part of his or her character.*

Take up the cudgel for

(1) defend something or someone strongly

Word Used in Sentence(s)

*(1) "In countries like France, where the peasants constitute far more than half of the population, it was natural that writers who sided with the proletariat against the bourgeoisie, should use, in their criticism of the bourgeois regime, the standard of the peasant and petty bourgeois, and from the standpoint of these intermediate classes should take up the **cudgels** for the working class."*

—Marx, Karl and Engles, Frederick. *The Communist Manifesto*, Communist League pamphlet, 1848.

Target

(1) aim; focus; reduce effort or cost to achieve objective
(2) establish as a target or goal

Word Used in Sentence(s)

*(1) **Targeting** new markets for existing products creates more profitable sales opportunities.*

*(2) "Scientists and the National Aeronautics and Space Administration's Jet Propulsion Laboratory in California said Tuesday that they have **targeted** a fine grained fractured slab of bedrock for the Mars Rover's first drilling attempt."*

—Lee Hotz, Robert. "Mars Rover Ready to Dig In," *Wall Street Journal*, January 16, 2013: pg. B4.

Team build

(1)   to create cooperative group dynamics

Word Used in Sentence(s)

*(1) "Although it is tempting to view the process of **team building** as something outside consultants or paid experts are hired to do, the fact is that it can and should be part of any team leader and manager's skill set."*

—Schermerhorn, John, Richard Osborn, Mary UHL-Bien, and James Hunt. *Organizational Behavior*, 12th Ed., NY: John Willey & Sons, Inc., 2012: pg. 172.

*(1) Our success was **team built**.*

*(1) It took four years and some personnel changes before we could say we were successful in **team building**.*

Teaming

(1)   gather and use experts in temporary work groups to solve problems that may only be encountered once; use of team work on the fly

Word Used in Sentence(s)

*(1) "The stable project management teams we grew up with still work beautifully in many contexts...Situations that call for **teaming** are, by contrast, complex and uncertain, full of unexpected events that require rapid changes in course. No two **teaming** projects are alike, so people must get up to speed quickly on brand-need topics, again and again. Because solutions can come from anywhere, team members do, too."*

*(1) "The concept of **teaming** helps individuals acquire knowledge, skills, and networks. And it lets companies accelerate the delivery of current products or services while responding to new opportunities. **Teaming** is a way to get work done while figuring how to do it better; it's executing and learning at the same time."*

—Edmondson, Amy C. "Teamwork on the Fly," *Harvard Business Review*, April 2012: pg. 74.

Undertake

(1)   assume duties, roles, or responsibilities; begin something; take on

(2)   guarantee; promise; to give a pledge

Word Used in Sentence(s)

*(1) Career development is not something someone should **undertake** just because he suddenly becomes unhappy in his position or loses his job.*

*(1) He always volunteered to **undertake** the most difficult tasks on the team.*

*(1) **Undertaking** difficult tasks demonstrates a willingness to take risks— a leadership trait.*

Unfetter

(1)   free from fetter or restraint; liberate

Word Used in Sentence(s)

*(1) "With just a few clicks on the management console, IT administrators can apply policies, applications, and settings to different sets of users. For example, schools may want to pre-install or block applications, extensions, or URLs for different grade levels of students and **unfetter** access for teachers."*

—CDW. "Google Partnership Turns a New Page for Enterprise Chromebook Solutions," *The Free Library*, February 5, 2013.

Wangle

(1)   get, make, or bring about by persuasion or adroit manipulation

(2)   wriggle

Word Used in Sentence(s)

*(1) The object of most prayers is to **wangle** an advance on good intentions.*

—Robert Brault, American operatic tenor (1963–)

Weigh in

(1)   argument; discussion; join in a cause; take part

Word Used in Sentence(s)

*(1) A true believer will **weigh in** and defend their beliefs against any opponent in any forum at any time.*

4

100 Top Action Verbs for Challenging Situations and Difficult Moments, Calumny, Comebacks, or When You Just Want to Get in the Last Word

Abase

(1) belittle; cause to feel shame; degrade; demean; humble; humiliate; lose esteem or self-worth; subjugate

(2) lower in grade or rank or prestige

Word Used in Sentence(s)

*(1) "Islam, too, favors self-effacement. 'Whoever humbles himself for the sake of Allah,' Mohammed teaches, 'Allah will exalt him and enhance his honor and dignity.' Christianity is the supreme champion of humility. St. Bernard defined it as 'a virtue by which, knowing ourselves as we truly are, we **abase** ourselves.' Thomas Aquinas adds: 'The virtue of humility consists in keeping oneself within one's own bounds, not reaching out to things above one, but submitting to one's superior.'"*

—Farrell, Michael J. "Humility: What's in It for Me?," *U.S. Catholic*, Volume 72, Issue 9, September 2007.

<u>**Collocates to:**</u> biofuels, himself, ourselves, themselves, worth

Abash

(1) chagrin; daunt; deflate; disconcert; embarrass; faze; humble; humiliate; make ill at ease or ashamed; mortify; rattle; shame

Word Used in Sentence(s)

*(1) Most people are **abashed** at their first attempt of public speaking.*

*(1) "**Abash'd** the Devil stood, And felt how awful goodness is, and saw Virtue in her shape how lovely."*

—John Milton, English poet, historian, and scholar (1608–1674)

Abhor

(1) be repulsed by; be revolted by; despise; detest; dislike; hate; loathe; shrink from; view with horror

Word Used in Sentence(s)

*(1) American patriots **abhor** the thought that elected representatives of our government would suggest or infer that there should be legislation to alter the first and second amendments.*

*(1) We **abhor** the thought of selling our 200-year-old family business.*

*(1) "'Could you please not scream at the officials?' my daughter would plead. My son, braver, shouted back at me from the basketball court: 'I am hustling! Leave me alone!' I couldn't. I just couldn't. They were the ones playing, but I was the one caring. I've read the same news stories you have, about the T-ball coach who paid a player to bean a subpar teammate, the parents who have done even worse. I clucked my tongue along with you. I **abhor** the emphasis America places on winning. I know what matters isn't the score but how you play the game. And yet... There's a fire that flares up in me when opponents square off. It doesn't matter what they're playing, or at what level-competition makes me come alive. ('My wife will watch any sport with me on television,' my husband once told an envious colleague. 'Even soccer.') I don't know how I got this way."*

—Hingston, Sandy. "Confessions of an Ugly Sports Mom," *Prevention*, Volume 59, Issue 11, November 2007: pg. 75.

Abstain

(1) deny; desist; do without; give up; go without; refrain; refuse to partake; sit on the fence; withdraw; withhold

Word Used in Sentence(s)

*(1) "As a general rule, I **abstain** from reading reports of attacks upon myself, wishing not to be provoked by that to which I cannot properly offer an answer."*

—Abraham Lincoln, 16th U.S. President (1609–1865)

*(1) "The people are the best guardians of their own rights and it is the duty of their executive to **abstain** from interfering in or thwarting the sacred exercise of the lawmaking functions of their government."*

—William Henry Harrison, 9th U.S. President (1773–1841)

*(1) "The companies that tried to keep pace by launching mergers of their own not only failed to usurp the leader Ericsson but also found themselves under assault by the only player that **abstained** from the M&A frenzy: the Chinese company Huawei."*

—Keil, Thomas and Tomi Laamanen. "When Rivals Merge, Think Before You Follow Suit," *Harvard Business Review*, December 2011: pg. 25.

Collocates to: alcohol, food, intentions, marriage, relations, sex, vote

Accost

(1) approach and speak to someone aggressively

(2) solicit for sex

(3) buttonhole; greet; hail; salute

Word Used in Sentence(s)

*(1) "Byrnes went 2-for-3 and drove in the winning run against USC later in the day, and the L.A. Times' headline read, 'Byrnes KOs intruder, then SC.' Byrnes spent this past winter in the Dominican Republic. He was immensely popular, earning the nickname 'Captain America,' and he was named MVP of the league after hitting .345 with 11 homers and 37 RBIs. But he also saw the lawless side of the island, where angry fans sometimes **accost** players in the dugout."*

—Slusser, Susan. "Byrnes Burns for Big-League Job: A's Are Giving Outfielder His Shot This Season," *San Francisco Chronicle*, March 17, 2002: pg. B9.

Acerbate

(1)   annoy or vex; irritate; make something taste bitter

Word Used in Sentence(s)

*(1) Alex knew how passionate and agitated the crowd was, so rather than **acerbate** them further, he tempered his remarks.*

*(1) His child-like actions **acerbate** his fellow classmates and make it hard to carry on a meaningful conversation.*

Admonish

(1)   caution; chide; give a warning; rebuke; reprimand; reprove; scold gently; tell off; warn

Word Used in Sentence(s)

*(1) Many people do not believe it is the federal government's role to **admonish** citizens for acts of personal behavior affecting no other person.*

Collocates to: correct, judge, jury, senator, sternly, them, wake

Adulterate

(1)   contaminate; make impure

Word Used in Sentence(s)

*(1) " 'Some importers are **adulterating** tequila, and they're doing great damage to our image,' said Jose Luis Gonzalez, president of the Tequila Regulatory Council, which governs the industry. The vast majority of imported mixto is by established companies like Cuervo and Sauza, and we have no doubt that their product is genuine. But some of the others **adulterate** it and even use silly, offensive brand names that make Mexico look ridiculous."*

—Collier, Robert, Chronicle Staff Writer, "Tequila Temptation," *San Francisco Chronicle*, November 19, 1997: pg. 1/Z1.

*(1) "The test of friendship is assistance in adversity, and that too, uncon-
ditional assistance. Co-operation which needs consideration is a commercial contract and not friendship. Conditional co-operation is like
adulterated cement which does not bind."*

—Mohandas Gandhi, Indian, preeminent leader of Indian nationalism in
British-ruled India (1869–1948)

Adumbrate

(1) foreshadow; give a general description of something but not the details;
prefigure; obscure; overshadow; predict; presage; summary

Word Used in Sentence(s)

*(1) The global political troubles **adumbrated** an eventual world—wide
economic recession.*

*(1) It is never good for a manager to **adumbrate** news of a partial layoff
to just a few employees.*

Affect

(1) change; concern; have an effect on; impact; impinge on; impress; influence; move; shape; strike; sway; touch

(2) distress; disturb; move; touch; upset

(3) assume; fake; imitate; pretend or have; put on

Word Used in Sentence(s)

*(1) How various countries attract or discourage import and export oper-
ations **affects** the way American firms structure their global operations.*

*(1) "Being fit matters...New research suggests that a few extra pounds or
a slightly larger waistline **affects** an executive's perceived leadership
ability as well as stamina on the job."*

—Kwoh, Leslie. "Marketing," *Wall Street Journal*, January 16, 2013:
pg. B1.

Collocates to: adversely, does, factor, how, negatively, performance, positive

Allege

(1) assert without proof; claim; cite as an authority; excuse; offer as a plea

Word Used in Sentence(s)

*(1) Given the ubiquity of social media, sometimes all it takes to ruin someone's reputation is for a person to **allege** a heinous act to have occurred.*

*(1) "'We need a healthy dose of real competition,' says John Anderson, president of the Electricity Consumers Resource Council. 'We were deregulation's first supporters. But all we've really done is go from one regulatory structure to a new one that is less customer-friendly.' He and other critics also **allege** that a key negative feature in each market is 'market power'—an oligopoly situation that may be allowing generating companies to whipsaw prices upward."*

—Clayton, Mark. "In Deregulation of Electric Markets, a Consumer Pinch," *Christian Science Monitor*, April 25, 2006.

Collocates to: authorities, courts, critics, defendants, documents, officials, lawsuits, plaintiffs, police, prosecutors

Arrogate

(1)   ascribe; assume; claim as own; take power that is not yours

Word Used in Sentence(s)

*(1) I won't **arrogate** to teach you about life.*

*(1) He is the type of man who will **arrogate**, assume, and ascribe such powers to himself.*

Back down

(1)   back off; bow out; give up; pull out; retreat from a position; surrender

Word Used in Sentence(s)

*(1) "Don't **back down** just to keep the peace. Standing up for your beliefs builds self-confidence and self-esteem."*

—Oprah Winfrey, American television personality, actress, and producer (1954–)

*(1) "You are a coward when you even seem to have **backed down** from a thing you openly set out to do."*

—Mark Twain, American humorist, writer, and lecturer (1835–1910)

*(1) "Officials tend to **back down** when the people get their backs up."*

—Unknown

Back out

(1) abandon; ; back off; back pedalbail out; cancel or renege on an arrangement; leave; pull back; retreat

Word Used in Sentence(s)

*(1) "When in doubt, **back out** on a technicality."*

—Walter Shapiro, American columnist

Bafflegab

(1) double-talk; gibberish talk; speak in an ambiguous or incomprehensible way; song and dance; speak tap dance around a straight answer; speak gobbledygook; use puffery

Word Used in Sentence(s)

*(1) The Play, "Death of a Salesman" could have easily been subtitled "the end of one man's **bafflegab**."*

Belie

(1) disprove; to give false impression or to contradict

Word Used in Sentence(s)

*(1) The small, unassuming building **belied** the global Internet business that was taking place inside.*

*(1) "Man is a creature of hope and invention, both of which **belie** the idea that things cannot be changed."*

—Tom Clancy, American novelist (1947–)

*(1) "Our very hopes **belied** our fears, our fears our hopes **belied**, we thought her dying when she slept, and sleeping when she died!"*

—Thomas Hood, English poet and humorist (1799–1845)

Collocates to: fact, image, notion, numbers, seem, words

Beset

(1)   attack; be snowed under; beleaguer; besiege; harass; inundate; overrun; overwhelm; plague; surround

Word Used in Sentence(s)

*(1) In spite of the toughest gun laws in the U.S., Chicago is **beset** by more gun violence than any other American city.*

Collocates to: by, delays, economy, financial, injuries, internal, problems, troubles

Besmirch

(1)   attack someone; blacken; cast aspersions on; charge falsely or with malicious intent; damage; defame; slander; sully; taint; tarnish

Word Used in Sentence(s)

*(1) Since being fired, he has been busy **besmirching** his former boss.*

*(1) Because of the ubiquity of social media, it is much easier to **besmirch** someone and not be held accountable.*

*(1) He **besmirched** her reputation with lies and untruths.*

*(1) "Men are nicotine-soaked, beer-**besmirched**, whiskey-greased, red-eyed devils."*

—Carrie Nation, American temperance activist (1848–1911)

Collocates to: anything, man, name, otherwise, reputation, would

Blandish

(1)   coax; cajole; induce or persuade by gentle flattery; influence

Word Used in Sentence(s)

*(1) A leader most likely would not attempt to **blandish** a follower into accepting his point of view but rather resort to the use of influence.*

Bowdlerize

(1) censor; edit; expurgate; remove obscenity or other inappropriate content

Word Used in Sentence(s)

*(1) "John Nance Garner, FDR's first vice president, famously said 'the job of second-in-command wasn't worth a warm bucket of spit.' Well, that's not exactly what Garner said, but in an era before hot microphones, newspapermen were kind enough to **bowdlerize** it for him."*

—Mark Hemingway, American writer for *The Washington Examiner*

Bullyrag

(1) dominate; force into agreement or compliance; intimidate

Word Used in Sentence(s)

*(1) This was the kind of neighborhood in which it was standard practice for young teens to be **bullyragged** into joining a street gang.*

Cadge

(1) ask; beg; get away with; rob; sneak; sponge by imposing on another's good nature; steal; take

Word Used in Sentence(s)

*(1) If people were not in such a good mood during the Christmas season, **cadging** by many charities would not be so successful.*

Collocates to: drinks, food, free, from, lift, try

Calumniate

(1) utter maliciously false statements, charges, or imputations; slander; traduce

Word Used in Sentence(s)

(1) "I am not to order the natural sympathies of my own breast, and of every honest breast to wait until the tales and all the anecdotes of the coffeehouses of Paris and of the dissenting meeting houses of London are

*scoured of all the slander of those who **calumniate** persons, that after-*
wards they may murder them with impunity. I know nothing of your Story
of Messalina. What, are not high rank, great splendour of descent, great
personal elegance and outward accomplishments ingredients of moment
in forming the interest we take in the misfortunes of men?"

—Bromwich, David. "The Context of Burke's Reflections," *Social
Research*, Volume 58, Issue 2, Summer 1991: pg. 313–354.

<u>**Collocates to:**</u> afterwards, person, slander, that, those, who

Capitulate

(1)   acquiesce; cede; give in; give up; give way; relent; submit; surrender;
yield

Word Used in Sentence(s)

*(1) When the company brought in nonunion workers, the union **capitu-
lated** and went back to work without a new contract.*

*(1) The union bargaining team was forced to **capitulate** on the pension
issue.*

*(1) "I will be conquered; I will not **capitulate**."*

—Samuel Johnson, English poet, critic, and writer (1709–1784)

*(1) Today, successful selling should produce a win-win outcome, not one
in which the buyer feels like she had to **capitulate**.*

Card stack

(1)   load an argument with evidence for one side while suppressing evidence
to the contrary

Word Used in Sentence(s)

*(1) **Card stacking** can be a tool of advocacy groups or of those groups
with specific agendas to manipulate perception of an issue by emphasizing the groups' beliefs over the opposition, over fact-based information,
even over reality.*

Cast back

(1)   drag or hold back; go back, search back, or refer back; impede

Word Used in Sentence(s)

*(1) He **cast back** to his Scottish heritage for themes in his poetry.*

Castigate

(1)   call down; chastise; criticize; punish; reprimand severely

Word Used in Sentence(s)

*(1) The consumer advocacy group **castigated** the online firm for not protecting the privacy of the customer database.*

*(1) Sometimes the political left will **castigate** the fundamentals of the free market concept.*

*(1) "You are quick to **castigate** those who dare to heap verbal or visual abuse upon liberals and the socialistic programs* The Chronicle*'s editorial policies endorse, but fail to acknowledge the one-sided news reporting and total unfairness in maligning 3.4 million NRA members, 60 to 100 million American gun owners, and most members of Congress, as something less than loyal Americans and patriotic citizens."*

—Letters to the editor, *San Francisco Chronicle*, May 17, 1995.

Collocates to: critics, female, find, publically, quick, those, unemployed

Caterwaul

(1)   brawl; make a loud wailing noise; protest or complain nosily; quarrel noisily

Word Used in Sentence(s)

*(1) In many cultures, people **caterwaul** to demonstrate their unhappiness with government policies.*

*(1) The attendees at the music festival **caterwauled** for hours when the main attraction cancelled.*

Cavil

(1)   raise petty and irritating objections; trivial and frivolous objection; quibble

Word Used in Sentence(s)

*(1) The lawyers never **caviled** throughout the entire proceedings.*

*(1) "Bluster, sputter, question, **cavil**; but be sure your argument be intricate enough to confound the court."*

—William Wycherley, English dramatist of the Restoration Period (1640–1715)

Challenge

(1)   brave; call something into question; confront; dare; defy; face up to; invite to compete; stimulate intellect; take exception to; test; throw down the gauntlet

Word Used in Sentence(s)

*(1) "Support and **challenge** clients to examine life-work roles, including the balance of work, leisure, family, and community in their careers."*

—National Career Development Association Career Counseling Competencies "Minimum Competencies, Individual and Group Counseling Skills," (Revised Version, http://ncda.org/aws/NCDA/pt/sd/news_article/37798/_self/layout_ccmsearch/true, December 14, 2012.)

*(1) Anyone serving as a manager or team leader faces a **challenging** and complicated job that just gets more complex and difficult as time goes on.*

*(1) "Accept the **challenges** so that you may feel the exhilaration of victory."*

—General George Patton, American General World Wars I and II (1885–1945)

*(1) "The greatest **challenge** to any thinker is stating the problem in a way that will allow a solution."*

—Bertrand Russell, English logician and philosopher (1872–1970)

Coax

(1)   cajole; charm; entice; inveigle; lure; persuade somebody gently; sweet
talk; tempt; urge gently; wheedle; win over

Word Used in Sentence(s)

*(1) "A few progressive companies have been able to **coax** better performance from their teams by treating their sales force like a portfolio of
investments that require different levels and kinds of attention."*

—Steenburgh, Thomas and Michael Ahearne. "Motivating Salespeople:
What Really Works," *Harvard Business Review*, July–August 2012:
pg. 71.

*(1) "Happiness is like a cat. If you try to **coax** it or call it, it will avoid
you. It will never come. But if you pay no attention to it and go about
your business, you'll find it rubbing up against your legs and jumping
into your lap."*

—William Bennett. American author and politician (1943–)

Coerce

(1)   bully; compel; dominate; drive; force; intimidate; persuade; pressurize

Word Used in Sentence(s)

*(1) In the eyes of the anti-war movement of the 1960s, the military draft
coerced men against their will to serve in the military.*

*(1) "A woman simply is, but a man must become. Masculinity is risky
and elusive. It is achieved by a revolt from woman, and it is confirmed
only by other men. Manhood **coerced** into sensitivity is no manhood at
all."*

—Camille Paglia, American author, teacher, and social critic (1947–)

Comprise

(1)   compose; comprehend; consist of; constitute; include; make up

Word Used in Sentence(s)

> *(1) "Self-professed conservatives __comprise__ about 40 percent to 45 percent of the electorate."*

—Paul Weyrich, American conservative political activist and commentator (1942–2008)

> *(1) "Remember, that of all the elements that __comprise__ a human being, the most important, the most essential, the one that will sustain, transcend, overcome, and vanquish obstacles is—Spirit!"*

—Buddy Ebsen, American character actor and dancer (1908–2003)

Confiscate

(1) forfeit; impound; seize; take

Word Used in Sentence(s)

> *(1) Many second amendment advocates believe that periodic legislative attempts at gun control are nothing more than thinly veiled attempts to __confiscate__ private weapons.*

Conflagrate

(1) enflame; enkindle; ignite; kindle; start to burn

Word Used in Sentence(s)

> *(1) "In fact, she was the one who got him the job with Janus. And he's the one who's supposed to investigate this. Dammit. By the time Rebecca arrived at the refinery, the automatic fire-suppression systems had dealt with the resultant __conflagration__—which barely had a chance to __conflagrate__. The different section chiefs started reporting in that their sections were okay, with the obvious exception of Yinnik regarding the refinery. One of T'Lis's assistants said the computer core was fine."*

—DeCandido, Keith R. A. *A Singular Destiny*, NY: Pocket Books Edition: 1st Pocket Books paperback ed., 2009.

Confute

(1) prove to be false; refute

(2) make useless

Word Used in Sentence(s)

(1) "Certain terms referring to emotion do not translate across cultures. 'They have a word for it that we lack.' Or, 'they' use a word that seems to mean something like our word, but just don't apply it in the same way. English lacks a clear translation for the Malaysian term marah—*a word that to English speakers seems to **confute** anger and envy."*

—Eaton, Marcia Muelder. "Instilling Aesthetic Values," *Arts Education Policy Review*, Volume 95, Issue 2, November/December 1993: pg. 30.

Connive

(1) avoid noticing something; cooperate secretly or have a secret understanding; encounter or assent to an illegal or criminal act; form intrigue in an underhanded manner; pretend ignorance or fail to take action; look the other way; plot a secret plan

Word Used in Sentence(s)

*(1) "God cannot alter the past; that is why he is obliged to **connive** at the existence of historians."*

—Samuel Butler, British author (1835–1902)

Connote

(1) imply meanings or ideas beyond the explicit meaning; suggest or convey a meaning

(2) involve as a condition or accompaniment

Word Used in Sentence(s)

*(1) "Hal Rothman explained how Las Vegas was built on industries of vice by offering visitors something they could not have at home, and it thus took on the label of 'Sin City.' Las Vegas, he wrote, 'is a code for self-indulgence and sanctioned deviance' (2002, xviii). Indeed, 'vice' is common in the local vernacular in reference to the activities for which the city is known. Of course, 'vice' and 'sin' **connote** different things to different religions and cultures."*

—Rowley, Rex. "Religion in Sin City," *Geographical Review*, Volume 102, Issue 1, January 2012: pg. 76–92.

Collocates to: came, differently, does, names, necessarily, status, term, uses

Consternate

(1)   deprive of courage or power to act out of fear or anxiety; dismay;
      unnerve

Word Used in Sentence(s)

*(1) "But if we had to trade with a Europe dominated by the present
German trade policies, we might have to change our methods to some
totalitarian form. This is a prospect that any lover of democracy must
view with **consternation**."*

—Wendell Willkie, corporate lawyer and politician (1882–1944)

Contradistinguish

(1)   contrast; reveal differences; show disparity

Word Used in Sentence(s)

*(1) "These are our complex ideas of soul and body, as
contradistinguished."*

—John Locke, English philosopher and physician (1632–1704)

Contravene

(1)   be in breach of; breach; break; contradict; deny; disobey; disregard;
      flout; violate

Word Used in Sentence(s)

*(1) "Sometimes it leads me even to hesitate whether I am strictly correct
in my idea that all men are born to equal rights, for their conduct seems
to me to **contravene** the doctrine."*

—Benjamin F. Wade, American lawyer and United States Senator
(1800–1878)

*(1) "Yates has denied wrongdoing and said that, with the benefit of hind-
sight, he would have reopened an inquiry into electronic eavesdropping
of voicemail messages. After the hearing, Rupert Murdoch sent News
International staff an email saying that the company has taken responsibility, and that the allegations 'directly **contravene** our codes*

of conduct and do not reflect the actions and beliefs of our many employees.'"

—Dodds, Paisley. "Murdoch Rejects Blame for Hack Scandal at Hearing," *Associated Press*, July 20, 2011.

Convolute

(1) coil; draw out; make complex

Word Used in Sentence(s)

(1) "And how many models and actresses do you see on magazine covers who have brand-new faces and have had plastic surgery, while I myself have never had any plastic surgery? I am an artist, and I have the ability and the free will to choose the way the world will envision me. 'But can she acknowledge that some people will misinterpret a woman putting horns on her face?' Trust me, I know that. I think a lot of people love to **convolute** *what everyone else does in order to disempower women."*

—Blasberg, Derek. "Going Gaga," *Harper's Bazaar*, May 2011.

Countervail

(1) avail against; balance; compensate; equalize; make up for

Word Used in Sentence(s)

(1) "In doctrinal form, this is known as the universal destination of goods, which fixes a social mortgage or claim on all property, tangible or intellectual. It is not collectivism, which has never produced enough wealth to distribute. Universal destination calls, rather, for a broader view of wealth and a robust array of forces and institutions to **countervail** *pure capitalism. The anti-debt crusade, which seemed almost utopian a few years ago, has given us a useful sketch of that new global vision."*

—Bole, William. "Forgiving Their Debts," *America*, Volume 182, Issue 10, March 2000: pg. 17.

Cross the Rubicon

(1) decision that cannot be reversed; die is cast; no turning back; pass a point of no return; take the plunge

Word Used in Sentence(s)

*(1) International pressure may be able to prevent non-nuclear countries from **crossing the Rubicon** to become nuclear-armed countries.*

*(1) "A great statesman **crosses the Rubicon** without considering the depth of the river. Once he or she declares to cross it, they must face any challenges and risks during the journey. Fretting on the shore won't make the dangers go away."*

—"North Korean Negotiating Behavior: A Cultural Approach," *East Asian Review*, Volume 15, No. 2, Summer 2003, pg. 87–104.

Curtail

(1)   abridge; cut short; make less; scale back; shorten

Word Used in Sentence(s)

*(1) Many school districts have had to **curtail** the non-core classes and add that time to science and math courses.*

*(1) We were forced to **curtail** the grand opening celebration due to power failure.*

*(1) "The budget should be balanced. Public debt should be reduced. The arrogance of officialdom should be tempered, and assistance to foreign lands should be **curtailed**, lest Rome become bankrupt."*

—Marcus Tullius Cicero, ancient Roman lawyer, writer, scholar, orator, and statesman (106 BC–43 BC)

Daunt

(1)   deprive of courage or power to act out of fear or anxiety; intimidate; make fearful; to dismay

Word Used in Sentence(s)

*(1) For many college freshmen, the sheer size of the campus is the most **daunting** thing about college.*

*(1) The goals presented by the executive committee were **daunting**.*

*(1) "Do not doubt a woman's power to aid; no toil can **daunt** a pure affection."*

—Silius Italicus, Roman council and poet (ca. 28–ca. 103)

Collocates to: did, does, even, may, others, would

Debase

(1) adulterate; bastardize; contaminate; corrupt; debauch; defame; degrade; demean; deprave; downgrade; pervert; ruin in character or quality; vitiate

Word Used in Sentence(s)

*(1) "With enough 'bad apples' in the system, judges may develop a grudging attitude towards all prisoner claims. Indeed, as some scholars have admonished, overextension of constitutional protection may dilute and thus **debase** constitutional values."*

—Juceam, Daniel. "Recent Developments," *Harvard Journal of Law & Public Policy*, Volume 21, Issue 1, Fall 1997: pg. 251.

Collocates to: currency, demean, dilute further, myself, our, tended, threaten, values

Debauch

(1) corrupt; debase; degrade; deprave; lead astray morally; lower in character; ruin

Word Used in Sentence(s)

*(1) "The best way to destroy the capitalist system is to **debauch** the currency."*

—Vladimir Lenin, Russian communist revolutionary, politician, and political theorist (1870–1924)

Decimate

(1) annihilate; destroy; devastate; great destruction or harm on a tenth; select by lot to harm or kill a tenth; vacate

Word Used in Sentence(s)

(1) New taxes and government regulations will __decimate__ job growth in small businesses.

(1) Hurricane Sandy __decimated__ the New Jersey coastal communities.

Deep six

(1)   dump; hide or destroy evidence; reject something

Word Used in Sentence(s)

(1) With the advent of the Internet, it has become much harder to hide white-collar crime by __deep sixing__ evidence.

(1) When the U.S. Marshalls arrived, the accountants tried to __deep six__ the books.

Defy

(1)   challenge; confront; dare; disobey; disregard; dissent; face front; flout; hurl defiance; mutiny; out dare; rebel; resist; revolt; rise up; stand up to

Word Used in Sentence(s)

(1) "You must not fear death, my lads; __defy__ him, and you drive him into the enemy's ranks."

—Napoleon Bonaparte, French general, politician, and emperor (1769–1821)

Deign

(1)   condescend; lower oneself; unsuitable role for one's position

Word Used in Sentence(s)

(1) She would not __deign__ to discuss the matter in a public forum.

(1) "__Deign__ on the passing world to turn thine eyes, and pause awhile from learning to be wise. There mark what ills the scholar's life assail— toil, envy, want, the patron, and the jail."

—Samuel Johnson, English writer (1709–1784)

Collocates to: answer, did, does, even, give, look, notice, themselves, would

Denigrate

(1) belittle; defame; degrade; disparage; insult; loss or lessoning of virtue;
malign; pour scorn on; put down; slander

Word Used in Sentence(s)

*(1) The audience **denigrated** the speaker with shouts and insults.*

*(1) Our current elected representatives have been **denigrating** the concept of the public servant conceived by the founding fathers.*

Deplete

(1) consume; eat up; exhaust; use up completely; wipe out

Word Used in Sentence(s)

*(1) "Time and health are two precious assets that we don't recognize and appreciate until they have been **depleted**."*

—Denis Waitley, American motivational speaker, writer, and consultant (1933–)

Collocates to: layer, protocol, resources, substances

Depreciate

(1) belittle; derogate; disparage; lower the value of

Word Used in Sentence(s)

*(1) "Today people who hold cash equivalents feel comfortable. They shouldn't. They have opted for a terrible long-term asset, one that pays virtually nothing and is certain to **depreciate** in value."*

—Warren Buffet, American business magnate, investor, and philanthropist (1930–)

*(1) "Those who profess to favor freedom, and yet **depreciate** agitation, are men who want crops without plowing up the ground."*

—Frederick Douglass, American social reformer, orator, writer, and statesman (1818–1895)

Derail

(1) interrupt; throw off course

Word Used in Sentence(s)

*(1) He managed to **derail** the proposed merger.*

*(1) "I put less stock in others' opinions than my own. No one else's opinions could **derail** me."*

—Judd Nelson, American actor, screenwriter, and producer (1959–)

Disabuse

(1) correct; enlighten; free one from an incorrect assumption or belief

Word Used in Sentence(s)

*(1) Our foreign policy must come from the strength to **disabuse** despots and dictators of allusions of grandeur at the expense of peace.*

Disavow

(1) deny knowledge or approval of; disassociate; disclaim; disown; recant; refuse to acknowledge or accept; reject; renounce; repudiate; turn your back on; wash one's hands of

Word Used in Sentence(s)

*(1) The board of directors **disavowed** the actions of the CEO.*

*(1) "One may **disavow** and disclaim vices that surprise us, and whereto our passions transport us; but those which by long habits are rooted in a strong and powerful will are not subject to contradiction. Repentance is but a denying of our will, and an opposition of our fantasies."*

—Michel Eyquem De Montmainge, French Renaissance writer (1533–1592)

Discombobulate

(1) confuse; disconcert; disrupt thinking; upset the composure

Word Used in Sentence(s)

*(1) His thinking was **discombobulated** as a result of all the problems and issues he faced.*

*(1) Trying to make the best choice for a college can be **discombobulating** because there are so many excellent options.*

*(1) Too many fancy words will just **discombobulate** simple people.*

*(1) The frenzied pace of commodities trading can leave one **discombobulated**.*

Disparage

(1) belittle; criticize; demean; denigrate; deride; laugh at; lower in esteem or discredit; mock; pour scorn on; ridicule; run down; slight; sneer; think of something or someone as small or insignificant; underestimate; vilify

Word Used in Sentence(s)

*(1) "When men are full of envy, they **disparage** everything, whether it be good or bad."*

—Publius Cornelius Tacitus, Roman senator and a historian of the Roman Empire (56–117 AD)

*(1) "But the **disparaging** of those we love always alienates us from them to some extent. We must not touch our idols; the gilt comes off in our hands."*

—Gustave Flaubert, French writer (1821–1880)

Dissipate

(1) blow; disappear; disintegrate; dissolve; fade; fritter away; spread out; thin out; throw away; waste

Word Used in Sentence(s)

*(1) "Beware of **dissipating** your powers; strive constantly to concentrate them. Genius thinks it can do whatever it sees others doing, but it is sure to repent every ill-judged outlay."*

—Johann Wolfgang von Goethe, German playwright, poet, novelist, and dramatist (1749–1832)

*(1) "To penetrate and **dissipate** these clouds of darkness, the general mind must be strengthened by education."*

—Thomas Jefferson, American founding father, 3rd U.S. President (1743–1826)

Dither

(1)   falter; flap; fuss; hesitate; shiver; shutter; tizzy; wait

Word Used in Sentence(s)

*(1) "Practice easing your way along. Don't get het up or in a **dither**. Do your best; take it as it comes. You can handle anything if you think you can. Just keep your cool and your sense of humor."*

—Smiley Blanton, American psychiatrist and psychoanalyst (1882–1966)

Do a one-eighty

(1)   to radically reverse one's decision, ideas, or opinions; to turn around and go in the opposite direction

Word Used in Sentence(s)

*(1) He **did a one-eighty** in his political beliefs when he grew a little older.*

Don't fly too close to the sun

(1)   don't become over exuberant; don't become self-centered; don't get carried away with success; don't try to be more than you are

Word Used in Sentence(s)

*(1) Because of our arrogance that our technology can solve almost any problem, we are deaf to the warnings of "**don't fly too close to the sun**," and we could initiate our own destruction.*

Enervate

(1) debilitate; deprive of strength force or vigor; devitalize; disturb the composure of; run down; unnerve; weaken physically, morally, or spiritually

Word Used in Sentence(s)

*(1) Being a POW will **enervate** the best man, and repatriation requires a long recuperation.*

*(1) "Reformers sought to strengthen certain measures while their opponents sought to repeal or **enervate** some provisions of the 1985 Defense Authorization Act. This fight became part of the work on defense authorization in 1986."*

—Wirls, Daniel. "Congress and the Politics of Military Reform," *Armed Forces & Society*, Transaction Publishers, Volume 17, Issue 4, Summer 1991: pg. 487–512.

Enmesh

(1) catch; embroil; ensnare; entangle; implicate; involve; trap

Word Used in Sentence(s)

*(1) "No matter how **enmeshed** a commander becomes in the elaboration of his own thoughts, it is sometimes necessary to take the enemy into account."*

—Winston Churchill, British politician, best known for his leadership of the United Kingdom during World War II (1874–1965)

*(1) "They come here, they don't know the can'ts because they're fleeing things that are generally worse. And they see this place as the land of opportunity, and they come here and they—they—they **enmesh** themselves in it, and many of them do quite well—much better, in many cases, than some who are born and raised here."*

—Rush Limbaugh radio discussion, EIB network, January 18, 1996.

Equivocate

(1) ambiguous; evasive; hedge; mince words; palter; prevaricate; pussyfoot; quibble; shuffle; waffle

(2) use equivocal terms or language in order to be devisive, mislead, hedge, or otherwise be deliberately ambiguous

Word Used in Sentence(s)

(1) It is not a sound strategy for a witness to __equivocate__ before a grand jury.

(1) "I am in earnest—I will not __equivocate__—I will not excuse—I will not retreat a single inch—and I will be heard!"

—William Lloyd Garrison, U.S. abolitionist (1805–1879)

Exacerbate

(1)   aggravate; annoy; bilious; embitter; exasperate; intensify; irate; make more bitter or severe; to be cantankerous; to be contentious; to worsen an already bad or difficult situation or condition

Word Used in Sentence(s)

(1) One cannot escape an eventual empty and __exacerbated__ life if one's existence consists of bilious and embittered efforts to engage in self-pity.

(1) "By speaking, by thinking, we undertake to clarify things, and that forces us to __exacerbate__ them, dislocate them, schematize them. Every concept is in itself an exaggeration."

—Jose Ortega y Gasset, Spanish philosopher and humanist (1883–1955)

Collocates to: conflicts, differences, difficulties, dilemmas, discrimination, fears, feelings, issues, injustices, problems, situations, tendencies, threats, violence

Fight on death ground

(1)   deliberately choose a strategy that leaves no options other than winning

Word Used in Sentence(s)

(1) "When it comes to the carbon pricing agenda, PM Gillard and her Labor Government are fighting on __death ground__—the terrain that the military strategist Sun Tzu described more than 2,000 years ago in The Art of War.*"*

—Eubank, Leigh. "Carbon Price Fight on Death Ground," *ABCnews.net*, March 17, 2011.

Get crosswise with someone

(1) to be in conflict with another

Word Used in Sentence(s)

*(1) Tim **got himself crosswise** with his supervisor over the work rules.*

Gild the lily

(1) add unnecessary decoration or ornamentation that is already pleasing;
attempt to improve something that is already fine

Word Used in Sentence(s)

*(1) "One may **gild the lily** and paint the rose, but to convey by words
only an adequate idea of the hats and bonnets now exhibited absolutely
passes human ability."*

—Version of Shakespeare's *King John, Newark Daily Advocate*, 1895.

Hagride

(1) afflict with worry, dread, need, or the like; harass; torment

Word Used in Sentence(s)

*(1) "A man **hagridden** by the future haunted by visions of an imminent
heaven or hell upon earth."*

—C.S. Lewis, Irish novelist, poet, academic, medievalist, literary critic,
and essayist (1898–1963)

Hamstring

(1) fetter; hamper; render powerless or useless; unable to perform some
action

Word Used in Sentence(s)

*(1) The civic group's efforts to gentrify the park were **hamstrung** by
political greed and incompetence.*

Harangue

(1)   accost verbally; berate or yell at someone or something; deliver a passionate, forceful, or vehement diatribe; give a loud blustering rant

Word Used in Sentence(s)

*(1) "Bay area water agencies seem to be winning their long battle to **harangue** customers into consuming less."*

—John Upton, American writer for the *New York Times*

*(1) Under the scathing criticism of the opposition, the pent-up fury of the original speaker vented itself into a fiery **harangue**.*

*(1) "Ayn Rand's popularity on the street is at odds with her standing in the academic world. Some critics have called her interminable, tone-deaf, blind to human reality, a writer who creates not dialogue but **harangue**."*

—John Timpane, American writer for the *Philadelphia Inquirer*

Collocates to: began, continues, evils, husband, political, scorching, simultaneous

Hector

(1)   bait; bully; heckle; intimidate; swagger; treat with insolence

Word Used in Sentence(s)

*(1) Political debate should be an opportunity for voters to learn the candidates' views on issues, but instead it has become a chance to heckle and **hector** the opponent more.*

Impede

(1)   block; delay; encumber; get in the way; hamper; hinder; hold back; hold up; inhibit; obstruct progress; slow down

Word Used in Sentence(s)

*(1) "Human folly does not **impede** the turning of the stars."*

—Tom Robbins, American novelist (1936–)

*(1) It is the manager's job to see that nothing **impedes** the progress of the company's objectives.*

Collocates to: ability, development, efforts, growth, investigation, progress

Impel

(1)   drive; fling; force; hurl; propel; provoke; push; set or keep going; thrust; throw

(2)   coerce; compel; drive; force; induce; make; require; urge

Word Used in Sentence(s)

*(1) "Surely you've noticed. You're in a testy mood, but when the phone rings you feign cheer while talking to a friend. Strangely, after hanging up, you no longer feel so grumpy. Such is the value of social occasions— they **impel** us to behave as if we were happy, which in fact helps free us from our unhappiness."*

—Myers, D.G., "The Secrets of Happiness," *Psychology Today*, Volume 25, Issue 4, July 1992.

Collocates to: action, behave, causes, declare, goals, may, separation, toward, us

Impugn

(1)   attack as false or wrong by argument or criticism; challenge something as false or wrong; express doubts about the truth or honesty of someone

Word Used in Sentence(s)

*(1) Once you publish, you open yourself to critics who sometimes love to **impugn** your work.*

*(1) "I am thankful to God for this approval of the people. But while deeply grateful for this mark of their confidence in me, if I know ... my heart, my gratitude is free from any taint of personal triumph. I do not **impugn** the motives of any one opposed to me. It is no pleasure to me to triumph over anyone."*

—Abraham Lincoln, 16th U.S. President (1809–1865)

Collocates to: anybody, character, might, motives, patriotism

Insinuate

(1)   allude; creep in; hint; imply; indicate; intimate; suggest indirectly at something unpleasant; whisper

Word Used in Sentence(s)

*(1) "This commission has rule-making power that carries the force of law. The Senate, it is true, will have the power to override its decisions— but only with a three-fifths majority. There are no procedures that allow citizens or doctors to appeal the Board's decisions. The administrative state—here in the guise of providing health care for all—surely will reduce the people under a kind of tyranny that will **insinuate** itself into all aspects of American life, destroying liberty by stages until liberty itself becomes only a distant memory."*

—Erler, Edward. "Supreme Decisions Ahead," *USA Today*, November 2011.

*(1) "It is precisely the purpose of the public opinion generated by the press to make the public incapable of judging, to **insinuate** into it the attitude of someone irresponsible, uninformed."*

—Walter Benjamin, German theologian, writer, and essayist (1892–1940)

Collocates to: herself, himself, into, itself, themselves, tried, trying

Interpose

(1)   aggressive; arbitrate; insert; intercept; interfere; intermediate; meddle; mediate; offer assistance or presence; put between; unsolicited opinion

Word Used in Sentence(s)

*(1) "Finish each day before you begin the next, and **interpose** a solid wall of sleep between the two. This you cannot do without temperance."*

—Ralph Waldo Emerson, American poet, lecturer, and essayist (1803–1882)

Jack it

(1)   loaf; malinger; work half-heartedly

Word Used in Sentence(s)

*(1) If an unhappy worker demonstrates his or her discontentment by **jacking it** or other visible signs, it is symbolic of a deeper character flaw.*

Jump the shark

(1)   reach the point where one has maxed his or her high point and now he or she is on the down side

Word Used in Sentence(s)

*(1) Jack Welch might very well have **jumped the shark**.*

Jump ugly

(1)   react quickly and harshly insult someone

Word Used in Sentence(s)

*(1) Donald Trump has a quick temper and will **jump ugly** when he feels someone has spoken ill of him or his business tactics.*

Kick someone to the curb

(1)   do away with; disregard; dump someone; eliminate; fire someone; reject someone; throw under the bus

Word Used in Sentence(s)

*(1) "Only hang around people that are positive and make you feel good. Anybody who doesn't make you feel good, **kick them to the curb** and the earlier you start in your life the better. The minute anybody makes you feel weird and not included or not supported, you know, either beat it or tell them to beat it."*

—Amy Poehler, American actress, comedienne, producer, and writer (1971–)

*(1) "**Kicked to the Curb**"*

—Headline from *New York Post*, Sunday, November 11, 2012.

Lament

(1) be sad; cry; dirge; express grief or sorrow; howl; lament; mourn; weep

(2) annoyance; express regret or disappointment about something

Word Used in Sentence(s)

*(1), (2) "The public generally applauds recent 'Shock of Order' policing and commercial revitalization, although critics **lament** the loss of traditional freedoms for informal beach vendors and casual sports. These paradoxes highlight enduring tensions between social order and hierarchy on one hand, and democratic rights and equality on the other."*

—Godfrey, Brian, and M. Oliva Arguinzoni. "Regulation Public Space on the Beachfronts of Rio de Janeiro," *Geographical Review*, Volume 102, Issue 1, January 2012: pg. 17–34.

Lampoon

(1) charade; mockery; parody; satirize

Word Used in Sentence(s)

(1) The program, Saturday Night Live, *is an example of a comedy by **lampoon** model that has been successful over the long run.*

Loathe

(1) detest; disinclined; reluctant; unwilling

Word Used in Sentence(s)

*(1) "But the tide (which stays for no man) calling them away, that were thus **loathe** to depart, their Reverend Pastor, falling down on his knees, and they all with him, with watery cheeks commended them with the most fervent prayers unto the Lord and his blessing."*

—Nathaniel Morton, Keeper of Records, Plymouth Colony (1620–1685)

Misconstrue

(1) get the wrong idea; get the wrong impression; miscomprehend; misinterpret; misread; ; understand incorrectly

Word Used in Sentence(s)

(1) "Peer nominations are not a perfect criterion of victim status because students might be unaware that a classmate is being bullied or they might __misconstrue__ peer conflict between students of comparable strength or status as bullying. However, the virtue of peer report is that information is based on multiple observers, which should produce a more reliable overall measure (Pellegrini, 2001)."

—Cornell, Dewey and Sharmila Mehta. "Counselor Confirmation of Middle School Student Self-Reports of Bullying Victimization," *Professional School Counseling*, Volume 14, Issue 4, April 2011: pg. 261–270.

Collocates to: conflict, dismiss, easy, gesture, magisterium, might, ordinary, students, peer

Negate

(1)   cancel; contradict; counteract; go against; make ineffective; nullify; reverse; undo; wipe out

(2)   deny; exclude; refuse; repudiate

Word Used in Sentence(s)

(1) "Once you label me, you __negate__ me."

—Soren Kierkegaard, Danish philosopher and theologian (1813–1855)

Nettle

(1)   annoy; exasperate; grate; irritate; provoke; vex

Word Used in Sentence(s)

(1) "Out of this __nettle__—danger—we pluck this flower—safety."

—William Shakespeare, English dramatist, playwright, and poet (1564–1616)

Nullify

(1)   abolish; annul; bring to nothing; cancel out; invalidate; make valueless; make void or ineffective; quash

Word Used in Sentence(s)

(1) "Many attempts to communicate are __nullified__ by saying too much."

—Robert Greenleaf, American writer (1904–1990)

Obfuscate

(1) complicate; conceal; confuse; disguise; make dim, dark, or indistinct; obscure

Word Used in Sentence(s)

(1) It is better to face the consequences of telling the truth than to try to __obfuscate__ and face the consequences of the original crime and lying.

(1) "It's __obfuscation__. There is no attempt to be clear and concise and to describe the product for what it is."

—Don Catlin, American scientist and one of the founders of modern drug-testing in sports (1938–)

Obligate

(1) bind by contract; coerce; compel legally or morally; force; make; necessitate; oblige; require

Word Used in Sentence(s)

(1) "The Roots of the Palestine-Israel Conflict, the course catalog warns students: 'This course is NOT designed to present an objective account of a two-sided conflict.' The fact that there are supposedly two sides does not __obligate__ us to portray each as equally right and/or equally wrong. The goal, rather, is to understand why the conflict arose, and what sorts of power inequalities have made it continue."

  —Wisse, Ruth. "Now, About That," *Strength and Tolerance*, Volume 127, Issue 3, March 2009: pg. 27–30.

Collocates to: bacteria, does, facultative, intracellular scavengers, species, states, united, vertebrae

Obtrude

(1) become obtrusive; impose or force on someone

(2) extrude; force one's self or one's ideas on others; thrust out

Word Used in Sentence(s)

*(1) "As a theory of mass communication, agenda setting asserts that while media may not tell us exactly what to think, they frequently tell us what to think about, when the issues at hand do not otherwise **obtrude** into our lives."*

—Denham, Bryan. "Effects of Mass Communication on Attitudes Toward Anabolic Steroids: An Analysis of High School Seniors." *Journal of Drug Issues,* Volume 36, Issue 4, Fall 2006: pg. 809–829.

*(1) "I can't do with mountains at close quarters—they are always in the way, and they are so stupid, never moving, and never doing anything but **obtrude** themselves."*

—D.H. Lawrence, British poet, novelist, and essayist (1885–1930)

Obtund

(1)   blunt; deaden; dull something; paralyze; quell; reduce; stupefy

Word Used in Sentence(s)

*(1) Drugs and liquor will **obtund** the sense that problems are no longer an immediate concern, but when the narcotic and alcohol veil is lifted, the problems are still there.*

Occlude

(1)   block or obstruct something such as a passageway; close or shut; conceal, hide, or obscure something

Word Used in Sentence(s)

*(1) To **occlude** the light, the windows were covered with heavy, dark drapes.*

Open Pandora's box

(1)   to open a can of worms; unleash a stream of unforeseen problems

Word Used in Sentence(s)

(1) "At some point, this century or next, we may well be facing one of the major shifts in human history—perhaps even cosmic history—when intelligence escapes the constraints of biology, nature didn't anticipate us,

and we in our turn shouldn't take artificial general intelligence (AGI) for granted. We need to take seriously the possibility that there might be an **opening of Pandora's box** *moment with AGI that, if missed, could be disastrous. With so much at stake, we need to do a better job of understanding the risks of potentially catastrophic technologies."*

—Shedlock, Mike. "Rise of Intelligent Machines Will Open 'Pandora's Box,' Threatening Human Extinction," *Business News, Favstocks.com*, November 29, 2012.

Oscillate

(1)   change one's mind frequently about beliefs and opinions; move back and forth

Word Used in Sentence(s)

(1) "There is nothing in the world more pitiable than an irresolute man, **oscillating** *between two feelings, who would willingly unite the two and who does not perceive that nothing can unite them."*

—Johann Wolfgang von Goethe, German playwright, poet, novelist, and dramatist (1749–1832)

Ostracize

(1)   banish; exclude; exclude from normal activities; ignore; shun; snub

Word Used in Sentence(s)

(1) "The situation decayed further, the lawsuit charges, when Kasprowicz and several colleagues filed complaints with their office's equal opportunity officer. Many of those who filed complaints, according to the suit, were retaliated against by being included in the transfer to the new division, where work was scarce. The suit alleges that managers yelled at workers who complained, urged other workers to **ostracize** *who complained, and that 35 workers were pressured to sign a petition upholding management's actions."*

—Golab, Art. "Ready to Work, but Nothing to Do All Day," *Chicago Sun Times*, July 14, 2002: pg. 14.

Collocates to: further, humiliate, them, themselves, those, Russians, scapegoat, why

Patronize

(1) belittle; condescend; demean; denigrate; talk down to; treat one in inferior manner

(2) be a regular customer of a store or business; frequent; sponsor; use; utilize

Word Used in Sentence(s)

*(1) "Preferential affirmative action **patronizes** American blacks, women, and others by presuming that they cannot succeed on their own. Preferential affirmative action does not advance civil rights in this country."*

—Alan Keyes, American conservative political activist, author, and former diplomat (1950–)

*(1) "A **patronizing** disposition always has its meaner side."*

—George Eliot (pseudonym of Mary Ann Evans), English Victorian novelist (1819–1880)

Persuade

(1) cause someone to believe something; convince; induce someone to do something through reasoning or argument; reason; urge

Word Used in Sentence(s)

*(1) By **persuading** his boss to take that step, Jeff demonstrated his skill in managing upwards.*

*(1) "Companies work hard to **persuade** existing customers to buy additional products. Often that is a money losing proposition."*

—Shah, Denish and V. Kumar. "The Dark Side of Cross-Selling, Idea Watch," *Harvard Business Review*, December 2012: pg. 21.

*(1) "**Persuading** institutional investors to actively exercise oversight control would be useful—and would reduce fixations on quarterly results."*

—Forester de Rothschild, Lynn and Adam Posen. "How Capitalism Can Repair its Bruised Image," *Wall Street Journal*, January 2, 2013: pg. A17.

(1) "We need to try harder to __persuade__ one another—to try to get people to change their minds. There isn't nearly enough persuasion going on in America today, and there was too little, in the view of many citizens, in the past presidential campaign."

—Jenkins, John. "Persuasion as the Cure for Incivility," *Wall Street Journal*, January 9, 2013: pg. A11.

Pervade

(1)   defuse; infuse; permeate; saturate; spread throughout; suffuse; transfuse

Word Used in Sentence(s)

(1) "Sincerity is impossible, unless it __pervade__ the whole being, and the pretense of it saps the very foundation of character."

—James Russell Lowell, American poet, critic, essayist, editor, and diplomat (1819–1891)

(1) "The illusion that times that were are better than those that are, has probably __pervaded__ all ages."

—Horace Greeley, American newspaper editor (1811–1872)

Purloin

(1)   make off with the possessions or belongings of others; steal

Word Used in Sentence(s)

(1) "It is curious how sometimes the memory of death lives on so much longer than the memory of the life it __purloined__."

—Roy Arundhati, Indian author of *The God of Small Things* and political activist (1961–)

Quash

(1)   annul; put down; repress; set aside; subdue; suppress; quell something completely; reject as not valid

Word Used in Sentence(s)

(1) Sales managers should __quash__ the concept of the written sales quote or bid unless the product is an undifferentiated commodity.

Quell

(1) conquer; control; crush; defeat; extinguish; overwhelm; put an end to; put down; repress; subdue; suppress something

(2) allay; alleviate; assuage; calm; disperse; mitigate; mollify

Word Used in Sentence(s)

*(1) "Machines were, it may be said, the weapon employed by the capitalists to **quell** the revolt of specialized labor."*

—Karl Marx, German political philosopher and revolutionary (1818–1883)

Rankle

(1) aggravate; annoy; bother; cause bitter and lasting annoyance or resentment; exasperate; gall; have long-lasting anger; inflame; infuriate; irate; irk; needle; rile; rub the wrong way

Word Used in Sentence(s)

*(1) "In the Midwest, where less of the chill has been felt, critics call this a 'media recession,' overplayed by myopic New Yorkers—especially financial journalists, who are seeing their profession weaken and the value of their own assets drop. Yet, as much as it might **rankle** the rest of the nation, there's little doubt that when New York gets a chill, the rest of the country shivers along with it."*

—Schwartz, J. and D. Tsiantar, "How Safe Is Your Job?" *Newsweek*, Volume 116, Issue 19, November 5, 1990: pg. 44, 4p.

Collocates to: continue, does, land, might, much, must, potential, still, tactics, those

Scheme

(1) conspire; devise; machinate; plot; to plan in a deceitful way

Word Used in Sentence(s)

*(1) "It is easy to hate and it is difficult to love. This is how the whole **scheme** of things works. All good things are difficult to achieve; and bad things are very easy to get."*

—Socrates, classical Greek Athenian philosopher (470 BC–399 BC)

Screw the pooch

(1)   foul up; make a mistake; mess up

Word Used in Sentence(s)

*(1) One of the worst foul ups a player can make in a rugby match is badly muff a kick or **screw the pooch**.*

Sow dragon's teeth

(1)   to plant seeds of future conflict

Word Used in Sentence(s)

*(1) "If the Republican policy is to **sow dragon's teeth** instead of the golden grain of conciliation, they may be prepared to reap accordingly."*

—Editorial, *The Constitution* (Atlanta, Georgia), 13 January 2012: pg. 4.

Stymie

(1)   get in the way of; hinder; stump; thwart

Word Used in Sentence(s)

*(1) A problem in thermodynamics **stymied** half the class.*

(1) "President Harry Cotterell said: 'We have long campaigned for the closure of the loophole whereby residents try to have development land suddenly designated inappropriately as a village green to stymie sustainable building projects."

—Knighton, John. "Move to End Green Space Law 'Abuse,'" *Huddersfield Daily Examiner*, October 19, 2012.

Subjugate

(1)   dominate; subdue

Word Used in Sentence(s)

(1) "Strange as may be the historical account of how some king or emperor, having quarreled with another, collects an army, fights his enemy's army, gains a victory by killing three, five, or ten thousand men,

*and **subjugates** a kingdom and an entire nation of several millions, all
the facts of history (as far as we know it) confirm the truth of the statement that the greater or lesser success of one army against another is the
cause, or at least an essential indication, of an increase or decrease in
the strength of the nation—even though it is unintelligible why the defeat
of an army—a hundredth part of a nation—should oblige that whole
nation to submit."*

—Leo Tolstoy, Russian writer and author of *War and Peace* (1828–1910)

Vacillate

(1) be indecisive; waver

Word Used in Sentence(s)

*(1) "'At this moment,' said Porthos, 'I feel myself pretty active; but at
times I **vacillate**; I sink; and lately this phenomenon, as you say, has
occurred four times. I will not say this frightens me, but it annoys me.
Life is an agreeable thing. I have money; I have fine estates; I have
horses that I love; I have also friends that I love: D'Artagnan, Athos,
Raoul, and you.'"*

—Alexandre Dumas, French writer and author of *The Man in the Iron
Mask* (1802–1870)

Vex

(1) be aggravated, angry, annoyed, or bugged; be displeased; be exasperated;
confuse someone; irk or pester someone; put one's nose out of joint

Word Used in Sentence(s)

*(1) "**Vexed** sailors cursed the rain, for which poor shepherds prayed
in vain."*

—Edmund Waller, English poet and politician (1607–1679)

*(1) "I'll walk where my own nature would be leading: It **vexes** me to
choose another guide."*

—Emily Bronte, English novelist and poet (1818–1848)

*(1) "A very good part of the mischief that **vex** the world arises from
words."*

—Edmund Burke, British statesman and philosopher (1729–1797)

*(1) "Action and affection both admit of contraries and also of variation of degree. Heating is the contrary of cooling, being heated of being cooled, being glad of being **vexed**. Thus they admit of contraries. They also admit of variation of degree: for it is possible to heat in a greater or less degree; also to be heated in a greater or less degree. Thus action and affection also admit of variation of degree. So much, then, is stated with regard to these categories."*

—Aristotle, Greek philosopher and polymath, author of *The Categories* (384–322 BC)

Vilify

(1)   belittle; criticize; defame; do a hatchet job on; disparage; insult; libel; malign; pillory; pull to pieces; run down; slander; speak ill of; use abusive slanderous language

Word Used in Sentence(s)

*(1) Political elections have become less about issues and more about who can **vilify** their opponent more.*

*(1) "To **vilify** a great man is the readiest way in which a little man can himself attain greatness."*

—Edgar Allan Poe, American author, poet, editor, and literary critic (1809–1849)

*(1) "**Vilify, Vilify, Vilify,** some of it will always stick."*

—Pierre-Augustin Caron de Beaumarchais, French playwright, watchmaker, inventor, musician, diplomat, fugitive, spy, publisher, horticulturalist, arms dealer, satirist, financier, and revolutionary (1732–1799)

*(1) "Now, as both of these gentlemen were industrious in taking every opportunity of recommending themselves to the widow, they apprehended one certain method was, by giving her son the constant preference to the other lad; and as they conceived the kindness and affection which Mr. Allworthy showed the latter, must be highly disagreeable to her, they doubted not but the laying hold on all occasions to degrade and **vilify** him, would be highly pleasing to her; who, as she hated the boy, must love all those who did him any hurt."*

—Henry Fielding, English novelist and dramatist, author of *The History of Tom Jones, A Foundling* (1707–1754)

5

100 Top Action Verbs for Mind Games, Mental Panache, Mastermind Monkey Business, Meeting MENSAs, or Just Showing Off

Abnegate

(1) extremely sad; surrender or deny oneself

(2) give up rights; reject; relinquish; renounce;

(3) hopeless; servile

Word Used in Sentence(s)

> *(1) "Scientists, being people of cognitive complexity, must start making their own decisions as to whether what they're doing adds to human happiness or detracts from it, and not **abnegate** moral responsibility."*

> —Weldon, Fay. "A 'Profile' of the Creator," *Washington Post*, July 19, 1992.

<u>**Collocates to:**</u> <u>moral, otherwise, responsibility, serve</u>

Abrogate

(1) abolish; get rid of; negate; nullify by authority; repeal

Word Used in Sentence(s)

*(1) "[On love:] I have no respect for anyone who says they've given up, or that they're not looking or that they're tired. That is to **abrogate** one's responsibility as a human being."*

—Harlan Ellison, American writer (1934–)

(1) "The reports of Kim Jong Eun's base visits follow more than a week of aggressive rhetoric from Pyongyang, which on Monday said it had abrogated the 1953 armistice that suspended the Korean War…"

—Gale, Alastair. "Kim's Visit to Bases Raises Tensions," *Wall Street Journal*, March 13, 2013.

*(1) He should not **abrogate** that responsibility, which is inherent to the Chairman of the Board.*

Collocates to: contracts, laws, rights, states, treaties

Abjure

(1) disown; reject or disavow a previously held belief or view usually under pressure or oath; renounce or turn one's back on a position once held; repudiate; to formally recant

(2) foreswore; give up one's rights under oath; profess to abandon; reject; renounce

Word Used in Sentence(s)

*(1) Foreign-born individuals who want to become U.S. citizens must take an oath of allegiance in which they swear to absolutely and entirely renounce and **abjure** all allegiance and fidelity to any foreign prince, potentate, state, or sovereignty.*

*(1) "Criticism of the King, let us begin with the colonists' criticism of monarchy, for this also furnishes us with a commentary about how men in a republican democracy should embrace civility and **abjure** hyper-masculinity. Thomas Paine delivered the most incisive criticisms against monarchic rule. Paine denied that kings began from 'an honorable origin,' (n222) for theirs is founded on an arrogant and dangerous masculinity."*

—Kang, John M. "Manliness and the Constitution," *Harvard Journal of Law and Public Policy*, Volume 32, Issue 1, Winter 2009: pg. 261–332.

Collocates to: allegiance, forced, renounced, should, sort, test

Absquatulate

(1) abscond; bolt; decamp; depart in a hurry; escape; flee; hurry off; leave; make off; run off; take flight

Word Used in Sentence(s)

*(1) In the early days of fire insurance, the insurance companies also ran fire houses and would sometimes show up at a fire. If the burning home wasn't a policyholder, the fire brigade would try to sell a policy. If the policy couldn't be sold, many instances the fire brigade would **absquatulate**, leaving the building to burn.*

Abjure

(1) disavow or reject a formerly held belief; swear off or to foreswear something

Word Used in Sentence(s)

*(1) "'I **abjure** you,' Alcide said. Colonel Flood winced, and young Sid, Amanda, and Culpeper looked both astonished and impressed, as if there were a ceremony they'd never thought to witness. 'I see you no longer, I hunt with you no longer. I share flesh with you no longer.'"*

—Charlaine Harris in the Sookie Stackhouse novel, *Dead to the World*, New York: Berkley Publishing, 2004.

*(1) "I have from an early age **abjured** the use of meat, and the time will come when men such as I will look upon the murder of animals as they now look upon the murder of men."*

—Leonardo Da Vinci, Italian Renaissance polymath: painter, sculptor, architect, and musician (1452–1519)

Collocates to: allegiance, forced, renounced, sort, test

Acquiesce

(1) accept; agree; assent; comply with passively; concede; concur; consent; give in; go along with; submit; yield

Word Used in Sentence(s)

*(1) "No man can sit down and withhold his hands from the warfare against wrong and get peace from his **acquiescence**."*

—Woodrow Wilson, 28th U.S. President (1856–1924)

*(1) "Men **acquiesce** in a thousand things, once righteously and boldly done, to which, if proposed to them in advance, they might find endless objections."*

—Robert Dale Owen, American politician (1801–1877)

Collocates to: choice, compelled, council, demands, forced, must, refused, quietly

Adumbrate

(1) foreshadow; give a general description of something but not the details; obscure; overshadow; predict; prefigure; presage; summary

Word Used in Sentence(s)

*(1) The global political troubles **adumbrated** an eventual world-wide economic recession.*

*(1) It is never good for a manager to **adumbrate** news of a partial layoff to just a few employees.*

Agglomerate

(1) accumulate; cluster; gather together; jumbled collection

Word Used in Sentence(s)

*(1) "Common property campesino communities fit very uncomfortably in the neoliberal discourse, but in the Mexican context, ejidos and comunidades agrarias are irrevocable, at least in the short and medium term. The reformers, therefore, also created new legal mechanisms for private capital to associate with common property through joint ventures, made it easier to **agglomerate** land within ejidos, and established new mechanisms for associations of individuals within ejidos and comunidades to exploit common properties (Wexler and Bray 1996; Cornelius and Myhre 1998; World Bank 1995, 69)."*

—Koolster, Dan. "Campesinos and Mexican Forest Policy During the Twentieth Century," *Latin American Research Review*, Volume 38, Issue 2, 2003: pg. 94.

Ameliorate

(1) correct a mistake; improve; make better; tolerate

(2) correct a deficiency or defect; take action that makes up for one's negative or improper actions; to make right a wrong

Word Used in Sentence(s)

*(1) Kathy demonstrated her strength of character by **ameliorating** the errors in the project that she caused before anyone else discovered them.*

*(1) Phillip **ameliorated** the issues in the business plan prior to the meeting with the investors.*

*(1) "For more than 100 years, psychologists have attempted, with modest success, to **ameliorate** mental problems from depression to low intelligence by changing patients' attitudes and by exploring their childhood angst. Now, pharmacological approaches are used, also with only moderate success. Recent evidence suggests a more fruitful path tied to the fact that human behavior—sexual orientation, alcoholism, intelligence, the propensity for violence—has a genetic component."*

—Nemko, Marty. "Choosing the Career Path Less Traveled: Many Jobs Look Great on the Big Screen," *U.S. News & World Report*, Volume 146, Issue 4, May 1, 2009: pg. 22.

Collocates to: conditions, economic effects, efforts, help, might, prevent, problems

Analyze

(1) consider; dissect; evaluate; examine; explore; interpret; investigate; probe; question; scrutinize; study

Word Used in Sentence(s)

*(1) Randi **analyzed** the situation from all positions before making her decision.*

*(1) Rick will be given the responsibility of **analyzing** the impact of the new quotas on the sales department's budget.*

*(1) "You are a product of your environment. So choose the environment that will best develop you toward your objective. **Analyze** your life in terms of its environment. Are the things around you helping you toward success—or are they holding you back?"*

—W. Clement Stone, American author (1902–2002)

(1) "There is nothing to fear except the persistent refusal to find out the truth, the persistent refusal to __analyze__ the causes of happenings."

—Dorothy Thompson, American writer (1893–1961)

(1) "The method of nature: who could ever __analyze__ it?"

—Ralph Waldo Emerson, American poet, lecturer, and essayist (1803–1882)

Collocates to: ability, collect, data, evaluate, identify, information, results, sample, situation, used

Anodyne

(1) capable of showing comfort; eliminating pain

Word Used in Sentence(s)

(1) *"Illusion is an __anodyne__, bred by the gap between wish and reality."*

—Herman Wouk, American author (1915–)

Collocates to: connotations, dominance, imagined, less, making, nothing, rather

Articulate

(1) convey; enunciate; express thoughts, ideas, or feelings coherently; pronounce; put into words; say; speak clearly; speech; utter

Word Used in Sentence(s)

(1) "For the past 30 years, a group of social scientists around the world—from pioneers like Edward Deci and Richard Ryan, at the University of Rochester, to a new generation of scholars such as Adam Grant, at Wharton—have __articulated__ a more subtle view of what motivates people in a variety of settings, including work."

—Pink, Daniel. "A Radical Prescription for Sales," *Harvard Business Review*, July–August 2012: pg. 77.

(1) "Leaders __articulate__ a lucid sense of purpose, create effective leadership teams, prioritize, and sequence their initiatives carefully, redesign organizational structures to make good execution easier, and most importantly, integrate these tactics into one coherent strategy."

—Wheeler, Steven, Walter McFarland, and Art Kleiner. "A Blueprint for Strategic Leadership," *Strategy+Business*, Issue 49, Winter 2007: pg. 46.

Arrogate

(1)   ascribe; assume; claim as own; take power that is not yours

Word Used in Sentence(s)

*(1) I won't **arrogate** to teach you about life.*

*(1) He is the type of man who will **arrogate**, assume, and ascribe such powers to himself.*

Assuage

(1)   appease; erase doubts and fears; mollify; pacify; satisfy; soothe

Word Used in Sentence(s)

*(1) Judy was extremely annoyed, angry, and fearful that Tom showed up unannounced. She had previously kept him away by a restraining order and to avoid further trouble and to **assuage** her, Tom left.*

*(1) I worked to **assuage** my own guilt over the incident.*

*(1) "I've never known any trouble than an hour's reading didn't **assuage**."*

—Arthur Schopenhauer, German philosopher (1788–1860)

Collocates to: anger, anguish, anxiety, concerns, consciences, curiosity, doubt, fears, feelings, guilt, hunger, hurt, loneliness, pride, worries

Augur

(1)   betoken; bode; divine; forebode; foreshadow; foretell; portend; predict

Word Used in Sentence(s)

*(1) The improved weather **augured** for a better hunting season.*

*(1) A growing third-party movement is **auguring** for a far greater voter turnout in the next election.*

*(1) "These readings **augur** well in the very near term for supportive bond price action. We, however, still look for core inflation to tick up modestly and for overall labor market conditions to improve gradually."*

—Chris Sullivan, chief investment officer at the United Nations Federal Credit Union and UNFCU Financial Advisors

Collocates to: does, future, might, not, poorly, well

Aver

(1) affirm; assert the truthfulness of something; avow; claim; declare; maintain; profess; state; swear

Word Used in Sentence(s)

*(1) Some philosophers **aver** that both moral blame and legal responsibility should be based on prior behavior.*

*(1) President Bill Clinton **averred** that he smoked grass in college but did not inhale.*

*(1) "The anti-reformer is Chuck Schumer, the Senator from Wall Street, New York, who **averred** at the National Press Club last week that his party will have nothing to do with tax reform of the kind that Ronald Reagan negotiated with Democrats in 1989, or that the Simpson-Bowles deficit commission proposed in 2010, or that the Gang of Six Senators have been working on. It's Chuck's way or no way."*

—"Schumer to Tax Reform: Drop Dead," editorial, *Wall Street Journal*, October 15, 2012.

(1) "I know the thing that's most uncommon

(Envy be silent and attend!);

I know a reasonable woman,

Handsome and witty, yet a friend.

Not warped by passion, awed by rumor,

Not grave through pride, or gay through folly;

An equal mixture of good humor

And sensible soft melancholy.

'Has she no faults, then (Envy says), sir?'

*Yes, she has one, I must **aver**:*

When all the world conspires to praise her,

The woman's deaf, and does not hear."

—Alexander Pope, British poet, taken from "On a Certain Lady at Court" (1688–1744)

Bafflegab

(1) double-talk; gibberish talk; song and dance; speak gobbledygook; speak in an ambiguous or incomprehensible way; speak tap dance around a straight answer; use puffery

Word Used in Sentence(s)

*(1) The Play, "Death of a Salesman" could have easily been subtitled "the end of one man's **bafflegab**."*

Be Argus-eyed

(1) In Greek mythology, Argus was a giant with one hundred eyes, each looking in a different direction. Argus was employed by the goddess Hera as a watchman to guard the nymph Io. Zeus had Argus killed by Hermes so he could pursue his passionate love, Io.

(2) having keen eyes; keenly watchful for danger; sleepless; vigilant; wary; watchful; wide awake

Word Used in Sentence(s)

*(2) Corporate espionage costs firms billions of dollars, so it is imperative that all employees **be Argus-eyed** and report any suspicious activity.*

Belie

(1) disprove; to give false impression or to contradict

Word Used in Sentence(s)

*(1) The small, unassuming building **belied** the global Internet business that was taking place inside.*

*(1) "Man is a creature of hope and invention, both of which **belie** the idea that things cannot be changed."*

—Tom Clancy, American novelist (1947–)

*(1) "Our very hopes **belied** our fears, our fears our hopes **belied**—we thought her dying when she slept, and sleeping when she died!"*

—Thomas Hood, English poet and humorist (1799–1845)

<u>**Collocates to:**</u> fact, image, notion, numbers, seem, words

Bifurcate

(1)   branch; divide; fork; split into two sections or pieces

Word Used in Sentence(s)

*(1) "Labor also has started to **bifurcate**, as minimum-wage workers have begun to see their interests as distinct from—and often opposed to—those of relatively well-paid unionized workers in industry and the public sector."*

—Armijo, Leslie Elliott. "Inflation and Insouciance: The Peculiar Brazilian Game," *Latin American Research Review*, Volume 31, Issue 3, 1996: pg. 7, 40p.

*(1) "We **bifurcate** the society, with people who are so-called 'smart' getting pushed toward book learning, and everyone else getting pushed toward the trades. Ever since the Industrial Revolution, the guys who owned things wore suits, and the guys who ran the lathes wore work clothes. If an engineer wanted something made, he'd draw it and give the drawing to a machinist who then made it. I wanted to be the guy who designed it and made it."*

—Sulkis, Brian. "Oakland: Sculpting a Hands-on Life," *San Francisco Chronicle*, May 20, 2005: pg. F1.

Collocates to: expressed, margining, may, occurrence, or, terminology

Blandish

(1)   cajole; coax; induce or persuade by gentle flattery; influence

Word Used in Sentence(s)

*(1) A leader most likely would not attempt to **blandish** a follower into accepting his point of view but rather resort to the use of influence.*

*(1) When Susan stood and **brandished** the by-laws, everyone knew the executive session was going to be a long one.*

Bloviate

(1)   speak pompously and at length; to hold forth in a pompous self-centered way; to orate verbosely

Word Used in Sentence(s)

*(1) It seems as though elected officials are really good at only one thing—they love to **bloviate**.*

*(1) To **bloviate** is not recommended when you are among experts on the current topic.*

*(1) "Warren Harding invented the word 'normalcy', and the lesser known '**bloviate**' meaning one imagines, to spout, to spew aimless verbiage."*

—John Ashbery, U.S. poet and critic (1927–)

Bowdlerize

(1) censor; edit; expurgate; remove obscenity or other inappropriate content

Word Used in Sentence(s)

*(1) "John Nance Garner, FDR's first vice president, famously said 'the job of second-in-command wasn't worth a warm bucket of spit.' Well, that's not exactly what Garner said, but in an era before hot microphones, newspapermen were kind enough to **bowdlerize** it for him."*

—Mark Hemingway, American writer for *The Washington Examiner*

Bullyrag

(1) dominate; force into agreement or compliance; intimidate

Word Used in Sentence(s)

*(1) It was the kind of neighborhood in which it was standard practice for young teens to be **bullyragged** into joining a street gang.*

Cachinnate

(1) laugh convulsively or hard; laugh loudly or immoderately

Word Used in Sentence(s)

*(1) "He looked in at the door and snickered, then in at the window, then peeked down from between the rafters and **cachinnated** till his sides must have ached."*

—John Burroughs, American author of *A Bed of Boughs* (1837–1921)

Calumniate

(1)   charges or imputations; slander; traduce; utter maliciously false statements

Word Used in Sentence(s)

*(1) "I am not to order the Natural Sympathies of my own Breast, and of every honest breast to wait until the Tales and all the anecdotes of the Coffeehouses of Paris and of the dissenting meeting houses of London are scoured of all the slander of those who **calumniate** persons, that afterwards they may murder them with impunity. I know nothing of your Story of Messalina. What, are not high Rank, great Splendour of descent, great personal Elegance and outward accomplishments ingredients of moment in forming the interest we take in the misfortunes of Men?"*

—Bromwich, David. "The Context of Burke's Reflections," *Social Research*, Volume 58, Issue 2, Summer 1991: pg. 313–354.

Collocates to: afterwards, person, slander, that, those, who

Cavil

(1)   quibble; raise petty and irritating objections; trivial and frivolous objection

Word Used in Sentence(s)

*(1) The lawyers never **caviled** throughout the entire proceedings.*

*(1) "Bluster, sputter, question, **cavil**; but be sure your argument be intricate enough to confound the court."*

—William Wycherley, English dramatist of the Restoration period (1640–1715)

Cogitate

(1)   consider; deliberate; meditate; muse; ponder; reflect; ruminate

Word Used in Sentence(s)

*(1) "While I thus **cogitate** in disquiet and perplexity, half submerged in dark waters of a well in an Arabian oasis, I suddenly hear a voice from the background of my memory, the voice of an old Kurdish nomad: If water stands motionless in a pool it grows stale and muddy, but when it*

moves and flows it becomes clear: so, too, man in his wanderings.
Whereupon, as if by magic, all disquiet leaves me. I begin to look upon
myself with distant eyes, as you might look at the pages of a book to read
a story from them; and I begin to understand that my life could not have
taken a different course. For when I ask myself, 'What is the sum total of
my life?' something in me seems to answer, 'You have set out to exchange
one world for another—to gain a new world for yourself in exchange for
an old one which you never really possessed.' And I know with startling
clarity that such an undertaking might indeed take an entire lifetime."

—Muhammad Asad, journalist, traveler, writer (*Road to Mecca*), social
critic, linguist, thinker, reformer, diplomat (1900–1992)

Concatenate

(1)   integrate; link together; unite or join in a series or chain

Concinnate

(1)   show skill and harmony especially in a literary work; to show an elegant
arrangement

Confabulate

(1)   chat, converse, or talk informally

Word Used in Sentence(s)

*(1) "I shall not ask Jean Jacques Rousseau—If birds **confabulate***
or no?"

—William Cowper, English poet (1731–1800)

Conflagrate

(1)   enflame; enkindle; ignite; kindle; start to burn

Word Used in Sentence(s)

(1) "In fact, she was the one who got him the job with Janus. And he's
the one who's supposed to investigate this. Dammit. By the time Rebecca
arrived at the refinery, the automatic fire-suppression systems had dealt
*with the resultant **conflagration**—which barely had a chance to*
***conflagrate**. The different section chiefs started reporting in that their*

sections were okay, with the obvious exception of Yinnik regarding the refinery. One of T'Lis's assistants said the computer core was fine."

—DeCandido, Keith R. A. *A Singular Destiny*, NY: Pocket Books, Edition: 1st Pocket Books paperback ed. 2009.

Confute

(1)   prove to be false; refute

(2)   make useless

Word Used in Sentence(s)

(1) "Certain terms referring to emotion do not translate across cultures. 'They have a word for it that we lack.' Or, 'they' use a word that seems to mean something like our word, but just don't apply it in the same way. English lacks a clear translation for the Malaysian term marah—*a word that to English speakers seems to **confute** anger and envy."*

—Eaton, Marcia Muelder. "Instilling Aesthetic Values." *Arts Education Policy Review*, Volume 95, Issue 2, November/December: pg. 30.

Conjure

(1)   appeal; beg; make earnest or urgent appeal

(2)   bring or summon into being as by magic

Word Used in Sentence(s)

*(1) She **conjured** him to give up the life of drugs.*

*(2) "No one who, like me, **conjures** up the most evil of those half-tamed demons that inhabit the human beast, and seeks to wrestle with them, can expect to come through the struggle unscathed."*

—Sigmund Freud, Austrian neurologist who became known as the founding father of psychoanalysis (1856–1939)

Connote

(1)   imply meanings or ideas beyond the explicit meaning; suggest or convey a meaning

(2)   involve as a condition or accompaniment

Word Used in Sentence(s)

*(1) "Hal Rothman explained how Las Vegas was built on industries of vice by offering visitors something they could not have at home, and it thus took on the label of 'Sin City.' Las Vegas, he wrote, 'is a code for self-indulgence and sanctioned deviance' (2002, xviii). Indeed, 'vice' is common in the local vernacular in reference to the activities for which the city is known. Of course, 'vice' and 'sin' **connote** different things to different religions and cultures."*

—Rowley, Rex. "Religion in Sin City," *Geographical Review*, Volume 102, Issue 1, January 2012: pg. 76–92.

Collocates to: came, differently, does, names, necessarily, status, term, uses

Coruscate

(1) brilliant in style; flashy; showy; sparkle

Cross the Rubicon

(1) decision that cannot be reversed; die is cast; no turning back; pass a point of no return; take the plunge

Word Used in Sentence(s)

*(1) "A great statesman **crosses the Rubicon** without considering the depth of the river. Once he or she declares to cross it they must face any challenges and risks during the journey. Fretting on the shore won't make the dangers go away."*

—Chang Dal-Joong, *Korea JoongAng Daily*

Debauch

(1) corrupt; debase; degrade; deprave; lead astray morally; lower in character; ruin

Word Used in Sentence(s)

*(1) "The best way to destroy the capitalist system is to **debauch** the currency."*

—Vladimir Lenin, Russian Communist revolutionary, politician, and political theorist (1870–1924)

Declaim

(1) recite or read in public with studied or artful elegance

Word Used in Sentence(s)

*(1) "The fact that I couldn't recall the last name of even one of our daughter's so-called friends made me feel guiltier than ever. How can you call yourself a good mother, I could already hear the police **declaim**, when you don't even know who your daughter's friends are?"*

—Fielding, Joy. *Missing Pieces*, NY: Bantam Books, 1997.

Collocates to: against, banners, here, honeyed, now-grown, orations, scantly, soliloquy, vainly

Deign

(1) condescend; lower oneself; unsuitable role for one's position

Word Used in Sentence(s)

*(1) She would not **deign** to discuss the matter in a public forum.*

*(1) "**Deign** on the passing world to turn thine eyes, and pause a while from learning to be wise. There mark what ills the scholar's life assail— Toil, envy, want, the patron, and the jail."*

—Samuel Johnson, English writer (1709–1784)

Collocates to: answer, did, does, even, give, look, notice, themselves, would

Demur

(1) balk; be reluctant; doubt; express doubts; object on the grounds of scruples; protest; raise objections; voice opposition to

(2) delay decision or action because of doubts

Word Used in Sentence(s)

*(1) Those more likely to **demure** would probably be older and more conservative.*

Collocates to: accepted, carried, does, felt, made, surely, tried, without

Descant

(1) talk freely without inhibition

(2) play a melody or part different than the main

Word Used in Sentence(s)

> *(1) "These to their nests,*
>
> *Were slunk, all but the wakeful nightingale;*
>
> *She all night long her amorous **descant** sung."*

—John Milton, English poet, polemicist, scholar, and author of *Paradise Lost* (1608–1674)

> *(1) "The police amusingly **descant** on these jottings: 'I can't believe he'd ever write a sentence like 'I shall be compelled to take steps to silence you!'"*

—Christopher Buckley, "The Chekhov of Coldsands-on-Sea," *New York Times,* November 16, 1997.

Descry

(1) catch sight of something others missed; discern something difficult to catch sight of; notice; see what other's miss

Word Used in Sentence(s)

> *(1) "All that you may achieve or discover you will regard as a fragment of a larger pattern of the truth which from the separate approaches every true scholar is striving to **descry**."*

—Abbott L. Lowell, American educator and legal scholar (1856–1943)

> *"I **descried** a sail."*

—Jonathan Swift, Anglo-Irish satirist, essayist, political pamphleteer, poet, and cleric (1167–1745)

Devolve

(1) become someone else's obligation; pass on to a deputy or successor; transfer to another

(2) deteriorate

Word Used in Sentence(s)

*(1) "My desire to **devolve** authority has nothing to do with a wish to shirk responsibility."*

—Dalai Lama, Tibean, high lama in the Gelug or "Yellow Hat" school of Tibetan Buddhism (1935–)

*(1) "When a detailed prototype was built, the discussion rapidly **devolved** into arguments. Everyone kept saying 'why doesn't it have this feature or that feature?' One participant said the haggling went on for years."*

—Leonardi, Paul. "Early Prototypes Can Hurt a Team's Creativity," *Harvard Business Review*, December 2011: pg. 28.

Collocates to: authority, into, power, responsibility, soon, upon

Discomfit

(1) confuse; deject; disconcert; foil; frustrate; mix-up; thwart

Word Used in Sentence(s)

*(1) The protesters can continue to argue, but their points will not **discomfit** me—my mind is made up.*

Divagate

(1) digress; diverge; lose clarity; stray; turn aside from the main point; wander off the ranch

Word Used in Sentence(s)

*(1) It is important for the speaker to not **divagate** from the critical point with too many side issues.*

Drink from the waters of the River Lethe

(1) have no memory of something; to be in oblivion; to forget absolutely

Word Used in Sentence(s)

*(1) In Virgil's Aeneid, the souls of the dead **drank from the waters of the River Lethe** to erase the traces of their past lives before they could be born again into new bodies.*

Dulcify

(1) ease someone's anger; pacify; make pleasant or agreeable; mollify; sweeten

Word Used in Sentence(s)

*(1) His soothing tone **dulcified** the rising panic within the crowd.*

Educe

(1) come to a conclusion; derive; evoke; solve a problem based on thoughtful consideration of facts

(2) deduce; draw out; elicit; infer

(3) bring out or develop; elicit from

Word Used in Sentence(s)

*(1) "In other words, apartheid becomes shorthand for the most egregious instances of systemic and overt racism that necessarily and automatically **educe** (or should **educe**) severe international condemnation."*

—Editors. "The Ethnicity of Caste," *Anthropological Quarterly*, Volume 78, Issue 3, Summer 2005: pg. 543–584, 42p.

Edify

(1) educate; enlighten; illuminate; improve; inform; instruct; teach

(2) to uplift morally, spiritually, or intellectually

Word Used in Sentence(s)

*(1) To **edify** students is one of the most important goals of a teacher.*

Effectuate

(1) bring about; cause or accomplish something; effect

Word Used in Sentence(s)

(1) "...opportunity for all persons in the armed services without regard to race, color, religion, or national origin. This policy shall be put into

effect as rapidly as possible, having due regard to the time required to ***effectuate*** *any necessary changes without impairing efficiency..."*

—Morris J. MacGregor Jr., Integration of the Armed Forces (1940–1965)

(1) "...when it is such as we have been more accustomed to contemplate. This opinion is indeed plausible at the first view, because it may be said that we go half-way to meet that Author, who proposeth to reach an end by means which have an apparent probability to ***effectuate*** *it; but it will appear upon reflection, that this very circumstance, instead of being serviceable, is in reality detrimental..."*

—John Ogilvie, Scottish Roman Catholic Jesuit martyr and author of "An Essay on the Lyric Poetry of the Ancients" (1579–1615)

Collocates to: able, design, intent, justice, necessary, policy, purpose

Elucidate

(1) clarify; explain to make something clear; explicate; expose; expound; illuminate; lucid; reveal; throw light on it

(1) "The recognition of dynamic urban spatial restructuring enables two significant actions for sustainability. First, understanding the urban historical geography of a city allows the contemporary investigator to identify key points or moments in the past where opportunities in the development path might have enabled or enhanced sustainability options. And second, once those past points or moments are recognized and appreciated, they might help ***elucidate*** *current or future opportunities for sustainability planning efforts."*

—Solecki, William D. and Robim M. Leichenko. "Urbanization and the Metropolitan Environment: Lessons from New York and Shanghai," *Environment*, Volume 48, Issue 4, May 2006: pg. 8–23, 16p.

Collocates to: help, further nature, needed, order, relationship, research, role, study

Envisage

(1) create a mental picture; envision; foresee; form an image in the mind; imagine; visualize

(2) confront; face

Word Used in Sentence(s)

*(1) "I did **envisage** being this successful as a player, but not all the hysteria around it off the golf course."*

—Tiger Woods, American pro golfer (1975–)

*(1) "Running for President is physically, emotionally, mentally, and spiritually the most demanding single undertaking I can **envisage** unless it's World War III."*

—Walter F. Mondale, American politician, lawyer, and U.S. Vice President (1928–)

Collocates to: ability, difficult, impossible, situation, seems

Eschew

(1)   abstain; avoid; distain; give up; have nothing to do with; keep away from; shun; steer clear of; turn your back on

Word Used in Sentence(s)

*(1) Sandra **eschewed** vendors that gave even a hint that bribes were part of their plan.*

*(1) In today's reform-minded political climate, elected officials are **eschewing** lobbyists with poor reputations.*

*(1) "An important part of Chief Executive Ron Johnson's Strategy at JC Penney has been to **eschew** sales and promotions in favor of everyday low prices."*

—Lahart, Justin. "Penney Must Endure Pain Before Gain," *Wall Street Journal Money & Investing*, November 9, 2012.

*(1) "In their own ways, Mayor Bloomberg and President Obama embody the obsessions of modern liberalism. Each holds an advanced Ivy League degree. Each believes he would make better choices for others than they could for themselves. Each has consequently **eschewed** the gradual and modest—the unglamorous improvements that might have better prepared Staten Island, for a dangerous storm."*

—McGurn, William. "Sandy and the Failures of Blue-Statism," *Wall Street Journal*, November 6, 2012.

Etiolate

(1) cause to become pale, unhealthy, weak, or appear sickly

(2) deprive of strength; weaken

(3) blanch or bleach by depriving of sunlight

Word Used in Sentence(s)

*(1) Sitting indoors playing games and becoming addicted to social media can easily lead one to appear **etiolated**.*

Evince

(1) reveal or indicate the presence of a particular feeling or condition; show plainly

(2) indicate; make manifest without a doubt

Word Used in Sentence(s)

*(1") "Most community colleges **evince** a strong interest in how their various publics view their program offerings. However, for an organization like a community college, both shaping and changing an image are difficult tasks."*

—Cowles, Deborah. "Understanding and Measuring the Public's Image of a Community College," *Community College Review*, Volume 18, Issue 4, Spring 1991: pg. 21.

Excogitate

(1) contrive; devise; discover; find; invent; study or think something through carefully and in detail

Word Used in Sentence(s)

*(1) "By evening, there were still groups fighting in the outlying neighborhoods. Fires and looting were involved and a certain amount of gunfire. Nobody could say when it began to quieten, but by nine P.M. the streets were silent and the fires had been extinguished. White billowy clothes, sheets mainly, blew around the streets for a few days before they were all picked up. Need I **excogitate** upon this?"*

—Wightman, Wayne. "A Foreign Country," *Fantasy & Science Fiction*, Volume 115, Issue 6; December 2008: pg. 7, 31p.

Exculpate

(1)   absolve; clear; declare or prove guiltless; discharge; dispense; exempt; free from blame; let off; pardon; relieve; spare

Word Used in Sentence(s)

*(1) "I'm disappointed we won't get the witnesses, because they **exculpate** my client."*

—Frank Dunhan, American lawyer (1946–2006)

Collocates to: also, any, client, defendants, people, responsibility

Execrate

(1)   hate; regard with extreme dislike; swear; use profane language

(2)   curse or call evil down upon

(3)   be contemptuous of; denounce scathingly; speak abusively of

(4)   abhor; detest; loathe

Word Used in Sentence(s)

*(1) "Whenever we encounter the Infinite in man, however imperfectly understood, we treat it with respect. Whether in the synagogue, the mosque, the pagoda, or the wigwam, there is a hideous aspect which we **execrate** and a sublime aspect which we venerate. So great a subject for spiritual contemplation, such measureless dreaming—the echo of God on the human wall!"*

—Victor Hugo, French romantic poet, novelist, and dramatist (1802–1885)

Expatiate

(1)   cover a wide scope of topics; elaborate

(2)   add details to an account or an idea

(3)   roam or wander freely

(4)   speak or write in great detail

Word Used in Sentence(s)

*(1) "Now, as the business of standing mast-heads, ashore or afloat, is a very ancient and interesting one, let us in some measure **expatiate** here."*

—Herman Melville, American author of *Moby Dick* (1819–1891)

*(1) "When people are too well off they always begin to long for something new. And so it came to pass, that the bird, while out one day, met a fellow bird, to whom he boastfully **expatiated** on the excellence of his household arrangements. But the other bird sneered at him for being a poor simpleton, who did all the hard work, while the other two stayed at home and had a good time of it. For, when the mouse had made the fire and fetched in the water, she could retire into her little room and rest until it was time to set the table. The sausage had only to watch the pot to see that the food was properly cooked, and when it was near dinnertime, he just threw himself into the broth, or rolled in and out among the vegetables three or four times, and there they were, buttered, and salted, and ready to be served. Then, when the bird came home and had laid aside his burden, they sat down to table, and when they had finished their meal, they could sleep their fill till the following morning: and that was really a very delightful life."*

—Jacob (1785–1863) and Wilhelm (1786–1859) Grimm, German academics, linguists, cultural researchers, and authors, *The Mouse, the Bird, and the Sausage*

*(1) "Robert E. Lee was generally described as antislavery. This assumption rests not on any public position he took but on a passage in an 1856 letter to his wife. The passage begins: 'In this enlightened age, there are few I believe, but what will acknowledge, that slavery as an institution, is a moral & political evil in any Country. It is useless to **expatiate** on its disadvantages.'"*

—Blount, Roy. "Making Sense of Robert E. Lee," *Smithsonian*, Volume 34, Issue 4, July 2004: pg. 58, 8p, 2c, 6bw.

Expiate

(1)   apologize; atone; make amends; make up; pay the penalty for; redress; suffer

Word Used in Sentence(s)

*(1) "But, in order to **expiate** the sin of avarice, which was my undoing, I oblige each passer-by to give me a blow."*

—Andrew Lang, Scottish poet, novelist (*Arabian Nights*), literary critic, and contributor to the field of anthropology (1844–1912)

*(1) "Thou whose injustice hath supplied the cause that makes me quit the weary life I loathe, as by this wounded bosom thou canst see how willingly thy victim I become, let not my death, if haply worth a tear, cloud the clear heaven that dwells in thy bright eyes; I would not have thee **expiate** in aught the crime of having made my heart thy prey; but rather let thy laughter gaily ring and prove my death to be thy festival."*

—Miguel Cervantes, Spanish novelist, poet, and playwright (1546–1616) *Don Quixote*

*(1) "Some Republicans remain terminally uncomfortable with issues involving race. One can still find those who regard black Americans as a group apart—poor, exotic, faintly criminal, and not fully equipped for life in polite society. In the grips of remorse, these Republicans act like white liberals: anxious, guilt-besotted, stricken by low self-esteem. They try to **expiate** their sins by behaving like what Peggy Noonan once called 'low-rent Democrats.'"*

—Snow, Tony. "The Race Card," *New Republic*, Volume 207, Issue 25, December 14, 1992: pg. 17–20, 3p.

<u>Collocates to:</u> against, desire, helped, sins, guilt

Explicate

(1)   analyze logically; clarify; elucidate; explain; illuminate; interpret; make clear; spell out; write about something at great length

Word Used in Sentence(s)

(1) *The business plan components should **explicate** both the vision and mission of the firm.*

(1) *The term **explicate** means tell the whole truth. Make it plain to the reader and don't leave anything out; but also don't leave anything implied.*

<u>Collocates to:</u> cognition, findings, issues, orders, plans, social behavior, text

Expostulate

(1) admonish; argue; complain; object; protest
(2) to reason with someone earnestly, objecting to that one's actions or intentions

Word Used in Sentence(s)

(1) "The generous nature of Safie was outraged by this command; she attempted to __expostulate__ with her father, but he left her angrily, reiterating his tyrannical mandate."

—Mary Shelley, English novelist, short story writer, dramatist, essayist, biographer, and travel writer (1797–1851), *Frankenstein*

(1) "Caroline drew in a breath to __expostulate__, then let it out again slowly as the necessity for realism overtook her."

—Perry, Anne. *Farriers' Lane*, NY: Fawcett Crest, 1993.

Flummox

(1) bewildered; confounded; in mystery

Word Used in Sentence(s)

(1) "__Flummoxed__ by Failure or Focused"

—Bain, Ken. "Headlines," *Wall Street Journal Review*, July 14, 2012: pg. C3.

(1) Some new digital applications can __flummox__ even the savviest mobile users.

Fulminate

(1) expel; explode; turn against

Word Used in Sentence(s)

(1) "I confess that I do not see what good it does to __fulminate__ against the English tyranny while the Roman tyranny occupies the palace of the soul."

—James Joyce, Irish novelist and poet (1882–1941)

*(1)"He lets other **fulminate** on his behalf while he maintains his gentlemanly demeanor."*

—Sandomir, Richard. "Cablevision's Dolan Makes the Deal Only When He's Ready," *New York Times*, December 6, 1998.

Gainsay

(1) contradict; deny; dispute; refuse to believe or grant the truth of something

Word Used in Sentence(s)

*(1) She was a founding member of the religion, yet the church leaders wanted her to **gainsay** her faith.*

Glaver

(1) babble; complement excessively; flatter; jabber; prate; wheedle

Word Used in Sentence(s)

*(1) "Here many, clepid filosophirs, **glaver** diversely."*

—John Wycliffe, English Scholastic philosopher, theologian, lay preacher, translator, reformer, and university teacher at Oxford University (1328–1384)

*(1) "Yon **glavering** idiot has long ears to match his long tongue."*

—George W. Gough, author of *The Yeoman Adventurer* (1873–Unknown)

Gorgonize

(1) paralyze or mesmerize with one's looks or personality; petrify or stupefy with a look

Word Used in Sentence(s)

*(1) "**Gorgonised** me from head to foot with a stony British stare."*

—Alfred, Lord Tennyson, English Poet Laureate of Great Britain and Ireland (1809–1892)

Hie

(1) belt along; cannonball along; hurry or hasten; hotfoot; locomote; move very fast; pelt along; race; rush; speed; step on it

Word Used in Sentence(s)

*(1) You will need to **hie** through the areas with little traffic if you plan to arrive on time.*

Imbricate

(1) cover; overlap in layers

Word Used in Sentence(s)

*(1) **Imbricate** the roof tiles.*

Immure

(1) build into a wall; confine someone; detain; enclose; jail; imprison; incarcerate; intern; put someone in a place with no escape; seclude; shut away; shut in

Word Used in Sentence(s)

*(1) "He who possesses the divine powers of the soul is a great being, be his place what it may. You may clothe him with rags, may **immure** him in a dungeon, may chain him to slavish tasks. But he is still great."*

—William Ellery Channing, American moralist, Unitarian clergyman, and author (1780–1842)

*(1) "Few go to college, effectively sentencing most of them, Rabbi Arthur Hertzberg tells the filmmakers, to lives of penury. And women are reared to become Jewish mothers, again and again and again. To outsiders, this is degrading; to Hasidim, it is exalting. 'After 100 years who's going to remember who ran Westinghouse, and who cares?' explains Ms. Abromowitz, the haberdasher. 'Your children will be a legacy forever.' Of course, the Hasidim cannot **immure** themselves completely; the film is filled with scenes of them riding the subway, reading English-language newspapers, walking past X-rated-video stores."*

—Margolick, David. "Opening a Window on Hasidism," *New York Times*, July 20, 1997.

Impute

(1) accredit; ascribe a result or quality to anything or anyone; assign;
attribute; fix

(2) accuse; allege; assert; challenge; charge; cite; implicate

Word Used in Sentence(s)

*(1) "Steve Jobs wanted customers to have a tactile experience when
opening the box of an iPhone or iPad. Sometimes Jobs used the design of
a machine to '__impute__' a signal rather than to be merely functional."*

—Isaacson, Walter. "The Real Leadership Lessons of Steve Jobs,"
Harvard Business Review, April 2012: pg. 98.

Inculcate

(1) impress a belief or idea on someone by repeating it over and over again
until the idea is accepted

(2) teach by persistent urging

(3) implant ideas through constant admonishing

Word Used in Sentence(s)

*(1) "When schools fail to __inculcate__ American values, giving short shrift
to the history of the American Revolution, the American Civil War, and
the American Civil Rights Movement, while emphasizing the history of
Africa, Latin America, or Asia, they are severing the ties that bind
Americans together in the name of diversity."*

—Braceras, Jennifer. "Not Necessarily in Conflict: Americans Can Be
Both United and Culturally Diverse," *Harvard Journal of Law & Public
Policy*, Volume 29, Issue 1, Fall 2005: pg. 27–32, 6p.

*(1) "As a researcher, I am interested in the behavior of digital natives.
The question of privacy—even the illusion of it—does not appear to be a
concern. Research indicates that the early __inculcation__ to a digital inter-
face (for example, children using iPads) may result in people never even
thinking about privacy."*

—Lee Sr., Jim, Knowledge Management practice leader. "The Best
Leaders Have Short Resumes," *Harvard Business Review*, December
2012: pg. 19.

Ingratiate

(1)   bow to; crawl to; curry favor; defer to; gain favor or favorable acceptance
for by deliberate effort; grovel to; make acceptable to another; suck up
to; toddy

Word Used in Sentence(s)

*(1) "Politicians are aiming to **ingratiate** themselves with Hispanics."*

—Meadows, Bob. "Race (Still) Matters," *Essence*, Volume 41, Issue 7;
November 2010: pg. 132, 5 p.

*(1) "No book is perfect. But Sleeper's citation of minor mistakes, espe-
cially when accompanied by his crude and pejorative ideological label-
ing, is where the real dishonesty resides. His effort represents one of the
more unfortunate things a book critic can do: use a review to **ingratiate**
himself with a certain ideological camp or to be more strongly identified
with that camp's views."*

—Anonymous. "Letter to the Editors," in response to "The Next
Generation of Technology: 35 Innovators under 35," *The Washington
Monthly*, July/August 2011.

Collocates to: herself, himself, myself, themselves, trying, with

Interlard

(1)   diversify; insert something different; interpolate; interpose; intersperse;
intertwine; interweave; introduce; mix together; vary, punctuate, or interrupt speech or writing by interspersing contrasting material

Word Used in Sentence(s)

*(1) His speech pattern was colorful because he **interlarded** it with
metaphors, similes, and quirky but interesting idioms.*

Inveigle

(1)   convince or persuade someone through trickery deception, dishonesty, or
flattery

Word Used in Sentence(s)

*(1) Former President Clinton had a scheme to **inveigle** several big insurance firms to cover his legal costs of impeachment.*

Juxtapose

(1)   adjoining; place side by side or close together for purposes of comparison; put side by side to compare

Word Used in Sentence(s)

*(1) "There has rarely been a starker **juxtaposition** of evil and innocence than the moment George W. Bush received the news about 9/11 while reading the* Pet Goat *with second graders in Sarasota, Florida."*

—Padgett, Tim. "The Interrupted Reading: The Kids with George W. Bush on 9/11," *Time Magazine*, May 3, 2011.

*(1) "I'm very interested in the color of sound. And I'm very interested in the **juxtaposition** of different things, ethnic instruments **juxtaposed** with symphonic instruments, and I'm interested in the ancient and the modern. I don't know why, but it has always been something that's fascinated me, from when I first heard a symphony orchestra I wanted to know how those sounds were made."*

—Anne Dudley, English composer and pop musician (1956–)

Lucubrate

(1)   produce a written work through lengthy, intensive effort; work, write, or study laboriously, especially at night; write learnedly

Word Used in Sentence(s)

*(1) He **lucubrated** for years in order to complete the 20-volume work on Lord Byron.*

Meliorate

(1)   amend; improve; make something better or more tolerable; soften

Word Used in Sentence(s)

(1) "The book of Nature is the book of Fate. She turns the gigantic pages,—leaf after leaf,—never returning one. One leaf she lays down, a floor of granite; then a thousand ages, and a bed of slate; a thousand ages, and a measure of coal; a thousand ages, and a layer of marl and mud; vegetable forms appear; her first misshapen animals, zoophyte, trilobium, fish; then, saurians—rude forms, in which she has only

*blocked her future statue, concealing under these unwieldy monsters the fine type of her coming king. The face of the planet cools and dries, the races **meliorate**, and man is born. But when a race has lived its term, it comes no more again."*

—Ralph Waldo Emerson, American essayist, lecturer, and poet (1803–1882)

Natter

(1) babble or talk ceaselessly; blather; chatter; gossip; grumble; have a chat; jaw; talk; to chit chat

Word Used in Sentence(s)

*(1) We used to make fun of a few old women **nattering** across the backyard fence for a few minutes a couple times a week; now tens of millions of people of every age and type do the same thing for hours a day online.*

Objurgate

(1) blame; castigate; chasten; chide vehemently; correct; decry; denounce; limit to a certain type of behavior; revile; upbraid harshly

Word Used in Sentence(s)

*(1) Everyone is looking for someone to **objurgate** for the high gas prices.*

Obnubilate

(1) becloud; cloud; darken; make obscure, vague

Word Used in Sentence(s)

*(1) "In the room which Monsieur Jacques Parizeau vacated so suddenly, the 'body odor of race,' to quote Montreal poet A.M. Klein, will continue to **obnubilate** until a window breaks."*

—Reimann, Peter. *Monsieur's Lapse*, Toronto, Canada: The Globe and Mail, November 3, 1995.

Obsecrate

(1) beg; beseech; implore; plead; supplicate

Word Used in Sentence(s)

*(1) Sometimes you must **obsecrate** to get what you want.*

Opine

(1) discourse; go on; harangue; hold, express, or give an opinion; lecture; orate; preach; rant; speak out; stress something; suppose; think

Word Used in Sentence(s)

*(1) You can **opine** about what employers should care about, but their primary concern is if you will fit in.*

Oppugn

(1) challenge the accuracy, probity of

Word Used in Sentence(s)

*(1) Jorge had the audacity to **oppugn** the merits of the data privacy research, which is a subject he knows nothing about.*

Pettifog

(1) argue over the details; engage in legal trickery; quibble

Word Used in Sentence(s)

*(1) Politicians will **pettifog** and try to make it sound like they are doing the people's business.*

Pontificate

(1) be a blowhard; express opinions in a pompous and dogmatic way

Word Used in Sentence(s)

*(1) "We try, we fail, we posture, we aspire, we **pontificate**—and then we age, shrink, die, and vanish."*

—George Saunders, American writer of short stories, essays, novellas, and children's books (1958–)

Prate

(1) babble; blather; chatter in a childish way; gibber; jabber; prattle; rant;
talk foolishly or at tedious length

Word Used in Sentence(s)

*(1) "In the present system of the National Institute of Health grants,
there is no way to succeed. 'No matter how much they **prate** in public
about thinking outside the box and rewarding 'high-risk' proposals,' the
reviewers are the same and their self-interest is the same."*

—Bethell, Tom. "Challenging Conventional Wisdom," *American
Spector*, Volume 38, Issue 6, July/August 2005: pg. 50–53.

*(1) "All periods **prate** against one another in your spirits; and the
dreams and **pratings** of all periods were even realer than your awake-
ness!"*

—Friedrich Nietzsche, German philosopher, poet, composer, cultural
critic, and classical philologist (1844–1900)

*(1) "This I conceive to be no time to **prate** of moral influences. Our
men's nerves require their accustomed narcotics, and a glass of whiskey
is a powerful friend in a sunstroke, and these poor fellows fall senseless
on their heavy drills."*

—Clara Barton, American teacher, patent clerk, nurse, and humanitarian
(1821–1912)

Propitiate

(1) favor; gain approval; like best; placate; win over

Word Used in Sentence(s)

*(1) "The cloud was so dark that it needed all the bright lights that could
be turned upon it. But for four years there was a contagion of nobility in
the land, and the best blood North and South poured itself out a libation
to **propitiate** the deities of Truth and Justice. The great sin of slavery was
washed out, but at what a cost!"*

—M. E. W. Sherwood, U.S. author of *An Epistle to Posterity*, Ch. 5
(1826–1903)

Promulgate

(1) broadcast; circulate; publish or make known; spread; transmit

Word Used in Sentence(s)

(1) "The duty of criticism is neither to depreciate nor dignify by partial representations, but to hold out the light of reason, whatever it may discover; and to **_promulgate_** *the determinations of truth, whatever she shall dictate."*

—Samuel Johnson, English poet, critic, and writer (1709–1784)

(1) "Today Americans would be outraged if U.N. troops entered Los Angeles to restore order; tomorrow they will be grateful! This is especially true if they were told there was an outside threat from beyond whether real or **_promulgated_***, that threatened our very existence. It is then that all peoples of the world will pledge with world leaders to deliver them from this evil. The one thing every man fears is the unknown. When presented with this scenario, individual rights will be willingly relinquished for the guarantee of their well-being granted to them by their world government."*

—Henry Kissinger, American political scientist, in an address to the Bilderberger meeting at Evian, France, May 21, 1992 (1923–)

Proselytize

(1)   indoctrinate to another cause or idea; recruit converts to a cause

Word Used in Sentence(s)

(1) "We do not need to **_proselytize_** *either by our speech or by our writing. We can only do so really with our lives. Let our lives be open books for all to study."*

—Mohandas Gandhi, Indian, preeminent leader of Indian nationalism in British-ruled India (1869–1948)

Quaff

(1) drink with gusto and in large volume; guzzle; imbibe; swill

Word Used in Sentence(s)

*(1) "We **quaff** the cup of life with eager haste without draining it, instead of which it only overflows the brim, objects press around us, filling the mind with the throng of desires that wait upon them, so that we have no room for the thoughts of death."*

—Oscar Wilde, Irish poet, novelist, dramatist, and critic (1854–1900)

Recrudesce

(1) become active again after a period of latency; break out

Word Used in Sentence(s)

*(1) Extremist political movements **recrudesce** from time to time.*

Reify

(1) materialize; regard (something abstract) as a material or concrete thing

Word Used in Sentence(s)

*(1) There is an old saying that too many people **reify** the model and mis-understand the world, meaning that there is too much emphasis on models, causing people to miss what is really happening.*

Repine

(1) complain; express unhappiness; feel or express dejection or discontent; fret

Word Used in Sentence(s)

*(1) "Though love **repine**, and reason chafe, there came a voice without reply—'Tis man's perdition to be safe, When for the truth he ought to die."*

—Ralph Waldo Emerson, American poet, lecturer, and essayist (1803–1882)

Remonstrate

(1) complain or object; make objection; plead or protest; repine; say in protest or show disapproval

Word Used in Sentence(s)

*(1) It is part of our custom to **remonstrate** and pontificate; it is part of how we demonstrate freedom of speech.*

Reprove

(1) accuse; admonish; censure; chide; correct; criticize others; disapprove; hall over the coals; rebuke; reprimand; scold; take to task; tell off

Word Used in Sentence(s)

*(1) In years past, parents **reproved** their children for misdeeds, but today that would be deemed verbal abuse.*

Reshape

(1) change or restore; reform; reformat; remake; remodel; restructure; rewrite; shape anew or again

Word Used in Sentence(s)

*(1) "On October 25, 2005, the Swedish telecommunications equipment maker Erickson announced the acquisition of key parts of Marconi's telecom business—thus starting a wave of deals that would **reshape** the global industry."*

—Keil, Thomas and Tomi Llmanen. "When Rivals Merge, Think Before You Follow Suit," *Harvard Business Review*, December 2011: pg. 25.

*(1) "Business model innovations have **reshaped** entire industries and redistributed billions of dollars of value."*

—Johnson, Mark, Clayton Christensen, and Henning Kagermann. "Reinventing Your Business Model," *Harvard Business Review*, December 2008: pg. 51.

Stultify

(1) impair or make ineffective

Word Used in Sentence(s)

(1) "Lucas waited until the company had stopped laughing over this; then he began again: 'But look at it from the point of view of practical politics, comrade. Here is an historical figure whom all men reverence

*and love, whom some regard as divine; and who was one of us—who lived our life, and taught our doctrine. And now shall we leave him in the hands of his enemies—shall we allow them to stifle and **stultify** his example?'"*

—Upton Sinclair, American author of *The Jungle* (1878–1978)

Unbosom

(1) disclose; give vent to feelings; reveal; tell all; tell one's troubles and inner feelings

Word Used in Sentence(s)

*(1) "Don Quixote wrapped the bedclothes round him and covered himself up completely, leaving nothing but his face visible, and as soon as they had both regained their composure he broke silence, saying, 'Now, Senora Dona Rodriguez, you may **unbosom** yourself and out with everything you have in your sorrowful heart and afflicted bowels; and by me you shall be listened to with chaste ears, and aided by compassionate exertions.'"*

—Miguel Cervantes, Spanish novelist, poet, and playwright, and author of *Don Quixote* (1547–1616)

Vituperate

(1) berate; harsh; scold; speak viciously about

Word Used in Sentence(s)

*(1) "The Yugoslavian-born poet Charles Simic has said, 'There are moments in life when true invective is called for, when it becomes an absolute necessity, out of a deep sense of justice, to denounce, mock, **vituperate**, lash out, in the strongest possible language.' We have come to such a moment. Leaving aside invective, **vituperation,** and mockery, I believe that we need space for peaceful yet passionate outrage."*

—Tannen, Deborah. "We Need Higher Quality Outrage," *Christian Science Monitor*, 2004.

Vitiate

(1) faulty; imperfect; impure; invalidate; make corrupt or unclean; pollute; spoil

Word Used in Sentence(s)

(1) For years, so-called "Christian zealot" groups have campaigned against homosexuality, claiming it <u>vitiates</u> the morality of America.

(1) "Saint Augustine wished to exclude any necessarily illusory utopianism from human hope here below. Even with his full complement of secular pessimism, Augustine was not advocating cruel and arbitrary rule, for he knew well how wicked motives could <u>vitiate</u> an otherwise well-governed state."

—Russell, Fredrick. "Only Something Good Can Be Evil: The Secular Genesis of Augustine's Secular Ambivalence," *Theological Studies*, Volume 51, Issue 4, December 1990: pg. 698, 19p.

(1) "The fact is that we had absolutely incompatible dispositions and habits of thought and action, and our danger and isolation only accentuated the incompatibility. At Halliford, I had already come to hate the curate's trick of helpless exclamation, his stupid rigidity of mind. His endless muttering monologue <u>vitiated</u> every effort I made to think out a line of action, and drove me at times, thus pent up and intensified, almost to the verge of craziness."

—H.G. Wells, English writer, author of *The War of the Worlds* (1866–1946)

Vociferate

(1)   clamor; bawl; shout; speak or say loudly or nosily

Word Used in Sentence(s)

(1) The constitutional right of assembly does not include the right to <u>vociferate</u> and disturb a speaker with whom your group disagrees.

(1) "I <u>vociferated</u> curses enough to annihilate any fiend in Christendom; and I got a stone and thrust it between his jaws, and tried with all my might to cram it down his throat. A beast of a servant came up with a lantern, at last, shouting—'Keep fast, Skulker, keep fast!'"

—Emily Bronte, English novelist and poet (1818–1848) *Wuthering Heights*

Vouch safe

(1) deign; do or give; give or grant in a gracious manner

Word Used in Sentence(s)

*(1) "The Trojans were scared when they saw the two sons of Dares, one of them in fright and the other lying dead by his chariot. Minerva, therefore, took Mars by the hand and said, 'Mars, Mars, bane of men, bloodstained stormer of cities, may we not now leave the Trojans and Achaeans to fight it out, and see to which of the two Jove will **vouchsafe** the victory? Let us go away, and thus avoid his anger.'"*

—Homer, author of the *Iliad* and the *Odyssey*, revered as the greatest of ancient Greek epic poets (circa 800 BC–701 BC)

6

100 Top Action Verbs for Presenters, Professors, Preachers, Poets, Playwrights, and Pundits Searching for Savoir Faire

Abdicate

(1) abandon; cede; demit; discard; relinquish; renounce; repudiate; resign; surrender (especially from a powerful position)

Word Used in Sentence(s)

*(1) Many British kings **abdicated** their crowns.*

*(1) **Abdicating** the throne is a serious matter for a monarch.*

*(1) "Napoleon, pressured to **abdicate** by his marshals in 1814, declared, 'Why is it always Wellington?'"*

—Black, Jeremy. *Military History*, Volume 22, Issue 3, Spring 2010: pg. 66.

*(1) "Power **abdicates** only under the stress of counter-power."*

—Martin Buber, German Jewish Biblical translator, philosopher, and interpreter (1878–1965)

Collocates to: duties, office, position, responsibilities, throne

Aberrate

(1) diverge from the expected; diverge or deviate from the straight path

Word Used in Sentence(s)

*(1) A mentor should never **aberrate** from being a perfect gentleman.*

Abide

(1)   bear; continue; endure; go on being; put up with; stomach; take; tolerate
(2)   hold; remain; stand fast; stand for; stay
(3)   to remain with someone; to stay

Word Used in Sentence(s)

*(1) "Gadhafi's government had lost all legitimacy and lied when it declared Friday it would **abide** by a cease-fire."*

—Hillary Rodham Clinton, U.S. Secretary of State (1947–), qtd. in Associated Press 2011

*(1) "I am not liked as a President by the politicians in office, in the press, or in Congress. But I am content to **abide** the judgment the sober second thought of the people."*

—Rutherford B. Hayes, 19th U.S. President (1822–1893)

Collocates to: agreement, by, certain, law, longer, must, regulations, rules, shall, standards, terms

Abduce

(1)   allege; cite; to advance evidence for
(2)   draw away; to abduct

Word Used in Sentence(s)

*(1) "If we **abduce** the eye unto either corner, the object will not duplicate."*

—Sir Thomas Browne, English author (1605–1682)

*(1) The project management team must **abduce** reasons for the cost overruns when there was no indication at the last stage gate of any such overage.*

Absolve

(1) clear; exculpate; forgive; free of blame or guilt; pardon; release

(2) prove someone is not responsible for

Word Used in Sentence(s)

> *(1) "Enron's 'firing' of Arthur Andersen as its auditor on Thursday, and the finger-pointing leading to it, amounts to a lovers' quarrel. Andersen, we now know, had been troubled for some time by Enron's accounting, but not so troubled that it was willing to risk losing such a lucrative client. So it submissively signed off on deceptive earnings reports. Last week's dismissal by Andersen of its lead Enron auditor, David Duncan, and its attempt to blame him for the destruction of Enron-related documents do not begin to **absolve** the firm."*

—Editors. "The Enron Hearings: Cleaning Up After the Debacle," *New York Times*, February 1, 2002.

<u>**Collocates to:**</u> <u>blame, does, guild, himself, ourself, responsibility, sins, yourself</u>

Absterge

(1) clean; cleanse; purge; wipe away

Word Used in Sentence(s)

> *(1) Under this administration, there appears to be a belief that many terrorists can **absterge** their crimes in civil court with lenient sentences.*

Accentuate

(1) accent; emphasize; heighten; intensify

(2) make more noticeable; play up; stress something

(3) mark with an accent

Word Used in Sentence(s)

> *(1) "Delete the negative; **accentuate** the positive!"*

—Donna Karan, American fashion designer (1948–)

*(1) "A science is said to be useful if its development tends to **accentuate** the existing inequities in the distribution of wealth, or more directly promotes the destruction of human life."*

—Godfrey Harold Hardy, English mathematician (1877–1947)

Collocates to: differences, opportunities, positives, shapes

Adumbrate

(1) foreshadow; give a general description of something but not the details; obscure; overshadow; predict; prefigure; presage; summary

Word Used in Sentence(s)

*(1) The global political troubles **adumbrated** an eventual world-wide economic recession.*

*(1) It is never good for a manager to **adumbrate** news of a partial lay-off to just a few employees.*

Advocate

(1) advance; back; be in favor of; bolster; defend; encourage; promote; sponsor; support

Word Used in Sentence(s)

*(1) Occasionally **advocating** the minority position may be a good strategy.*

*(1) "Can one preach at home inequality of races and nations and **advocate** abroad good-will towards all men?"*

—Dorothy Thompson, American journalist and radio broadcaster (1893–1961)

*(1) "Those who **advocate** common usage in philosophy sometimes speak in a manner that suggests the mystique of the 'common man.'"*

—Bertrand Russell, English logician and philosopher (1872–1970)

Affirm

(1) acknowledge; affirm; announce; asseverate; assert; avow; confirm; establish; insist; pronounce; state; validate; verify

(2) encourage; support; sustain; uphold

Word Used in Sentence(s)

(1) "If you could do only one thing as a mentor, __affirm__ your protégé."

—Johnson, W. Brad and Charles R. Ridley. *The Elements of Mentoring*, NY: Palgrave Macmillan, 2004: pg.10.

(1) "The more I read, the more I meditate; and the more I acquire, the more I am enabled to __affirm__ that I know nothing."

—Voltaire, French philosopher and writer (1694–1778)

(1) "Man is born a predestined idealist, for he is born to act. To act is to __affirm__ the worth of an end, and to persist in affirming the worth of an end is to make an ideal."

—Oliver Wendell Holmes, American physician, poet, writer, humorist, and professor (1809–1894)

Agglomerate

(1) accumulate; cluster; gather together; jumbled collection

Word Used in Sentence(s)

(1) "Common property campesino communities fit very uncomfortably in the neoliberal discourse, but in the Mexican context, ejidos and comunidades agrarias are irrevocable, at least in the short and medium term. The reformers, therefore, also created new legal mechanisms for private capital to associate with common property through joint ventures, made it easier to __agglomerate__ land within ejidos, and established new mechanisms for associations of individuals within ejidos and comunidades to exploit common properties (Wexler and Bray 1996; Cornelius and Myhre 1998; World Bank 1995, 69)."

—Koolster, Dan. "Campesinos and Mexican Forest Policy During the Twentieth Century," *Latin American Research Review*, Volume 38, Issue 2, 2003: pg. 94.

Aggrandize

(1) exalt; increase; make greater; make larger; puffery

Word Used in Sentence(s)

(1) It is merely __aggrandizing__ when the firm's advertising is nothing more than puffery.

*(1) The firm's public statement of the incident appeared to be an **aggrandized** version of their mission statement.*

Alleviate

(1) assuage; ease; facilitate; improve; lessen; lighten; make bearable; to relieve

Word Used in Sentence(s)

*(1) "The new technologies that we see coming will have major benefits that will greatly **alleviate** human suffering."*

—Ralph Merkle, American inventor of cryptographic hashing and a researcher and speaker on molecular nanotechnology (1952–)

*(1) "We have discovered that the scheme of 'outlawing war' has made war more like an outlaw without making it less frequent and that to banish the knight does not **alleviate** the suffering of the peasant."*

—C.S. Lewis, British scholar and novelist (1898–1963)

Collocates to: concerns, pain, poverty, some, suffering

Ameliorate

(1) correct a mistake; improve; make better; tolerate
(2) correct a deficiency or defect; take action that make up for one's negative or improper actions; to make right a wrong

Word Used in Sentence(s)

*(1) Kathy demonstrated her strength of character by **ameliorating** the errors in the project which she caused before anyone else discovered them.*

*(1) Phillip **ameliorated** the issues in the business plan prior to the meeting with the investors.*

*(1) "For more than 100 years, psychologists have attempted, with modest success, to **ameliorate** mental problems from depression to low intelligence by changing patients' attitudes and by exploring their childhood angst. Now, pharmacological approaches are used, also with only moderate success. Recent evidence suggests a more fruitful path tied to the*

fact that human behavior—sexual orientation, alcoholism, intelligence, the propensity for violence—has a genetic component."

—Nemko, Marty. "Choosing the Career Path Less Traveled," *U.S. News & World Report*, Volume 146, Issue 4, May 1, 2009: pg. 22.

<u>**Collocates to:**</u> <u>conditions, economic effects, efforts, help, might, prevent, problems</u>

Articulate

(1) convey; enunciate; express thoughts, ideas, or feelings coherently; pronounce; put into words; say; speak clearly; speech; utter

Word Used in Sentence(s)

*(1) "For the past 30 years, a group of social scientists around the world—from pioneers like Edward Deci and Richard Ryan, at the University of Rochester, to a new generation of scholars such as Adam Grant, at Wharton—have **articulated** a more subtle view of what motivates people in a variety of settings, including work."*

—Pink, Daniel. "A Radical Prescription for Sales," *Harvard Business Review*, July–August 2012: pg. 77.

*(1) "Leaders **articulate** a lucid sense of purpose, create effective leadership teams, prioritize, and sequence their initiatives carefully, redesign organizational structures to make good execution easier, and most importantly, integrate these tactics into one coherent strategy."*

—Wheeler, Steven, Walter McFarland, and Art Kleiner. "A Blueprint for Strategic Leadership," *Strategy+Business*, Issue 49, Winter 2007: pg. 46.

Assuage

(1) appease; erase doubts and fears; mollify; pacify; satisfy; soothe

Word Used in Sentence(s)

*(1) Judy was extremely annoyed, angry, and fearful that Tom showed up unannounced. She had previously kept him away by a restraining order; to avoid further trouble and to **assuage** her, Tom left.*

*(1) I worked to **assuage** my own guilt over the incident.*

*(1) "I've never know any trouble that an hour's reading didn't **assuage**."*

—Arthur Schopenhauer, German philosopher (1788–1860)

Collocates to: anger, anguish, anxiety, concerns, consciences, curiosity, doubt, fears, feelings, guilt, hunger, hurt, loneliness, pride, worries

Attune

(1) accustom to; adjust; bring into accord with someone or something; regulate; standardize

Word Used in Sentence(s)

*(1) "Kantor makes the case that being **attuned** to the signals of a conversational system—an approach he calls "structural dynamics"—is the first step toward becoming a far more prescient and effective leader."*

—Kliener, Art. "Building the Skills of Insight," *Strategy + Business*, http://www.strategy-business.com/article/00154?gko=d4421&cid= TL20130117&utm_campaign=TL20130117, accessed January 17, 2013.

Collocates with: nature, ourselves, senses, themselves, tools, ways

Augur

(1) betoken; bode; divine; forebode; foreshadow; foretell; portend; predict

Word Used in Sentence(s)

*(1) The improved weather **augured** for a better hunting season.*

*(1) A growing third-party movement is **auguring** for a far greater voter turnout in the next election.*

*(1) "These readings **augur** well in the very near term for supportive bond price action. We, however, still look for core inflation to tick up modestly and for overall labor market conditions to improve gradually."*

—Chris Sullivan, chief investment officer at the United Nations Federal Credit Union and UNFCU Financial Advisors

Collocates to: does, future, might, not, poorly, well

Author

(1) created; pen; scribe; source; write

Balance

(1) assess; calculate; collate; compare; consider; equalize; evaluate; even out; keep upright; offset; settle; square; stabilize; stay poised; steady; tally; total; weigh; weight up

Word Used in Sentence(s)

*(1) Managing a global enterprise requires a CEO who is adept at **balancing** many interests.*

*(1) Managers need to use a **balanced** approach in handling worker disputes.*

Bestride something like a Colossus

(1) to be a giant in some endeavor or field; to be preeminent

Word Used in Sentence(s)

*(1) "Why man, he doth **bestride the narrow world like a Colossus**, and we petty men walk under his huge legs and peep about to find ourselves dishonorable graves."*

—William Shakespeare, English poet and playwright (1564–1516); excerpt from *Julius Caesar*

Bloviate

(1) speak pompously and at length; to hold forth in a pompous self-centered way; to orate verbosely

Word Used in Sentence(s)

*(1) It seems as though elected officials are really good at only one thing—they love to **bloviate**.*

*(1) To **bloviate** is not recommended when you are among experts on the current topic.*

*(1) "Warren Harding invented the word 'normalcy,' and the lesser known '**bloviate**,' meaning one imagines, to spout, to spew aimless verbiage."*

—John Ashbery, U.S. poet and critic (1927–)

Broach

(1)   bring up; discuss; introduce; mention; moot; open up a subject for dis-
      cussion; present; put forth; raise; suggest

Word Used in Sentence(s)

> *(1) **Broaching** the topic of addiction with a family member is heart-
> wrenching but an act of love.*

> *(1) "The essays as a whole reflect the influence of anthropological con-
> cepts as well as studies conducted since the early 1980s by cultural his-
> torians of Europe and the United States (such as Lynn Hunt's work on
> the French Revolution). They **broach** a wide range of topics: popular
> religious celebrations, the delightful subject of street songs and dance,
> work and labor conditions, the notion of public space and its use, educa-
> tional reform, civic festivals, and village bands."*

> —Murray, Pamela. "Diverse Approaches to Nineteenth-Century
> Mexican History," *Latin American Research Review*, Volume 32, Issue 3,
> 1997: pg. 187, 6p.

Burn one's boats

(1)   burn one's bridges; choose a killing ground; commit to a course of
      action; cut oneself off from all means or hope of retreat; go for broke;
      irreversible course of action; nail one's colors to the mast; to put oneself
      in a position from which there is no going back

Word Used in Sentence(s)

> *(1) In 310 BC, Agathocles of Syracuse sailed his army to Carthage and
> **burned his boats** so his soldiers knew that the price of failure would be
> their death.*

Cachinnate

(1)   laugh convulsively or hard; laugh loudly or immoderately

Word Used in Sentence(s)

> *(1) There are some unconfirmed eyewitness accounts that Joseph Stalin
> would **cachinnate** loudly after he had finished berating and verbally ter-
> rorizing someone he believed was a weakling or coward.*

Cadge

(1) ask; beg; get away with; rob; sneak; sponge by imposing on another's good nature; steal; take

Word Used in Sentence(s)

*(1) If people were not in such a good mood during the Christmas season, **cadging** by many charities would not be so successful.*

Collocates to: drinks, food, free, from, lift, try

Calumniate

(1) charges or imputations; slander; traduce; utter maliciously false statements

Word Used in Sentence(s)

*(1) "I am not to order the natural sympathies of my own breast, and of every honest breast to wait until the tales and all the anecdotes of the coffeehouses of Paris and of the dissenting meeting houses of London are scoured of all the slander of those who **calumniate** persons, that afterwards they may murder them with impunity. I know nothing of your story of Messalina. What, are not high rank, great splendour of descent, great personal elegance and outward accomplishments ingredients of moment in forming the interest we take in the misfortunes of men?"*

—Bromwich, David. "The Context of Burke's Reflections," *Social Research*, Volume 58, Issue 2, Summer 91: pg. 313–354.

Collocates to: afterwards, person, slander, that, those, who

Captivate

(1) enchant; enthrall; fascinate; infatuate; intense romantic attraction

Word Used in Sentence(s)

*(1) "All kinds of beauty do not inspire love; there is a kind that only pleases the sight but does not **captivate** the affections."*

—Cervantes, Spanish novelist, poet, and playwright (1547–1616) *Don Quixote*

Champion

(1) advocate; back; campaign for; crusade for; excel; fight for; stand up for; support; uphold; to be a winner

Word Used in Sentence(s)

*(1) Sharon was the **champion** for the new compensation plan.*

*(1) "We cannot be both the world's leading **champion** of peace and the world's leading supplier of the weapons of war."*

—Jimmy Carter, 39th U.S. President (1924–)

*(1) "**Champion** the right to be yourself; dare to be different and to set your own pattern; live your own life and follow your own star."*

—Wilfred Peterson, American author (1900–1995)

Cogitate

(1) consider; deliberate; meditate; muse; ponder; reflect; ruminate

Concinnate

(1) show skill and harmony, especially in a literary work; to show an elegant arrangement

Word Used in Sentence(s)

*(1) President John F. Kennedy demonstrated his communications skill with his ability to **concinnate**, especially when composing his speeches.*

Confabulate

(1) chat, converse, or talk informally

Word Used in Sentence(s)

*(1) "I shall not ask Jean Jacques Rousseau if birds **confabulate** or no."*

—William Cowper, English poet (1731–1800)

Conflagrate

(1) enflame; enkindle; ignite; kindle; start to burn

Word Used in Sentence(s)

*(1) "In fact, she was the one who got him the job with Janus. And he's the one who's supposed to investigate this. Dammit. By the time Rebecca arrived at the refinery, the automatic fire-suppression systems had dealt with the resultant **conflagration**, which barely had a chance to **conflagrate**. The different section chiefs started reporting in that their sections were okay, with the obvious exception of Yinnik regarding the refinery. One of T'Lis's assistants said the computer core was fine."*

—DeCandido, Keith R. A. *A Singular Destiny*, First Edition, New York: Pocket Books, 2009.

Conjure

(1) appeal; beg; make earnest or urgent appeal

(2) ring or summon into being as by magic

Word Used in Sentence(s)

*(1) She **conjured** him to give up the life of drugs.*

*(1) "No one who, like me, **conjures** up the most evil of those half-tamed demons that inhabit the human beast, and seeks to wrestle with them, can expect to come through the struggle unscathed."*

—Sigmund Freud, Austrian neurologist who became known as the founding father of psychoanalysis (1856–1939)

Connote

(1) imply meanings or ideas beyond the explicit meaning; suggest or convey a meaning

(2) involve as a condition or accompaniment

Word Used in Sentence(s)

(1) "Hal Rothman explained how Las Vegas was built on industries of vice by offering visitors something they could not have at home, and it thus took on the label of 'Sin City.' Las Vegas, he wrote, 'is a code for self-indulgence and sanctioned deviance' (2002, xviii). Indeed, 'vice' is common in the local vernacular in reference to the activities for which

*the city is known. Of course, 'vice' and 'sin' **connote** different things to different religions and cultures."*

—Rowley, Rex. "Religion in Sin City," *Geographical Review*, Volume 102, Issue 1, January 2012: p76–92.

Collocates to: came, differently, does, names, necessarily, status, term, uses

Countervail

(1) avail against; balance; compensate; equalize; make up for

Word Used in Sentence(s)

*(1) "In doctrinal form, this is known as the universal destination of goods, which fixes a social mortgage or claim on all property, tangible or intellectual. It is not collectivism, which has never produced enough wealth to distribute. Universal destination calls, rather, for a broader view of wealth and a robust array of forces and institutions to **countervail** pure capitalism. The anti-debt crusade, which seemed almost utopian a few years ago, has given us a useful sketch of that new global vision."*

—Bole, William. "Forgiving Their Debts," *America*, Volume 182, Issue 10, March 2000: pg. 17.

Declaim

(1) recite or read in public with studied or artful elegance

Word Used in Sentence(s)

*(1) "The fact that I couldn't recall the last name of even one of our daughter's so-called friends made me feel guiltier than ever. How can you call yourself a good mother, I could already hear the police **declaim**, when you don't even know who your daughter's friends are?"*

—Fielding, Joy. *Missing Pieces*, NY: Bantam Books, 1997.

Collocates to: against, banners, here, honeyed, now-grown, orations, scantly, soliloquy, vainly

Deem

(1) assess; hold; judge; regard; take for; view as

Word Used in Sentence(s)

*(1) "They **deem** him the worst enemy who tells them the truth."*

—Plato, Classical Greek philosopher and mathematician (472 BC–347 BC)

*(1) "I **deem** it the duty of every man to devote a certain portion of his income for charitable purposes; and that it is his further duty to see it so applied as to do the most good of which it is capable."*

—Thomas Jefferson, American founding father, 3rd U.S. President (1743–1826)

Defuse

(1) cease or ease danger of menacing situation

Word Used in Sentence(s)

*(1) The ability to **defuse** a potentially tense confrontation is not typically in a manager's job description.*

*(1) "Every once in a while, you meet someone who really knows how to 'read a room.' This is the individual, usually a seasoned executive leader, who can walk into a tense meeting and sense why two would-be collaborators are butting heads, why a third manager hardly speaks, and why a fourth seems to be protecting some unspoken priority. Then, with a few words, the room-reader can **defuse** the problem, get people back on track, and move the team to a new level of productivity."*

—Kliener, Art. "Building the Skills of Insight," *Strategy + Business*, http://www.strategy-business.com/article/00154?gko=d4421&cid=TL20130117&utm_campaign=TL20130117, accessed January 17, 2013.

*(1) "The House **defused** one potential debt crisis Wednesday, while a top Republican set the stage for a broader debate over whether it is possible to actually balance the U.S. budget in coming years."*

—Hook, Boles, and O'Connor. "Passing Debt Bill, GOP Pledges End to Deficits," *Wall Street Journal*, January 23, 2013.

Delimit

(1) define; demarcate; determine; fix boundaries; restrict; set limits; state clearly

Word Used in Sentence(s)

*(1) One of the steps a researcher should take is to **delimit** the scope of the study.*

*(1) "Speech sounds cannot be understood, **delimited**, classified, and explained except in the light of the tasks which they perform in language."*

—Roman Jakobson, Russian linguist and literary theorist (1896–1982)

Denote

(1) announce; designate; indicate; mean; represent; signify; symbolize

(2) allude to; convey; express; imply; mean; refer to

Word Used in Sentence(s)

*(1) "Accordingly, humanities has come to **denote** not just poems and stories but all refined art, including painting, music, sculpture, film, and the like. As a result, humanistic now means arty—in other words, refined, cultivated, and effete."*

—Hocutt, Max. "Humanities? No. Liberal Arts? Yes," *Springer,* Winter 90/91, Volume 4, Issue 1, pg. 59, 9p.

*(1) "In commercial circles, the term Power Center has come to **denote** strip malls dominated by large stores with little space for small merchants."*

—Morganfield, Robbie. "Faith and Finances: Power Center Seen as Model for Urban Life," *Houston Chronicle,* Sept 10, 1995: pg. 37.

Depict

(1) describe; get a picture of; give a picture of; illustrate; picture in words; portray; present a lifelike image; represent; show

Word Used in Sentence(s)

*(1) Robert **depicted** the story in his eloquent speech.*

Describe

(1) account; delineate; depict; explain something; outline; report; to give an account of something by giving details of its characteristics

Word Used in Sentence(s)

(1) "When people __described__ their personal best leadership experiences, they told of a time when they imagined an exciting, highly attractive future for their organization. They had visions and dreams of what could be."

—Kouzes, James and Berry Posner. *The Leadership Challenge,* San Francisco, CA: Jossey-Bass Publishers, 1995: pg. 10.

(1) "If you are out to __describe__ the truth, leave elegance to the tailor."

—Albert Einstein, American theoretical physicist (1879–1955)

(1) "In argument, similes are like songs in love; they __describe__ much, but prove nothing."

—Franz Kafka, German writer (1883–1924)

Designate

(1) assign; delegate; design; doom; indicate; intend; point out or specify

Word Used in Sentence(s)

(1) "God is the name by which I __designate__ all things which cross my path violently and recklessly, all things which alter my plans and intentions, and change the course of my life, for better or for worse."

—Carl Gustav Jung, Swiss psychiatrist and psychologist (1875–1961)

Discern

(1) behold; catch; descry; differentiate; discriminate; distinguish; have insight; make out; perceive; pick out; recognize; see things clearly; separate mentally from others; spot

Word Used in Sentence(s)

(1) "As far as we can __discern__, the sole purpose of human existence is to kindle a light in the darkness of mere being."

—Carl Gustav Jung, Swiss psychotherapist and psychiatrist who founded analytical psychology (1875–1961)

*(1) "The first point of wisdom is to **discern** that which is false; the second, to know that which is true."*

—Lactantius Caecilius Firmianus Lactanius, North Africa, early Christian author (240–320)

Disclose

(1) bring into view; communicate; divulge; make known; release; reveal; unveil

Word Used in Sentence(s)

*(1) "In Atlanta, Delta, Newell-Rubbermaid, and Equifax have boosted contributions to defined contribution plans such as 401(k)s. Coca-Cola and SunTrust are among companies replacing their traditional pensions with cash-balance plans. Coca-Cola and SunTrust say the moves aren't pension freezes since they're switching to cash-balance plans, which are also defined-benefit plans. However, in filings with the Securities Exchange Commission, both companies **disclose** that they have frozen or are freezing portions of their older pension plans."*

—Grantham, Russell. "Traditional Pensions All But Retired: Financial Crisis Forces Firms to Freeze Plans," *Atlanta Constitution and Journal*, July 5, 2009: pg. 1A.

Collocates to: companies, declined, details, failed, information, required, status

Disseminate

(1) broadcast; circulate; distribute; propagate; publish; scatter; spread

Word Used in Sentence(s)

*(1) "Propaganda has a bad name, but its root meaning is simply to **disseminate** through a medium, and all writing therefore is propaganda for something. It's a seeding of the self in the consciousness of others."*

—Elizabeth Drew, American political journalist and author (1935–)

*(1) "The actions performed by great souls to spread, promote, and **disseminate** knowledge to every strata of society is a great service to mankind."*

—Sam Veda, American yoga wear designer (1945–)

Dissuade

(1) advise against; deter; discourage; divert; put off; talk out of

Word Used in Sentence(s)

*(1) **Dissuading** the protesters was the priority of the police.*

*(1) "The shortness of life cannot **dissuade** us from its pleasures, nor console us for its pains."*

—Marquis de Vauvenargues, French moralist and essayist (1715–1747)

*(1) "Cultures contain many cues and inducements to **dissuade** the individual from approaching ultimate limits, in much the same way that a special warning strip of land around the edge of a baseball field lets a player know that he is about to run into a concrete wall when he is preoccupied with catching the ball. The wider that strip of land and the more sensitive the player is to the changing composition of the ground under his feet as he pursues the ball, the more effective the warning. Romanticizing or lionizing as individualistic those people who disregard social cues and inducements increases the danger of head-on collisions with inherent social limits. Decrying various forms of social disapproval is in effect narrowing the warning strip."*

—Thomas Sowell, American writer and economist (1930–)

Educe

(1) come to conclusion; derive; evoke; solve a problem based on thoughtful consideration of facts

(2) deduce; draw out; elicit; infer

Word Used in Sentence(s)

*(1) "In other words, 'apartheid' becomes shorthand for the most egregious instances of systemic and overt racism that necessarily and automatically **educe** (or should **educe**) severe international condemnation."*

—Editors. "The Ethnicity of Caste," *Anthropological Quarterly*, Volume 78, Issue 3, Summer 2005: pg. 543–584, 42p.

Edify

(1) educate; enlighten; illuminate; improve; inform; instruct; teach

(2) to uplift morally, spiritually, or intellectually

Word Used in Sentence(s)

*(1) To **edify** students is one of the most important goals of a teacher.*

Elaborate

(1)   complex; complicate; convolute; detail on; dilate; expatiate on; fancy; intricate

(2)   amplify; develop; enlarge; expand on

(3)   produce by effort

(4)   develop in great detail; work out carefully

Word Used in Sentence(s)

*(1) "The more **elaborate** our means of communication, the less we communicate."*

—Joseph Priestley, English chemist and clergyman (1733–1804)

Collocates to: an, ceremony, costumes, declines, expensive, network, rituals, schemes, system

Elicit

(1)   bring out; call forth something; extract; obtain

(2)   cause to be revealed; draw forth; evoke

Word Used in Sentence(s)

*(1) "The test of leadership is not to put greatness into humanity, but to **elicit** it, for the greatness is already there."*

—James Buchanan, 15th U.S. President (1791–1868)

*(1) "When you make speeches, you **elicit** expectations against which you will be held accountable. "*

—Bill Bradley, American retired NBA basketball player and senator (1943–)

Collocates to: design, information, likely, questions, response, sympathy

Embody

(1)   exemplify; express; personify; represent; represent abstract; stand for; symbolize

Word Used in Sentence(s)

*(1) "Alexander the Great **embodies** the 'my way or the highway' brand of leadership, something different than the Xenophon's style. With this approach, you are either an ally or an enemy. There is no middle ground."*

—Forbes, Steve and John Prevas. *Power, Ambition, Glory*, NY: Crown Business Press, 2009: pg. 6.

*(1) "Laws that do not **embody** public opinion can never be enforced."*

—Elbert Hubbard, American editor, publisher, and writer (1856–1915)

*(1) "If we want the world to **embody** our shared values, then we must assume a shared responsibility."*

—William Jefferson Clinton, 42nd U.S. President (1946–)

Collocates to: culture, essence, ideals, institutions, principles, spirit, values

Emulate

(1) copy; follow; imitate; work or strive to copy something admired

(2) try often by copying or imitating a model

(3) rival successfully

Word Used in Sentence(s)

*(1) If you want to **emulate** someone, pick a role model whom society, and not just you, admires.*

*(1) Many foreign companies attempt to **emulate** American manufacturing but never manage to match the quality.*

*(1) "What do we lose by another's good fortune? Let us celebrate with them or strive to **emulate** them. That should be our desire and determination."*

—Sri Sathya Sai Baba, Indian spiritual leader (1926–2011)

*(1) "When you see a worthy person, endeavor to **emulate** him. When you see an unworthy person, then examine your inner self."*

—Confucius, Chinese teacher, editor, politician, and philosopher

*(1) "Former Deloitte & Touche chairman Michael Cook courageously resigned from a males-only club frequented by his customers when he made a public commitment to the advancement of women. Other firms later **emulated** Deloitte's women's initiative."*

—Kanter, Rosabeth. "Courage in the C-Suite," *Harvard Business Review*, December 2011: pg. 38.

Ensure

(1) follow; guarantee; make certain; make sure
(2) make safe; protect; secure

Word Used in Sentence(s)

*(1) "Despite genuine efforts to **ensure** fairness, some businesses may be inadvertently overlooking bias that creeps in at initial job placement. Others may underestimate early managers' impact on employees' career trajectories. And others may have neglected the topic of gender equality in recent years, considering it an issue of the past."*

—Carter, Nancy and Christine Silva. "Women in Management: Delusions of Progress," *Harvard Business Review*, March, 2010: pg. 21.

Envision

(1) conceive; conjure; dream; fancy; feature; ideate; imagine; picture; see; vision; visualize

Word Used in Sentence(s)

*(1) If you could **envision** the best customer service operation, what would it be like?*

*(1) "The mind is the limit. As long as the mind can **envision** the fact that you can do something, you can do it, as long as you really believe 100 percent."*

—Arnold Schwarzenegger, Austrian-born American actor and governor (1947–)

*(1) "The heroes of the world community are not those who withdraw when difficulties ensue, not those who can **envision** neither the prospect of success nor the consequence of failure—but those who stand the heat of battle, the fight for world peace through the United Nations."*

—Hubert H. Humphrey, 38th American U.S. Vice President and U.S. Senator from Minnesota (1911–1978)

*(1) "The world is changing...Networks without a specific branding strategy will be killed...I **envision** a world of highly niched services and tightly run companies without room for all the overhead the established networks carry."*

—Barry Diller, American media executive (1942–)

Evince

(1) reveal or indicate the presence of a particular feeling or condition; show plainly

(2) indicate; make manifest without a doubt

Word Used in Sentence(s)

*(1) "Most community colleges **evince** a strong interest in how their various publics view their program offerings. However, for an organization like a community college, both shaping and changing an image are difficult tasks."*

—Cowles, Deborah. "Understanding and Measuring the Public's Image of a Community College," *Community College Review*, Spring 91, Volume 18, Issue 4, pg. 21.

Exalt

(1) animate; boost; elevate; enliven; glorify; inspire; intensify; invigorate; laud; proclaim; raise high; to praise or worship somebody or something

Word Used in Sentence(s)

*(1) "Whatever enlarges hope will also **exalt** courage."*

—Samuel Johnson, English writer (1709–1784)

*(1) "Just once in a while let us **exalt** the importance of ideas and information."*

—Edward R. Murrow, American broadcast journalist (1908–1965)

Exhort

(1) admonish; encourage earnestly by advice or warning; give serious warning; goad; insist; inspire; press; prod; push; spur; urge strongly

Word Used in Sentence(s)

*(1) "The most excellent and divine counsel, the best and most profitable advertisement of all others, but the least practiced, is to study and learn how to know ourselves. This is the foundation of wisdom and the highway to whatever is good. God, Nature, the wise, the world, preach man, **exhort** him both by word and deed to the study of himself."*

—Pierre Charron, French 16th-century Catholic theologian and philosopher (1541–1603)

*(1) "I **exhort** you also to take part in the great combat, which is the combat of life, and greater than every other earthly combat."*

—Plato, Classical Greek philosopher and mathematician (424–327 BC)

*(1) In spite of the legal status in some states, most medical experts **exhort** people to avoid marijuana.*

Extol

(1) admire; command; eulogize; exalt; laud; praise; worship

Word Used in Sentence(s)

*(1) "Many are always praising the by-gone time, for it is natural that the old should **extol** the days of their youth; the weak, the time of their strength; the sick, the season of their vigor; and the disappointed, the spring-tide of their hopes."*

—George Caleb Bingham, American realist and artist (1811–1879)

*(1) "That sign of old age, **extolling** the past at the expense of the present."*

—Sydney Smith, English clergyman and essayist (1771–1845)

Extrapolate

(1) conclude; deduce; induce; infer; generalize; posit; project; reason; suspect

Word Used in Sentence(s)

(1) "My hope is that I will take the good from my experiences and ***extrapolate*** *them further into areas with which I am unfamiliar. I simply do not know exactly what that difference will be in my judging. But I accept there will be some based on my gender and my Latina heritage."*

—Sonia Sotomayor, Associate Justice Supreme Court (1954–)

<u>**Collocates to:**</u> <u>can, data, findings, from, motion, results, track</u>

Forge

(1) come up with a concept, explanation, idea, theory, principle, or theory; contrive; create

(2) beat; make out of components

(3) move ahead or act with sudden increase in motion or speed

Word Used in Sentence(s)

(1) "People are more inclined to be drawn in if their leader has a compelling vision. Great leaders help people get in touch with their own aspirations and then help them ***forge*** *those aspirations into a personal vision."*

—John Kotter, former professor at the Harvard Business School and an acclaimed author (1947–)

(1) "The President's offer is very much in keeping with the history of insisting that negotiation consists of the other side giving him everything he wants. That approach has given him the reputation as the modern president least able to ***forge*** *a consensus."*

—Strassel, Kimberley. "This Unserious White House, Opinion," *Wall Street Journal*, November 30, 2012: pg. A13.

(1) "We ***forge*** *the chains we wear in life."*

—Charles Dickens, English writer and social critic (1812–1870)

(1) "Bad men cannot make good citizens. It is when a people forget God that tyrants __forge__ their chains. A vitiated state of morals, a corrupted public conscience, is incompatible with freedom. No free government, or the blessings of liberty, can be preserved to any people but by a firm adherence to justice, moderation, temperance, frugality, and virtue; and by a frequent recurrence to fundamental principles."

—Patrick Henry, American lawyer, patriot, orator, and symbol of the American struggle for liberty (1736–1799)

Galvanize

(1)   activate; animate; electrify; fire up; incite; motivate; rouse; spur; stimulate into action; stir up

Word Used in Sentence(s)

(1) "Fear has a lot of flavors and textures. There is a sharp, silver fear that runs like lightning through your arms and legs, __galvanizes__ you into action, power, motion."

—Jim Butcher, American author of *Grave Peril* (1971–)

(1) "There are some men whom a staggering emotional shock, so far from making them mental invalids for life, seems, on the other hand, to awaken, to __galvanize__, to arouse into an almost incredible activity of soul."

—William McFee, English writer (1881–1961)

Guide

(1)   channel; conduct; direct; funnel; point
(2)   escort; lead; pilot; route; show; steer; supervise; surround; usher

Word Used in Sentence(s)

(1) A true leader both __guides__ and follows.

(1) "The only __guide__ to man is his conscience; the only shield to his memory is the rectitude and sincerity of his actions. It is very imprudent to walk through life without this shield, because we are so often mocked by the failure of our hopes and the upsetting of our calculations; but with

this shield, however the fates may play, we march always in the ranks of honor."

—Winston Churchill, British orator, author, and prime minister (1874–1965)

Go down the line

(1) all in; all out; compete with dead earnest; do whatever is necessary; full steam; give or take no quarter; go balls out; go down swinging; go for broke; go for the fences; go for gold; go for all the marbles; go full bore; go great guns; go the distance; go the limit; go toe to toe; go to the wall; make the maximum effort; valiant try

Word Used in Sentence(s)

*(1) A manager's dream team includes members who would **go down the line**.*

Hang tough

(1) don't back down; hold to one's position; stick to one's position on something no matter what

Word Used in Sentence(s)

*(1) Taking a controversial position is lonely so make sure you're right, and then go ahead and **hang tough**.*

Hunker down

(1) assume a defensive position to resist difficulties; become determined not to budge from an opinion or position; circle the wagons; get in defensive position; prepare for bad news or prolonged assault; prepare for siege; take shelter, literally or figuratively

Word Used in Sentence(s)

*(1) "While many businessmen were **hunkering down** for another bust after the lean years of the Second World War and the Great Depression before it, Taylor and company correctly reckoned it was the dawn of an era of prosperity and growth."*

—Richard Siklos, American newspaper writer and author

Hypothesize

(1) educated guess of some outcome

Word Used in Sentence(s)

(1) "In the last five years, though, an expanding number of computer scientists have embraced developmental psychology's proposal that infants possess basic abilities, including gaze tracking, for engaging with others in order to learn. Social interactions, combined with sensory experiences gained as a child explores the world, set off a learning explosion, researchers __hypothesize__."

—Bower, Bruce. "Meet the Growbots," *Science News*, Volume 179, Issue 3, January 29, 2011: pg. 18.

(1) "I __hypothesize__ that the Katrina event has made people think pretty seriously about infrastructure and its vulnerability."

—Stuart Elway, American business executive

Collocates to: led, may, might, reasonable, researchers, therefore, we

Ignite

(1) burn; combust; conflagrate; flare up; glow; inflame; kindle; light up; stimulate or provoke

Word Used in Sentence(s)

(1) "Leaders can't __ignite__ the flame of passion in others if they don't express enthusiasm for the compelling vision of their group."

—Kouzes, James and Berry Posner. *The Leadership Challenge*, San Francisco, CA: Jossey-Bass Publishers, 1995, pg. 11.

(1) "Without inspiration, the best powers of the mind remain dormant; [there] is a fuel in us which needs to be __ignited__ with sparks."

—Johann Gottfried Von Herder, German poet, critic, theologian, and philosopher (1744–1803)

Collocates to: fire, help, inflation, passion, spark, war

Imagine

(1) assume; conjecture; form a mental image of something; guess; suppose; think, believe, or fancy

Word Used in Sentence(s)

*(1) **Imagine** what our business would be like if we achieved just a fraction of our goals.*

*(1) He **imagined** the entire project before committing it to paper.*

*(1) "The best way to appreciate your job is to **imagine** yourself without one."*

—Oscar Wilde, Irish poet, novelist, dramatist, and critic (1854–1900)

*(1) "**Imagination** is everything. It is a preview of life's coming attractions."*

—Albert Einstein, American theoretical physicist (1879–1955)

Imbue

(1) indoctrinate; instill

(2) drink; endow; fill; infuse; permeate or take in moisture

Word Used in Sentence(s)

*(1) "Education would be so much more effective if its purpose were to ensure that by the time they leave school, every boy and girl should know how much they don't know and be **imbued** with a lifelong desire to know it."*

—Sir William Haley, British newspaper editor and broadcasting administrator (1901–1987)

*(1) "Many companies, of course, benefit greatly from the mental and emotional investment of their creators. They thrive on the founders' passion and on the passion of like-minded employees. Their products or services—born of extreme attention to detail—are often of the highest quality. And founders with strong personalities may **imbue** their progeny with distinctive identities that can be exploited in marketing."*

—Singer, Thea. "Our Companies, Ourselves," *Inc.*, Volume 28, Issue 11, November 2006: pg. 38–40, 3p.

Collocates to: consciousness, life, meaning, personality, significance, with

Imply

(1) connote; hint; mean; signify; suggest strongly

Word Used in Sentence(s)

*(1) "Convictions do not **imply** reasons."*

—Margaret Deland, American novelist, short-story writer, and poet (1857–1945)

*(1) "But the fact that some geniuses were laughed at does not **imply** that all who are laughed at are geniuses. They laughed at Columbus, they laughed at Fulton, and they laughed at the Wright brothers. But they also laughed at Bozo the Clown."*

—Dr. Carl Sagan, American astronomer, writer, and scientist (1934–1996)

Implore

(1) appeal; ask for; beg; beseech; entreat; implore; make earnest or urgent request; plead; pray; press; request; solicit; supplicate

Word Used in Sentence(s)

*(1) "When Lacy's not in meetings, he's on the phone trying to motivate people to get involved. He appears on television news shows and on radio talk shows to sound off about youth violence. He appears at City Council meetings to **implore** city leaders to make the city's children a priority."*

—Walker, Thaai. "In the Name of the Daughter: The Murder of an Oakland Teenager Spurs Her Father to Fight for Change," *San Francisco Chronicle*, March 13, 1993: pg. 1.

Collocates to: admit, aid, god, eyes, forgiveness, guilt, leaders, members, stop

Improve

(1) ameliorate; amend; better; build up; develop; employ; enhance in value; enrich; expand; further; help; increase; make better; meliorate; perfect; raise to a better quality; upgrade use

(2) convalesce; get better; get stronger; get well; make progress; mend; perk up; rally; recover

Word Used in Sentence(s)

*(1) "The research shows that in almost every case, a bigger opportunity lies in **improving** your performance in the industry you're in, by fixing your strategy, and strengthening the capabilities that create value for customers and separate you from your competitors. This conclusion was reached after analyzing shareholder returns for 6,138 companies in 65 industries worldwide from 2001 to 2011."*

—Hirsh, Evan and Kasturi Rangan. "The Grass Isn't Greener," *Harvard Business Review,* January–February 2013: pg. 23.

*(1) Sam found two ways of **improving** the efficiency of the CAD software.*

*(1) Engineering **improved** upon the original design of the device.*

*(1) "When you are through **improving**... you are through."*

—Arab Proverb

*(1) "The 'inside-out' approach to personal and interpersonal effectiveness means to start first with self; even more fundamentally, to start with the most inside part of self—with your paradigms, your character, and your motives. The inside-out approach says that private victories precede public victories, that making and keeping promises to ourselves recede making and keeping promises to others. It says it is futile to put personality ahead of character, to try to **improve** relationships with others before **improving** ourselves."*

—Stephen R. Covey, American educator, author, businessman, and keynote speaker (1932–2012)

Infer

(1) assume; conclude or suppose; conjecture; deduce; extrapolate; gather; judge; reason; reckon; surmise; understand

Word Used in Sentence(s)

*(1) "From a drop of water, a logician can **infer** the possibility of an Atlantic or a Niagara without having seen or heard of one or the other."*

—Arthur Conan Doyle, Sr., Scottish writer (1859–1930)

*(1) "It is long ere we discover how rich we are. Our history, we are sure, is quite tame: We have nothing to write, nothing to **infer**. But our wiser years still run back to the despised recollections of childhood, and*

always we are fishing up some wonderful article out of that pond; until, by and by, we begin to suspect that the biography of the one foolish person we know is, in reality, nothing less than the miniature paraphrase of the hundred volumes of the Universal History."

—Ralph Waldo Emerson, American poet, lecturer, and essayist (1803–1882)

Infuse

(1) bathe; fill; fix an emotion or feeling; fortify; imbue; immerse; impart; implant; inculcate; inspire; instill; introduce; penetrate; permeate

(2) brew; saturate; soak; souse; steep; suffuse

Word Used in Sentence(s)

*(1) "Words mean more than what is set down on paper. It takes the human voice to **infuse** them with shades of deeper meaning."*

—Maya Angelou, American poet (1928–)

*(1) "An occupation earns the right to be a profession only when some ideals, such as being an impartial counsel, doing no harm, or serving the greater good, are **infused** into the conduct of people in that occupation. In like vein, a business school becomes a professional school only when it **infuses** those ideals into its graduates."*

—Barker, Richard. "No, Management Is Not a Profession," *Harvard Business Review*, July–August 2012: pg. 54.

Inspire

(1) breathe life into; encourage, give inspiration; have an exalting influence; influence or impel; invigorate; motivate; produce or arouse a feeling in others; stimulate

Word Used in Sentence(s)

*(1) "Shawn Kent Hayashi asks a profound question 'Are you **inspiring**?' Then through practical, real life examples, she demonstrates how leaders can develop from being motivational to **inspirational** through the power of conversations."*

—Seybold, Meghan. *Praise for Conversations for Creating Star Performers*, NY: McGraw-Hill, 2012.

*(1) Her courage **inspired** the other employees to work even harder.*

*(1) "Our chief want is someone who will **inspire** us to be what we know we could be."*

—Ralph Waldo Emerson, American poet, lecturer, and essayist (1803–1882)

*(1) "To **inspire** others, you have to know what motivates them, and you have to be inspired yourself about the topic you are discussing. To be a leader and developer of others, you have to be **inspiring**."*

—Hayashi, Shawn Kent. *Conversations for Creating Star Performers*, NY: McGraw-Hill, 2012: pg. 7.

*(1) "Leadership is the ability to **inspire** confidence and support among people who are needed to achieve organizational goals."*

—DuBrin, Andrew. *Leadership Research Findings, Practice, and Skills*, Boston: Houghton Mifflin Company, 1998: pg. 2.

*(1) "Few business narratives are more evocative that that of the **inspired** leader boldly pursuing an extraordinary innovative idea."*

—Gaovondarajan, Vijay and Chris Trimbla. "Building Breakthrough Businesses Within Established Organizations," *Harvard Business Review*, May 2005, pg. 58.

Collocates to: ability, awe, confidence, continue, educate, fear, generation, helped, motivate, others, trust

Instigate

(1) cause a process to start; enkindle; enkindle action; ignite; initiate change; spark

(2) cause trouble; provoke; stir up things

Word Used in Sentence(s)

*(1) "Change is inevitable. This much we know. But don't we occasionally feel the urge to **instigate** change rather than simply let it happen, as if we had no say in the matter?"*

—Editors. "Time for a Change," *Town and Country*, Volume 164, Issue 5360, May 2010.

*(1) "Indeed heresies are themselves **_instigated_** by philosophy."*

—Quintus Septimius Florens Tertullian, Christian author from Carthage in the Roman province of Africa (660AD–220 AD)

Collocates to: change, conflicts, investigation, social reform

Iterate

(1)   say or utter again; repeat

Word Used in Sentence(s)

*(1) To **_iterate_** a point made previously, customer retention is our main marketing priority.*

Jawbone

(1)   using persuasion rather than force to get someone to do what you want

Word Used in Sentence(s)

*(1) The U.S. has tried continually to **_jawbone_** the government of Pakistan to weed out Al-Qaida supporters within its military.*

Kindle

(1)   arouse; fire; light; provoke; stir to action

Word Used in Sentence(s)

*(1) "The fire you **_kindle_** for your enemy often burns yourself more than them."*

—Chinese Proverb

*(1) "Originality is nothing but judicious imitation. The most original writers borrowed from one another. The instruction we find in books is like fire. We fetch it from our neighbors, **_kindle_** it at home, communicate it to others, and it becomes the probe."*

—Voltaire, French philosopher and writer (1694–1778)

Laud

(1)   acknowledge; applaud; celebrate; extol; praise

Word Used in Sentence(s)

*(1) "And give to dust that is a little gilt, More **laud** than gilt o'er-dusted."*

—William Shakespeare, English dramatist, playwright, and poet (1564–1616)

Manumit

(1)   emancipate; free; set at liberty

Mentor

(1)   give assistance in career or business matters; provide advice or guidance

Collocates to: assigned, became, coach, facility, former, friend, long time, mentee, relationship, role, served, spiritual, student, teacher

Militate

(1)   contend; have a substantial effect on; make war or fight against; weigh heavily on

Mitigate

(1)   appease; change from one point or position; make less serious, severe, or intense; to soften one's position

Word Used in Sentence(s)

*(1) "The GOP would have to swallow hard on the defense cuts, though Mr. Obama will be under huge pressure to take action to **mitigate** the damage to the military."*

—Strassel, Kimberly. "Potomac Watch," *Wall Street Journal*, December 7, 2012: pg. A15.

Collocates to: bad news, conflict, damage, danger, disaster, disruption, effect, harm, hazard, impact, loss, result, risk, threat, worst

Nuance

(1)   give nuance to; provide subtle difference or degree of distinction

Word Used in Sentence(s)

*(1) "A man with a scant vocabulary will almost certainly be a weak thinker. The richer and more copious one's vocabulary and greater one's awareness of the fine distinctions and subtle **nuances** of meaning, the more fertile and precise is likely to be one's thinking. Knowledge of things and knowledge of the words for them grow together. If you do not know the words, you hardly know a thing."*

—Henry Hazlitt, American philosopher, literary critic, and journalist (1894–1993)

Objectify

(1)   externalize; make objective or concrete; represent an abstraction as if in bodily form

Word Used in Sentence(s)

*(1) "The 'Thong Song,' a rap homage to butt-baring bikinis, was released in 1999, several years after I graduated from an ideologically feminist all-women's college. Still, I can imagine the predictable feminist reaction it would have caused among my classmates. They would have decried the song as a kind of chest-beating battle cry, a reprehensible demonstration of how men (or 'the patriarchy') **objectify** and humiliate women. In fact, many of my cohorts would have used very fancy socio-logical language to explain that the patriarchy designed the tether-like thong to represent a leash, collar, or strangulation device, bound tightly around women's genital regions, thus signifying male ownership of the female anatomy."*

—Voss, Katrina. "Evolution and the Thong-Burqa Continuum," *Humanist*, Volume 70, Issue 5, September–October: pg. 22–23.

Collocates to: decisions, difficulty, discourse, efforts, impartial, men, must, spectator, women

Obviate

(1)   anticipate to prevent difficulties or disadvantages; avert; hinder; pre-clude; prevent

Word Used in Sentence(s)

*(1) The legal department found a solution and they were able to **obviate** the problem, thus preventing a major crisis.*

Optimize

(1) make the best or most effective use of a situation or resource

Word Used in Sentence(s)

*(1) "Fully understanding a company requires knowledge of its social structure and informal networks, and **optimizing** performance requires social investments."*

—Kanter, Rosabeth. "How Great Companies Think Differently," *Harvard Business Review*, November 2011: pg. 75.

*(1) "I've heard claims that we can wish our way to perfect, permanent wellness, but I haven't seen any proof of that. Sickness and death are part of life. But you can **optimize** your life. You can make progress as you strive toward perfection."*

—Unknown

*(1) "India and China developed by being involved in the far end of the value chain. Instead, Africa will meet and may exceed the Asian experience by **optimizing** its resources and focusing on massive agricultural and energy (solar) projects that will primarily aid the food crisis."*

—Olusegun Femi-Ishola, human resource executive, excerpt from "The Best Leaders Have Short Resumes," Interaction, *Harvard Business Review*, December 2012: p. 19.

Palliate

(1) alleviate or calm the problem but not rid the problem; ameliorate; cure; heal; improve; relieve

Word Used in Sentence(s)

*(1) "Friends are often chosen for similitude of manners, and therefore each **palliate** the other's failings because they are his own."*

—Samuel Johnson, English poet, critic, and writer (1709–1784)

Parlay

(1) exploit an asset successfully; take a winning position and stake all on a subsequent effort; to build or increase from a small start

(2) talk or negotiate with someone

Word Used in Sentence(s)

*(1) "It was Ismail's first big order—$12,000. The money was enough to **parlay** into his first store, which opened in Dallas a year later."*

—Simons, John. "Living in America," *Fortune*, Volume 145, Issue 1; pg. 92, 3 p.

<u>**Collocates to:**</u> able, experience, hopes, into, success, trying

Parse

(1) create component parts of a sentence; give out in parts or sections

Word Used in Sentence(s)

*(1) "Constitutional Scholars **Parse** Pay Measures"*

—US News Headlines, *Wall Street Journal*, January 24, 2012: p.A4.

Pacify

(1) appease; calm down; ease anger or agitation; mollify; placate; soothe

Word Used in Sentence(s)

*(1) The latest pension enhancement management offering should **pacify** the union representatives.*

*(1)"The wrath of a king is as messengers of death, but a wise man will **pacify** it."*

—Biblical quote

Perseverate

(1) continue something; repeat something insistently or over and over again

Word Used in Sentence(s)

*(1) Leaders need to **perseverate** in reminding their followers of the mission.*

Persevere

(1) be steadfast in purpose; persist; to continue in some effort or course of action in spite of difficulty or opposition

Word Used in Sentence(s)

*(1) "Victory belongs to the most **persevering**."*

—Napoleon Bonaparte, French military and political leader (1769–1821)

Placate

(1) appease; blend together; calm; stop from being angry

Word Used in Sentence(s)

*(1) "Successful politicians are insecure and intimidated men. They advance politically only as they **placate**, appease, bribe, seduce, bamboozle, or otherwise manage to manipulate the demanding and threatening elements in their constituencies."*

—Walter Lipmann, American public intellectual, writer, reporter, and political commentator (1889–1974)

Posit

(1) assume; conceive; conjecture; hypothesize; imagine; postulate; put forward; speculate; state or assume as fact; suggest; theorize

Word Used in Sentence(s)

*(1) "Government, for the past 80 years or so, has seen its purpose as mainly to 'respond' to society's failures the moment they occur or whenever they are imagined. Adam Lanza killed with guns, so modern policy making logic **posits** that government must pass a law. Whether that law will accomplish its goal is…irrelevant."*

—Henninger, Daniel. "The Biggest Cliff of All," *Wall Street Journal*, December 27, 2012: pg. A11.

*(1) "It is the duty of the human understanding to understand that there are things which it cannot understand, and what those things are. Human understanding has vulgarly occupied itself with nothing but understanding, but if it would only take the trouble to understand itself at the same time, it would simply have to **posit** the paradox."*

—Soren Kierkegaard, Danish philosopher and theologian (1813–1855)

Postulate

(1) assume; claim; guess; hypothesize; look for a reason or take for granted without proof; propose; put forward; suggest

Word Used in Sentence(s)

*(1) "Once you abstract from this, once you generalize and **postulate** universals, you have departed from the creative reality and entered the realm of static fixity, mechanism, materialism."*

—D.H. Lawrence, British poet, novelist, and essayist (1885–1930)

Purport

(1) claiming to be something you are not; pretending to do something you are not doing

(2) give the appearance, often falsely of being something one is not

Word Used in Sentence(s)

*(1) "The Framers of the Bill of Rights did not **purport** to 'create' rights. Rather, they designed the Bill of Rights to prohibit our Government from infringing rights and liberties presumed to be preexisting.*

—William J. Brennan, Jr., American jurist who served as an Associate Justice of the United States Supreme Court (1906–1997)

Ratiocinate

(1) work toward a solution through logical thinking and reason

Word Used in Sentence(s)

*(1) When you come down to it, there is too much **ratiocination** in the debates and too few solutions based on practical common sense.*

Rationalize

(1) excuse; explanation for the action of

(2) interpret on the basis of some explainable reason

(3) make actions conform to reason

Word Used in Sentence(s)

*(1) "The very vehemence of outrage makes it a warped mirror, a roiling reflection of our values, exposing our contradictions as often as our convictions. To name a few: There's too little outrage. Bennett has been joined in his complaints by leaders of the religious right like James Dobson of the organization Focus on the Family, who writes that 'the willingness of my fellow citizens to **rationalize** the President's behavior' means that 'our greatest problem is not in the Oval Office. It is with the people of this land.'"*

—Paul, Annie M. "Outrage!" *Psychology Today*, Volume 32, Issue 1, February 1999: pg. 32.

<u>**Collocates to:**</u> <u>actions, attempt, behavior, efforts, justified, productions, tried, try</u>

Rebut

(1) argue in opposition; confute; contradict; deny; disprove; invalidate; oppose; refute

(2) show to be false

Word Used in Sentence(s)

*(1) In our legal system, the grand jury hears the prosecution testimony only and the defense does not get the opportunity to **rebut**.*

Recant

(1) abjur; disavow; withdraw formally

(2) withdraw or renounce beliefs or statements in public

Word Used in Sentence(s)

> *(1) "They may attack me with an army of six hundred syllogisms; and if I do not **recant**, they will proclaim me a heretic."*

—Desiderius Erasmus, Dutch priest, humanist, and editor of the *New Testament* (1469–1536)

Recapitulate

(1) repeat in more concise form or briefly as in an outline; summarize

Word Used in Sentence(s)

> *(1) "Adolescence [is] the time when an individual **recapitulates** the savage stage of the race's past."*

—Granville Stanley Hall, American psychologist and educator (1844–1924)

Reiterate

(1) repeat, say, or do the same thing; state again

Word Used in Sentence(s)

> *(1) "Mr. Obama plans to **reiterate** Monday at an event in Michigan his call for the House to pass an extension of the Bush-era tax cuts for households making under $250,000 in annual income."*

—Bendavid, Naftali and Carol Lee. "Obama, Boehner Meet as Urgency Over Talks Increases," *Wall Street Journal*, December 10, 2012: pg. A4.

Ruminate

(1) chew over; cogitate; contemplate; mull over; ponder; reflect on; think over

(2) meditate; to turn over in one's mind

Word Used in Sentence(s)

> *(1) "I may revolve and **ruminate** my grief."*

—William Shakespeare, English poet and playwright (1564–1516), excerpt from *King Henry VI, Part 1*

*(1)" 'True,' " replied Danglars, 'The French have the superiority over the Spaniards, that the Spaniards **ruminate**, while the French invent.' "*

—Alexandre Dumas, French writer (1802–1870), excerpt from *The Count of Monte Cristo*

Satiate

(1) glut with an excess of something; gratify completely; provide with more than enough; satisfy an appetite fully

Word Used in Sentence(s)

*(1) "But, emulating the patience and self-denial of the practiced native warriors, they learned to overcome every difficulty; and it would seem that, in time, there was no recess of the woods so dark, nor any secret place so lovely, that it might claim exemption from the inroads of those who had pledged their blood to **satiate** their vengeance, or to uphold the cold and selfish policy of the distant monarchs of Europe."*

—James Fennimore Cooper, American writer (1789–1851), excerpt from *The Last of the Mohicans*

Scintillate

(1) flash; sizzle; sparkle

(2) be brilliant and witty; sparkle intellectually

(3) twinkle, as a star

Word Used in Sentence(s)

*(1) We watched contentedly as our campfire **scintillated** in the darkness.*

Strike the right note

(1) say or do something suitable or appropriate

Tailor

(1) adjust; create; customize; fashion; fit; specify; style to fit

Word Used in Sentence(s)

> *(1) "Rather than assuming that there is one 'best' or universal answer to questions about such things as job design, resistance to change, the best compensation plans, how to design teams, what are the causes of unethical behavior, organizational behavior recognizes that management practices must be **tailored** to fit the exact nature of each situation...."*

—Schermerhorn, John, Richard Osborn, Mary UHL-Bien, and James Hunt. *Organizational Behavior*, 12th edition, NY: John Wiley & Sons, Inc., 2012, pg. 4.

> *(1) "The Federal Reserve's decision to tie interest rate increases to specific unemployment and inflation levels...are decisions most **tailored** to the specific situation the economy is in."*

—Derby, Michael and Kristina Peterson. "Is the Fed Doing Enough—or Too Much—to Aid Recovery," *Wall Street Journal*, January 7, 2013: pg. A2.

Teach

(1)   coach; give lessons; instruct; mentor; provide knowledge or insight; show or help a person learn

Word Used in Sentence(s)

> *(1) "She had intended to **teach** Anne the childish classic, 'Now I lay me down to sleep.' But she had, as I have told you, the glimmerings of a sense of humor—which is simply another name for a sense of fitness of things; and it suddenly occurred to her that that simple little prayer, sacred to white-robed childhood lisping at motherly knees, was entirely unsuited to this freckled witch of a girl who knew and cared nothing bout God's love, since she had never had it translated to her through the medium of human love."*

—Lucy Maud Montgomery, Canadian author of *Anne of Green Gables* (1874–1922)

Train

(1)   coach; educate; guide; inform; instruct; mentor; prepare; school; teach

Word Used in Sentence(s)

*(1) "Companies that want to make better use of the data they gather should focus on two things: **training** workers to increase their data literacy and efficiently incorporate information into decision making and giving those workers the right tools."*

—Shah, Shvetank, Andrew Horne, and Jamie Capella. "Good Data Won't Guarantee Good Decisions," *Harvard Business Review*, April 2012: pg. 24.

*(1) New hires are **trained** on all the production equipment.*

Vindicate

(1) an act was justified or one was innocent despite opinion to contrary; prove opinion correct

(2) clear from blame, suspicion, guilt, or criticism; uphold by evidence or argument

(3) defend or maintain against opposition

(4) lay claim or establish possession of

Word Used in Sentence(s)

*(1) Dueling may have been bloody and deadly, but at least it provided one a way to very quickly **vindicate** themselves—or die trying.*

Visualize

(1) create mental impression or image of something; dream of; envisage; image; picture; see in one's mind's eye; think about

Word Used in Sentence(s)

*(1) "**Visualize** this thing that you want, see it, feel it, believe in it. Make your mental blueprint, and begin to build."*

—Robert Collier, American motivational author (1885–1950)

*(1) "Almost, it seemed, she could **visualize** the women who had kept their pretties and their family homespun in its drawers—the women of those wandering generations who were grandmothers and greater great grandmothers of her own mother."*

—Jack London, American author, journalist, and social activist (1876–1916), *The Valley of the Moon*

7

100 Top Action Verbs for Schooling, Sagacity, Shrewdness, and Other Times to Be Sharp and Serious

Abate

(1) die away; put an end to; reduce; slack; subside

Word Used in Sentence(s)

(1) "In striking contrast to Eisenhower, the young Democratic president secretly pledged to Chiang use of America's veto in the Security Council to keep the P.R.C. out of the United Nations. Kennedy believed his sympathies would eventually necessitate blocking China and so, against the advice of his experts, he chose to benefit from the inevitable by trading his veto for Chiang's cooperation on other issues. Kennedy's suspicion of China appeared to grow rather than __abate__ during his presidency. Although the split between Moscow and Beijing became increasingly obvious, Kennedy persistently dismissed it as an argument over how to bury the United States."

—Editors. "International Economics and National Security," *Foreign Affairs*, Volume 70, Issue 5, Winter 1991/1992: pg. 74–90.

(1) "The decision to restrict gasoline sales was a departure for Mayor Michael Bloomberg and Gov. Andrew Cuomo, who had said last week that they anticipated that fuel shortages would have __abated__ by now."

—York, Michael Howard. "Gas Rationing Put in Place in New York," *Wall Street Journal*, November 19, 2012: pg. A15.

*(1) "We should every night call ourselves to an account: What infirmity
have I mastered to-day? what passions opposed? what temptation resisted? what virtue acquired? Our vices will **abate** of themselves if they be
brought every day to the shrift."*

—Seneca, Roman philosopher (mid-first century AD)

Ablate

(1) become less in amount, force, or intensity; decline; decrease; diminish;
      dwindle; fade away; fall; make less of; remove; subside

(2) end; halt; put a stop to something; terminate

(3) grow less; make less active or intense

Word Used in Sentence(s)

*(1) "Don't turn dating into a project. Instead make it a part of your
social life, just as you would hanging out with the girls. 'When your consciousness is, I've got to find my husband, you're putting the need for a
man before everything else,' Wade says. Besides, it can make you seem
desperate and turn men away. So aim for a fully rounded social life in
which you routinely interact with men. And don't hesitate to take **ablate**
to events that include family and friends. The way a man interacts with
the people you love can speak volumes about the kind of person he is."*

—Saunders, Nicole. "Yes, There Is a Love Out There for You," *Essence*,
Volume 36, Issue 4, August 2005: pg. 142.

Collocates to: able, body, costs, energy, heat, impact, light, moister, shock,
water

Absorb

(1) acquire; assimilate; attract; consume; digest; endure; engulf; fascinate;
      imbibe; insure; sustain; soak up; take in; use up

(2) draw into oneself; grasp; realize; recognize; take in; understand

(3) become captivated, interested, engaged, or preoccupied in; fascinated

Word Used in Sentence(s)

> *(1) "Read, read, read. Read everything—trash, classics, good and bad, and see how they do it. Just like a carpenter who works as an apprentice and studies the master. Read! You'll **absorb** it. Then write. If it is good, you'll find out. If it's not, throw it out the window."*

—William Faulkner, American short-story writer and novelist (1897–1962)

> *(1) "When I am attacked by gloomy thoughts, nothing helps me so much as running to my books; they quickly **absorb** me and banish the clouds from my mind."*

—Michel de Montaigne, French philosopher and writer (1533–1592)

> *(1) "Lecturers should remember that the capacity of the mind to **absorb** is limited to what the seat can endure."*

—Unknown

> *(1) "Throw away all ambition beyond that of doing the day's work well. The travelers on the road to success live in the present, heedless of taking thought for the morrow. Live neither in the past nor in the future, but let each day's work **absorb** your entire energies, and satisfy your wildest ambition."*

—William Osler, Canadian physician (1849–1919)

Accelerate

(1) gather speed; go faster; hasten; hurry; increase speed; move increasingly quicker; pick up speed; pick up the pace; step up

(2) happen or develop faster; progress faster

Word Used in Sentence(s)

> *(1) "The rush shows the extent to which wrangling in Washington over deficit reduction already is affecting the way taxpayers are spending their money. In addition to rethinking their charitable giving, some tax-payers are **accelerating** large medical expenses, selling appreciated stock, and even prepaying mortgages."*

—Saunders, Laura and Hanna Karp. "Fiscal Talks Spur Charitable Giving," *Wall Street Journal*, December 7, 2012: pg. A1.

*(1) "The concept of teaming helps individuals acquire knowledge, skills,
and networks. And it lets companies **accelerate** the delivery of current
products of services while responding to new opportunities."*

—Edmondson, Amy C. "Teamwork on the Fly," *Harvard Business
Review*, April 2012: pg. 74.

Accentuate

(1) accent; emphasize; heighten; intensify

(2) make more noticeable; play up; stress something

(3) mark with an accent

Word Used in Sentence(s)

*(1) "Delete the negative; **accentuate** the positive!"*

—Donna Karan, American fashion designer (1948–)

*(1) "A science is said to be useful if its development tends to **accentuate**
the existing inequities in the distribution of wealth, or more directly promotes the destruction of human life."*

—Godfrey Harold Hardy, English mathematician (1877–1947)

Collocates to: differences, opportunities, positives, shapes

Acclimate

(1) acclimatize; accustom yourself; adapt; adjust; become accustomed to a
new environment or situation; familiarize; get used to

Word Used in Sentence(s)

*(1) **Acclimating** to a new country involves many social, cultural, and
political changes for immigrants.*

*(1) It took longer than he thought to become **acclimated** to the New York
City social life.*

Actualize

(1) make something actual or real; realize

(2) realize in action or make real

(3) fulfill the potential of

Word Used in Sentence(s)

*(1) "I think there is something more important than believing: Action!
The world is full of dreamers; there aren't enough who will move ahead
and begin to take concrete steps to **actualize** their vision."*

—W. Clement Stone, American author (1902–2002)

Collocates to: consummate, embody, help, individuals, potential, their

Actuate

(1)   activate; arouse to action; motivate; put into motion; start; trigger

Word Used in Sentence(s)

*(1) Great leaders can begin **actuating** a new movement just with his or
her vision.*

*(1) Toni's speech **actuated** the Congress to finally act on the bill.*

Adapt

(1)   acclimate; accommodate; adjust; change; conform; fashion; fit; get used
to; make suitable; reconcile; square; suit; tailor

(2)   make fit often by modification

(3)   cause something to change for the better

Word Used in Sentence(s)

*(1) "Intelligence is the ability to **adapt** to change."*

—Stephen Hawking, British theoretical physicist, cosmologist, and
author (1941–)

*(1) "The wise **adapt** themselves to circumstances, as water molds itself
to the pitcher."*

—Chinese Proverb

*(1) "**Adapt** yourself to the things among which your lot has been cast
and love sincerely the fellow creatures with whom destiny has ordained
that you shall live."*

—Marcus Aurelius, Roman emperor (121–180 AD)

*(1) "The key to success is often the ability to **adapt**."*

—Unknown

*(1) "Reasonable people **adapt** themselves to the world. Unreasonable
people attempt to **adapt** the world to themselves. All progress, therefore,
depends on unreasonable people."*

—George Bernard Shaw, Irish playwright and a cofounder of the London
School of Economics (1896–1950)

Collocates to: ability, able, change, conditions, environment, must, quickly

Adduce

(1) allege; bring forward; cite as evidence; lead to; present; put forward

Word Used in Sentence(s)

*(1) Let me **adduce** the following reasons for recommending the merger.*

*(1) "In an effort to defend against a hate crime charge, some defendants
may try to prove their lack of prejudice by introducing evidence of non-
racist speech, memberships, and activities. How could a judge rule such
evidence irrelevant? If the defendant is permitted to **adduce** such evidence, however, the prosecutor will almost certainly be allowed to introduce rebuttal evidence of the defendant's racism."*

—Jacobs, James B. "Should Hate Be a Crime?," *Public Interest*, Issue
113, Fall 1993: pg. 3–14, 12p.

Collocates to: can, evidence, link, might

Advise

(1) counsel; direct; give advice; give opinion; inform; let know; make aware;
notify; offer a personal opinion to somebody; opine; recommend; seek
advice or information; tell someone what has happened; warn

Word Used in Sentence(s)

*(1) A career counselor can **advise** but the client has to act.*

*(1) It is better not to decide on a career until somebody can **advise** you.*

*(1) "In every society some men are born to rule, and some to **advise**."*

—Ralph Waldo Emerson, American poet, lecturer, and essayist
(1803–1882)

Advocate

(1) advance; back; be in favor of; bolster; defend; encourage; promote; sponsor; support

Word Used in Sentence(s)

*(1) Occasionally **advocating** the minority position might be good strategy.*

*(1) "Can one preach at home inequality of races and nations and **advocate** abroad good-will towards all men?"*

—Dorothy Thompson, American journalist and radio broadcaster (1893–1961)

*(1) "Those who **advocate** common usage in philosophy sometimes speak in a manner that suggests the mystique of the 'common man.'"*

—Bertrand Russell, English logician and philosopher (1872–1970)

Affect

(1) change; concern; have an effect on; impact; impinge on; impress; influence; move; shape; strike; sway; touch

(2) distress; disturb; move; touch; upset

(3) assume; fake; imitate; pretend or have; put on

Word Used in Sentence(s)

*(1) How various countries attract or discourage import and export operations can **affect** the way American firms structure their global operations.*

*(1) "Being fit matters...New research suggests that a few extra pounds or a slightly larger waist line **affects** an executive's perceived leadership ability as well as stamina on the job."*

—Kwoh, Leslie. "Marketing," *Wall Street Journal*, January 16, 2013: pg. B1.

Collocates to: adversely, does, factor, how, negatively, performance, positive

Affirm

(1) acknowledge; affirm; announce; assert; asservate; avow; confirm; establish; insist; pronounce; state; validate; verify

(2) encourage; support; sustain; uphold

Word Used in Sentence(s)

*(1) "If you could do only one thing as a mentor, **affirm** your protégé."*

—Johnson, W. Brad and Charles R. Ridley. *The Elements of Mentoring*, NY: Palgrave Macmillan, 2004: pg. 10.

*(1) "The more I read, the more I meditate; and the more I acquire, the more I am enabled to **affirm** that I know nothing."*

—Voltaire, French philosopher and writer (1694–1778)

*(1) "Man is born a predestined idealist, for he is born to act. To act is to **affirm** the worth of an end, and to persist in affirming the worth of an end is to make an ideal."*

—Oliver Wendell Holmes, American physician, poet, writer, humorist, and professor (1809–1894)

Aggrandize

(1) exalt; increase; make greater; make larger; puffery

Word Used in Sentence(s)

*(1) It is merely **aggrandizing** when the firm's advertising is nothing more than puffery.*

*(1) The firm's public statement of the incident appeared to be an **aggrandized** version of their mission statement.*

Alert

(1) be watchful; intelligent; look out for; make aware of impending trouble or danger

Word Used in Sentence(s)

*(1) "Ordinary people think that talent must be always on its own level and that it arises every morning like the sun, rested and refreshed, ready to draw from the same storehouse, always open, always full, always abundant, new treasures that it will heap up on those of the day before; such people are unaware that, as in the case of all mortal things, talent has its increase and decrease, and that independently of the career it takes, like everything that breathes… it undergoes all the accidents of health, of sickness, and of the dispositions of the soul, its gaiety or its sadness. As with our perishable flesh, talent is obliged constantly to keep guard over itself, to combat, and to keep perpetually on the **alert** amid the obstacles that witness the exercise of its singular power."*

—Eugene Delacroix, greatest French romantic painter (1798–1863)

*(1) "With the exception of the instinct of self-preservation, the propensity for emulation is probably the strongest and most **alert** and persistent of the economic motives proper."*

—Thorstein Veblen, American economist (1857–1929)

*(1) "Great effort is required to arrest decay and restore vigor. One must exercise proper deliberation, plan carefully before making a move, and be **alert** in guarding against relapse following a renaissance."*

—Horace, ancient Roman poet (65 BC–8 BC)

Alleviate

(1) assuage; ease; facilitate; improve; lessen; lighten; make bearable; to relieve

Word Used in Sentence(s)

*(1) "The new technologies that we see coming will have major benefits that will greatly **alleviate** human suffering."*

—Ralph Merkle, American inventor of cryptographic hashing, and more recently a researcher and speaker on molecular nanotechnology (1952–)

*(1) "We have discovered that the scheme of 'outlawing war' has made war more like an outlaw without making it less frequent and that to banish the knight does not **alleviate** the suffering of the peasant."*

—C.S. Lewis, British scholar and novelist (1898–1963)

Collocates to: concerns, pain, poverty, some, suffering

Align

(1) adjust; be or come into adjustment; bring into proper or desirable coordination; correlate

(2) arrange something in reference with something else; place in line so as to arrange in a particular order

Word Used in Sentence(s)

*(1) As I consider this position, I want to be sure I am **aligned** with the values and culture of the organization.*

*(1) The firm's objectives and goals must be **aligned**.*

*(1) "Intuitional logic should be **aligned** with economic logic but need not be subordinate to it. For example, all companies require capital to carry out business activities and sustain themselves. However, at great companies, profit is not the sole end; rather, it is a way of ensuring that returns will continue."*

—Kanter, Rosabeth. "How Great Companies Think Differently,"
Harvard Business Review, November 2011: pg. 68.

*(1) "When you examine the lives of the most influential people who have ever walked among us, you discover one thread that winds through them all. They have been **aligned** first with their spiritual nature and only then with their physical selves."*

—Albert Einstein, American physicist (1879–1955)

*(1) "Parallels between ancient leaders and modern executives will never **align** perfectly, but there is definite value in making the comparisons, Ancient leaders obviously operated under different conditions and lacked many advantages that modern day CEOs take for granted, but they ran their empires by utilizing similar styles of leadership."*

—Forbes, Steve and John Prevas. *Power, Ambition, Glory*, NY: Crown Business Press, 2009: pg.10.

Allay

(1)   alleviate; calm; dispel; put to rest; relief; subside

Word Used in Sentence(s)

> *(1) "Defending the truth is not something one does out of a sense of duty or to __allay__ guilt complexes, but is a reward in itself."*

—Unknown

> *(1) "The animosities of sovereigns are temporary, and may be __allayed__; but those which seize the whole body of people, and of a people too, dictate their own measures, produce calamities of long duration."*

—Thomas Jefferson, 3rd U.S. President (1762–1826)

Amplify

(1)   augment; elevate; enlarge; expand; increase; intensify; magnify
(2)   add details to; clarify; develop; elaborate on; go into details

Word Used in Sentence(s)

> *(1) "Cross-selling generates marketing expenses; second, cross-buying, __amplifies__ costs by extending undesirable behavior to a greater number of products or services."*

—Shah, Denish and V. Kumar. "The Dark Side of Cross-Selling," *Harvard Business Review*, December 2012: pg. 22.

Analyze

(1)   consider; dissect; evaluate; examine; explore; interpret; investigate; probe; question; scrutinize; study

Word Used in Sentence(s)

> *(1) Randi __analyzed__ the situation from all positions before making her decision.*

> *(1) Rick will be given the responsibility of __analyzing__ the impact of the new quotas on the sales department's budget.*

*(1) "You are a product of your environment. So choose the environment
that will best develop you toward your objective. **Analyze** your life in
terms of its environment. Are the things around you helping you toward
success—or are they holding you back?"*

—W. Clement Stone, American author (1902–2002)

*(1) "There is nothing to fear except the persistent refusal to find out the
truth, the persistent refusal to **analyze** the causes of happenings."*

—Dorothy Thompson, American journalist and radio broadcaster
(1893–1961)

· *(1) "The method of nature: who could ever **analyze** it?"*

—Ralph Waldo Emerson, American poet, lecturer, and essayist
(1803–1882)

Collocates to: ability, collect, data, evaluate, identify, information, results,
sample, situation, used

Appertain

(1)   an attribute of; apply; be appropriate; be part of; belong; relate to

Word Used in Sentence(s)

*(1) "As Senator Trumbull noted, the 'bill has nothing to do with the
political rights or status of parties. It is confined exclusively to their civil
rights, such rights as should **appertain** to every free man.'"*

—Smith, Douglas. "A Lockean Analysis of Section One of the
Fourteenth Amendment," *Harvard Journal of Law & Public Policy*,
Volume 25, Issue 3, Summer 2002: pg. 1095.

Approve

(1)   accept; agree to; attest; back up; command; commend; endorse; favor;
praise; ratify; sanction; support
(2)   allow; authorize; consent; grant; pass; sanction

Word Used in Sentence(s)

*(1) "Most of us believe in trying to make other people happy only if they
can be happy in ways which we **approve**."*

—Robert Lynd, Irish essayist and journalist (1879–1949)

*(1) "They that **approve** a private opinion, call it opinion; but they that dislike it, heresy; and yet heresy signifies no more than private opinion."*

—Thomas Hobbes, English philosopher (1588–1679)

*(1) "Nothing should so much diminish the satisfaction which we feel with ourselves as seeing that we disapprove at one time of that which we **approve** of at another."*

—François de la Rochefoucauld, French classical author (1613–1680)

Ascertain

(1) determine; discover; establish; find out; learn; realize; uncover
(2) find out with certainty

Word Used in Sentence(s)

*(1) A manager can **ascertain** the cause of many problems by careful observation.*

Collocates to: able, difficult, extent, order, study, try, whether

Assess

(1) estimate; impose; judge; value
(2) to estimate the value, cost, benefit, or worth of

Word Used in Sentence(s)

*(1) In order to **assess** the pros and cons of this merger, we will need to assemble an ad hoc intradepartmental team.*

*(1) "A mid-career transition is a great opportunity for a leader to help an employee **assess** her current interest areas and identify areas of satisfaction as well as development opportunities. In addition, a leader can look at burnout areas and determine if there are opportunities to rekindle that interest."*

—Betty Karkau, Senior Consultant, Career Systems International, author of manuscript, "Stopping the Mid-Career Crisis," 2009

Collocates to: ability, designed, difficulty, effects, items, impact, order, situation, student, study, used, whether

Assuage

(1) appease; erase doubts and fears; mollify; pacify; satisfy; soothe

Word Used in Sentence(s)

*(1) Judy was extremely annoyed, angry, and fearful that Tom showed up unannounced. She had previously kept him away by a restraining order and to avoid further trouble and to **assuage** her, Tom left.*

*(1) I worked to **assuage** my own guilt over the incident.*

*(1) "I've never known any trouble that an hour's reading didn't **assuage**."*

—Arthur Schopenhauer, German philosopher (1788–1860)

Collocates to: anger, anguish, anxiety, concerns, consciences, curiosity, doubt, fears, feelings, guilt, hunger, hurt, loneliness, pride, worries

Augur

(1) betoken; bode; divine; forebode; foreshadow; foretell; portend; predict

Word Used in Sentence(s)

*(1) The improved weather **augured** for a better hunting season.*

*(1) A growing third-party movement is **auguring** for a far greater voter turnout in the next election.*

*(1) "These readings **augur** well in the very near term for supportive bond price action. We, however, still look for core inflation to tick up modestly and for overall labor market conditions to improve gradually."*

—Chris Sullivan

Collocates to: does, future, might, not, poorly, well

Authenticate

(1) confirm; endorse; serve to prove; substantiate; validate

Word Used in Sentence(s)

*(1) "Previous analysis of Douglas County indictment statistics revealed high interracial homicide rates for African Americans. However, when coroners' inquests are used to **authenticate** such rates, black interracial*

homicide rates dropped significantly from 32 to 21 percent, while white interracial homicide rates increased from 4 to 5.6 percent. The reason for this change is simple. African Americans who killed whites were almost always indicted, but if a black killed another black, the chances of being indicted declined. For white perpetrators, however, the ratio for killing outside of their race increased because police who shot African Americans or mobs who lynched blacks were virtually never indicted."

—McKanna, Jr., Clare. "Seeds of Destruction: Homicide, Race, and Justice in Omaha, 1880–1920," *Journal of American Ethnic History*, Volume 14, Issue 1, Fall 1994: pg. 65.

Collocates to: biometrics, document, further, identity, tape, used, validate

Aver

(1)   affirm; assert the truthfulness of something; avow; claim; declare; maintain; profess; state; swear

Word Used in Sentence(s)

*(1) Some philosophers **aver** that both moral blame and legal responsibility should be based on prior behavior.*

*(1) President Bill Clinton **averred** that he smoked grass in college but did not inhale.*

*(1) "The anti-reformer is Chuck Schumer, the Senator from Wall Street, New York, who **averred** at the National Press Club last week that his party will have nothing to do with tax reform of the kind that Ronald Reagan negotiated with Democrats in 1989, or that Simpson-Bowles deficit commission proposed in 2010, or that the Gang of Six Senators have been working on. It's Chuck's way or no way."*

—Opinion. "Schumer to Tax Reform: Drop Dead," *Wall Street Journal*, October 15, 2012.

(1) "I know the thing that's most uncommon

(Envy be silent and attend!);

I know a reasonable woman,

Handsome and witty, yet a friend.

Not warped by passion, awed by rumor,

Not grave through pride, or gay through folly;

An equal mixture of good humor

And sensible soft melancholy.

Has she no faults, then (Envy says), sir?'

*Yes, she has one, I must **aver**:*

When all the world conspires to praise her,

The woman's deaf, and does not hear."

—Alexander Pope, British poet (1688–1744), "On a Certain Lady at Court"

Avow

(1) acknowledge; admit publicly; affirm; aver; claim; declare boldly; maintain; state

Word Used in Sentence(s)

*(1) President Bill Clinton **avowed** that he "did not have sex with that woman."*

*(1) If you set out to **avow** something, then acknowledge you are pledging your name, affirming your consciousness, and admitting publically, you are asserting your honor.*

*(1) "Cautious, careful people always casting about to preserve their reputation or social standards never can bring about reform. Those who are really in earnest are willing to be anything or nothing in the world's estimation, and publicly and privately, in season and out, **avow** their sympathies with despised ideas and their advocates, and bear the consequences."*

—Susan B. Anthony, American civil rights leader (1820–1906)

Collocates to: both, many, others, should

Backcast

(1) describe something or sometime in the past without having seen or experienced it; to reconstruct past events on the basis of the study of events or other evidence

Word Used in Sentence(s)

> *(1) "The term '**Backcasting**' was coined by Robinson [Robinson, 1982] as a futures method to develop normative scenarios and explore their feasibility and implications. It became important in the sustainability arena for obvious reasons and is often used as a tool to connect desirable long-term future scenarios (50 years) to the present situation by means of a participatory process."*

—"Backcasting," http://forlearn.jrc.ec.europa.eu/guide/ 4_methodology/meth_backcasting.htm, accessed April 20, 2013.

Balance

(1)   assess; calculate; collate; compare; consider; equalize; evaluate; even out; keep upright; offset; settle; square; stabilize; stay poised; steady; tally; total; weigh; weight up

Word Used in Sentence(s)

> *(1) Managing a global enterprise requires a CEO who is adept at **balancing** many interests.*

> *(1) Managers need to use a **balanced** approach in handling worker disputes.*

Battle test

(1)   test something under the most difficult of conditions

Word Used in Sentence(s)

> *(1) New product development teams are **battle tested** by the unknown risks they will face.*

> *(1) An uncertain economic period may be the ideal condition for **battle testing** your inexperienced marketing team.*

Beguile

(1)   attract; charm into doing; deceive; divert; enthrall; entice; fascinate; lure; mesmerize; put under a spell; woo

Word Used in Sentence(s)

*(1) "I am not merry, but I do **beguile** that thing I am by seeming
otherwise."*

—William Shakespeare, English dramatist, playwright, and poet
(1564–1616)

Bifurcate

(1) branch; divide; fork; split into two sections or pieces

Word Used in Sentence(s)

*(1) "Labor also has started to **bifurcate**, as minimum-wage workers have
begun to see their interests as distinct from—and often opposed to—those
of relatively well-paid unionized workers in industry and the public
sector."*

—Armijo, Leslie Elliott. "Inflation and Insouciance: The Peculiar
Brazilian Game," *Latin American Research Review*, Volume 31, Issue 3,
1996: pg. 7, 40p.

*(1) "'We **bifurcate** the society, with people who are so-called 'smart'
getting pushed toward book learning, and everyone else getting pushed
toward the trades.' Ever since the Industrial Revolution, the guys who
owned things wore suits, and the guys who ran the lathes wore work
clothes. If an engineer wanted something made, he'd draw it and give the
drawing to a machinist who then made it. I wanted to be the guy who
designed it and made it."*

—Sulkis, Brian. "Oakland: Sculpting a Hands-on Life," *San Francisco
Chronicle*, May 20, 2005: pg. F1.

 Collocates to: expressed, margining, may, occurrence, or, terminology

Blaze

(1) be brilliant; flash; glare; rush; speed around

Word Used in Sentence(s)

*(1) The new product was announced with a **blaze** of adverting and promotions.*

*(1) "When beggars die there are no comets seen; but the heavens them-selves **blaze** forth the death of princes."*

—William Shakespeare, English dramatist, playwright, and poet (1564–1616)

*(1) "I would rather be ashes than dust! I would rather that my spark should burn out in a brilliant **blaze** than it should be stifled by dry-rot. I would rather be a superb meteor, every atom of me in magnificent glow, than a sleepy and permanent planet. The function of man is to live, not to exist. I shall not waste my days trying to prolong them. I shall use my time."*

—Jack London, American short-story writer and novelist (1876–1916)

*(1) "The **blaze** of reputation cannot be blown out, but it often dies in the socket; a very few names may be considered as perpetual lamps that shine unconsumed."*

—Samuel Johnson, English poet, critic, and writer (1709–1784)

Burnish

(1)   brighten; cause to glow; gloss; make lustrous or shiny; to polish or shine

Word Used in Sentence(s)

*(1) "Radio Sawa is hardly the first government-funded use of popular culture to **burnish** America's image. During the cold war, Voice of America radio beamed jazz into the Soviet bloc."*

—Bayles, Martha. "The Return of Cultural Diplomacy," *Newsweek*, December 31, 2008.

*(1) "In the Spring a livelier iris changes on the **burnish'd** dove; in the Spring and yon man's fancy turns to thoughts of love."*

—Alfred Lord Tennyson, English poet (1809–1892)

Collocates to: brand, credentials, image, opportunity, reputation, surface

Calibrate

(1)   to determine, rectify, or mark the graduations, *especially* to measure against a standard

Word Used in Sentence(s)

*(1) "Almost one in five American men between the ages of 25 and 54 doesn't have a job. Fiscal and monetary policy should be **calibrated** to get more of them working before they become permanently unemployable."*

—Wessel, David. "Long-Term Economic To-Do List," *Wall Street Journal*, November 8, 2012: pg. A8.

*(1) American secondary and collegiate education needs to be **calibrated** more toward providing students with educations that prepare them for knowledge-based work, which is what American industry needs now.*

<u>**Collocates to:** analyze, careful, data, difficult, model, properly, used</u>

Call the shots

(1)   direct the outcome of an activity or affair; to predict the outcome of something

Word Used in Sentence(s)

*(1) I've waited years for the opportunity to run an operation, to **call the shots**.*

*(1) "At the outset when Robert Eaton was named as CEO replacing Lee Iacocca at General Motors, he informed key staffers that he believed in participatory management, not consensus management. The message was that Eaton would be **calling the shots**."*

—DuBrin, Andrew. *Leadership Research Findings, Practice, and Skills*, Boston: Houghton Mifflin Company, 1998.

Cherry-pick

(1)   choose the best thing; choose something very carefully; hand pick; opt; elect; single out

Word Used in Sentence(s)

*(1) "I think you have every right to **cherry-pick** when it comes to moving your spirit and finding peace in God. You take whatever works from wherever you can find it, and you keep moving toward the light."*

—Elizabeth Gilbert, American author of *Eat, Pray, Love* (1969–)

*(1) "Quote mining is a form of **cherry-picking**, and the genuine points used in construction of straw man arguments are typically **cherry-picked**."*

—http://rationalwiki.org/wiki/, accessed, April 23, 2013.

Choreograph

(1) arrange; compose; design; direct

Word Used in Sentence(s)

*(1) "No matter what you write or **choreograph**, you feel it's not enough."*

—Alvin Ailey, American dancer and choreographer (1931–1989)

Circumscribe

(1) boundary line; confine; define limit; delineate; demarcate; draw a line around; mark out; restrict

Word Used in Sentence(s)

*(1) "Implicit in the distinction between career counseling and guidance is a sense of what career counseling is not. It is important to **circumscribe** the field by exclusion, but it is essential to distinguish the field from related activities that, particularly recently, have been confused with it."*

—Crites, John, O. *Career Counseling, Models, Methods, and Materials*, NY: McGraw Hill, 1981.

*(1) "George Bush will join John Quincy Adams as the only other son of a president to win the White House. He also joins Adams as one of only four men who won the job despite losing the popular vote. Bush also plunges head-on into political uncertainty that could **circumscribe** his success."*

—Sherman, Mark and Ken Herman. "Now the Work Begins; President-elect Bush Faces Big Building Job with Little Time," *Cox Washington Bureau, Atlanta Journal Constitution*, December 14, 2000.

Collocates to: activities, boundaries, power, social, tenure, trying

Circumvent

(1) avoid; dodge; elude; evade; frustrate by surrounding or going around; get around; go around; outwit; skirt; take another route; thwart

Word Used in Sentence(s)

*(1) The students **circumvented** the school's ban on displaying flags on clothing by painting flags on the soles of their shoes.*

Classify

(1) arrange; assort; catalog; categorize; class; distribute into groups; grade; group; list by some order or sequence; organize; sort

Word Used in Sentence(s)

*(1) "Giants exist as a state of mind. They are defined not as an absolute measurement but as a proportionality...So giants can be real, even if adults do not choose to **classify** them as such."*

—Edward O. Wilson, American biologist, researcher, theorist, naturalist, and author (1929–)

Cluster

(1) agglomerate; assemble; bunch up or crowd together; constellate; flock; forgather; form; gather together or grow in bunches; meet

Word Used in Sentence(s)

*(1) "Sometime soon, in some location on Planet Earth, an assortment of companies, research institutions, entrepreneurs, and scientists will **cluster** together in an industrial ecosystem. Their goal: to exploit the rapid discoveries about the human genome..."*

—Ghadar, Fariborz, John Sviokla, and Dietrich Stephan, "Why Life Science Needs its Own Silicone Valley," *Harvard Business Review*, July–August 2012: pg. 25.

*(1) "The Image is more than an idea. It is a vortex or **cluster** of fused ideas and is endowed with energy."*

—Ezra Pound, American editor, poet, translator, and critic (1885–1972)

Cogitate

(1)   consider; deliberate; meditate; muse; ponder; reflect; ruminate

Word Used in Sentence(s)

*(1) "While I thus **cogitate** in disquiet and perplexity, half submerged in dark waters of a well in an Arabian oasis, I suddenly hear a voice from the background of my memory, the voice of an old Kurdish nomad: If water stands motionless in a pool, it grows stale and muddy, but when it moves and flows it becomes clear: so, too, man in his wanderings. Whereupon, as if by magic, all disquiet leaves me. I begin to look upon myself with distant eyes, as you might look at the pages of a book to read a story from them; and I begin to understand that my life could not have taken a different course. For when I ask myself, 'What is the sum total of my life?' something in me seems to answer, 'You have set out to exchange one world for another—to gain a new world for yourself in exchange for an old one which you never really possessed.' And I know with startling clarity that such an undertaking might indeed take an entire lifetime."*

—Muhammad Asad, journalist, traveler, writer, social critic, linguist, thinker, and reformer (1900–1992), *Road to Mecca*

Communicate

(1)   be in touch; be in verbal contact; call; connect; converse; convey; correspond; e-mail; impart; interconnect; join; publish; reveal; share; speak; talk; text; transmit information, thoughts, or feelings; wire; write

Word Used in Sentence(s)

*(1) "Great companies have three sets of stakeholders: customers, employees, and shareholders—in order of importance…the board should **communicate** that formula to the shareholders so they understand the greater good that the company represents."*

—Horst, Gary. "CEOs Need a NEW Set of Beliefs," *Harvard Business Review Blog*, September, 21, 2012: pg. 22.

*(1) "Ninety percent of leadership is the ability to **communicate** something people want."*

—Dianne Feinstein, American senator (1933–)

*(1) "Start with good people, lay out the rules, **communicate** with your employees, motivate them, and reward them. If you do all those things effectively, you can't miss."*

—Lee Iacocca, American business executive (1924–)

*(1) "Mayor Bill Akers of Seaside Heights, NJ now removed from the whirlwind of Hurricane Sandy's ferocity, and with the benefit of hindsight, the major says he has his regrets. He could, he says, have stopped by one of the shelters to speak to residents personally. He would have **communicated** information sooner."*

—Goldberg, Dan. "Responses to Sandy: From Great to Galling," *Star Ledger*, November 11, 2012: pg. 1.

Collocates to: ability, able, effectively, information, language, ways

Concentrate

(1) direct one's attention; draw together; make central

Word Used in Sentence(s)

*(1) "Research conducted in the auto industry shows that when people see a detailed prototype, something odd happens: they **concentrate** on the prototype's form and function, forgetting to attend to any remaining ambiguities about the problem the product is meant to solve or the obstacles in the way."*

—Leonardi, Paul. "Early Prototypes Can Hurt a Team's Creativity," *Harvard Business Review*, December 2011: pg. 28.

Connote

(1) facts; imply meaning or ideas beyond the explicit; involve as a condition or accompaniment; suggest

Word Used in Sentence(s)

*(1) "Freedom is not worth having if it does not **connote** freedom to err. It passes my comprehension how human beings, be they ever so experienced and able, can delight in depriving other human beings of that precious right."*

—Mohandas Gandhi, Indian philosopher (1869–1948)

Construe

(1) analyze something in a certain way; explain; infer or deduce; interpret; translate

Word Used in Sentence(s)

*(1) The purpose of the court system is to **construe** the meaning of the written laws.*

Corroborate

(1) back; back up with evidence; confirm formally; make certain the validity of; strengthen; support a statement or argument with evidence

Word Used in Sentence(s)

*(1) I believed my argument was sound but was pleased when an expert such as Dr. Phillips **corroborated** it.*

Decide

(1) adopt; agree; conclude; elect; fix on; go for; make a choice or come to conclusion; make up your mind; opt; pick; resolve; select; settle on; take

Word Used in Sentence(s)

*(1) "Whatever you do, you need courage. Whatever course you **decide** upon, there is always someone to tell you that you are wrong. There are always difficulties arising that tempt you to believe your critics are right."*

—Ralph Waldo Emerson, American poet, lecturer, and essayist (1803–1882)

*(1) "The possibilities are numerous once we **decide** to act and not react."*

—George Bernard Shaw, Irish literary critic, playwright, and essayist (1856–1950)

Deduce

(1) assume; conclude from evidence; conjecture; figure out; hypothesize; infer; posit; presume; reason; suppose; surmise; suspect; work out

(2) trace the course of deviation

Word Used in Sentence(s)

*(1) Forensics can examine a crime scene and from the evidence collected, experts can **deduce** the likely sequence of events.*

*(1) "Beyond the obvious facts that he has at some time done manual labor, that he takes snuff, that he is a Freemason, that he has been in China, and that he has done a considerable amount of writing lately, I can **deduce** nothing else."*

—Arthur Conan Doyle, Sr., Scottish writer, creator of the detective Sherlock Holmes (1859–1930)

Collocates to: able, can, effects, possible

Deem

(1) assess; hold; judge; regard; take for; view as

Word Used in Sentence(s)

*(1) "They **deem** him the worst enemy who tells them the truth."*

—Plato, classical Greek philosopher and mathematician
(472 BC–347 BC)

*(1) "I **deem** it the duty of every man to devote a certain portion of his income for charitable purposes; and that it is his further duty to see it so applied as to do the most good of which it is capable."*

—Thomas Jefferson, American founding father, 3rd U.S. President
(1743–1826)

Define

(1) characterize; classify; describe; determine or set down boundaries; distinguish; identify; label; term
(2) circumscribe; delimit; delimitate; demarcate; mark out

Word Used in Sentence(s)

*(1) "The team members **define** why the job exists and how it fits into the organization's ongoing strategy (or determines if it is even necessary now given the changes that may have occurred over the past few years)."*

—Hayashi, Shawn Kent. *Conversations for Creating Star Performers*, NY: McGraw Hill, 2012: pg. 19.

*(1) Clearly **defining** the scope of the project will help prevent scope creep.*

*(1) The project manager should clearly **define** the scope of the project.*

Delimit

(1)   define; demarcate; determine; fix boundaries; restrict; set limits; state clearly

Word Used in Sentence(s)

*(1) One of the steps a researcher should take is to **delimit** the scope of the study.*

*(1) "Speech sounds cannot be understood, **delimited**, classified, and explained except in the light of the tasks which they perform in language."*

—Roman Jakobson, Russian linguist and literary theorist (1896–1982)

Delineate

(1)   describe accurately; determine; draw an outline; fix boundaries; identify or indicate by marking with precision; represent something

Word Used in Sentence(s)

*(1) I plan to **delineate** my ideas regarding the new product in my presentation to the executive committee.*

*(1) "Do you want to know who you are? Don't ask. Act! Action will **delineate** and define you."*

—Thomas Jefferson, American founding father, 3rd U.S. President (1743–1826)

*(1) His responsibility was to **delineate** the scope of internal audits for the board finance committee.*

<u>**Collocates to:**</u> <u>boundary, combinations, limit, scope, sections, used</u>

Demystify

(1)   clarify; clear up; eliminate or remove mystery; make rational or comprehensible

Word Used in Sentence(s)

*(1) "Some teachers who are able to **demystify** the compositional process by providing sequential instruction in how to compose which helps students capture the spirit."*

—Conway, Colleen. "The Implementation of the National Standards in Music Education: Capturing the Spirit of the Standards," *Music Educators Journal*, Volume 94, Issue 4, March 2008: pg. 34–39, 6p.

Collocates to: attempts, experience, help, process, research, trying

Demarcate

(1) separate clearly; set boundaries; set mark

Word Used in Sentence(s)

*(1) "The decision to create and **demarcate** the boundaries of those states was made neither in Africa, nor by Africans, nor in consultation with Africans, nor after considering how it would affect the Africans politically, socially, culturally, and economically. But the states thus created survive to this day. Peoples that in the past have had very little or nothing at all to do with one another politically, socially, culturally, and economically can be made to exist as a single polity."*

—Editors. "Prerequisites for Economic Integration in Africa," *Africa Today*, Volume 42, Issue 4, 1995, 4th Quarter: pg. 56.

Collocates to: area, between, border, boundaries, clearly, social, spaces, territories

Demonstrate

(1) display; express; lay bare; make obvious; prove or show with evidence or reason; reveal

(2) determine; establish; make evident or plain; prove; reveal; validate

Word Used in Sentence(s)

*(1) One way to differentiate yourself from others is to **demonstrate** what you have learned and how you have applied this knowledge effectively.*

Detect

(1)   ascertain; become aware of; descry; discover; distinguish; expose; find; identify; notice; perceive; reveal; sense; spot; uncover

Word Used in Sentence(s)

*(1) Great managers have a skill of quickly **detecting** the strengths in their people.*

*(1) "It's hard to **detect** good luck—it looks so much like something you've earned."*

—Frank A. Clark, English author and writer (1943–)

*(1) "The Center for Creative Learning staff collected hundreds of peer-performance reviews and health-screening results from CEOs and other senior-level managers. From this data, they **detected** a correlation that a leader's weight may indeed influence perceptions of leaders among subordinates, peers, and superiors."*

—Kwoh, Leslie. "Marketing," *Wall Street Journal*, January 16, 2013: pg. B1.

Determine

(1)   agree to; bound; decide; delimit; delimitate; demarcate; discover; establish; judge; limit; mark out; measure; resolve; settle on

(2)   ascertain; clarify; establish; find out; uncover

(3)   affect; control; govern; influence; mold; shape

Word Used in Sentence(s)

*(1) The success of a strategy will be **determined**, in larger part, by the manager's ability to be flexible in the tactics used.*

*(1) The results of the research are one factor in whether or not we **determine** to proceed with the new product.*

*(1) "Your attitude, not your aptitude, will **determine** your altitude."*

—Zig Ziglar, American author, salesman, and motivational speaker (1926–2012)

*(1) "Best practice companies such as Apple, Dell, HP, Honda, IBM, LGE, and Toyota do what we just advise: They have approved vendor lists but never completely relinquish decisions about a product's components and material to top-tier suppliers. They carefully **determine** which items they should directly source themselves and which they should totally delegate."*

—Choi, Thomas and Tom Linton. "Don't Let Your Supply Chain Control Your Business," *Harvard Business Review*, December 2011: pg. 113.

Diagnose

(1) analyze the cause or nature of something; detect; establish; identify a condition; make a diagnosis; spot

Word Used in Sentence(s)

*(1) First **diagnose** the problem and then devise a solution to get the equipment running again.*

*(1) "In India, the Ministry of Agriculture's watershed management program coordinates NGOs that train government and other NGO staff to evaluate social impacts and **diagnose** organizational problems."*

—Fisher, Julie. "Local and Global: International Governance and Civil Society," *Journal of International Affairs*, Volume 57, Issue 1, Fall 2003: pg. 19–39, 21p.

Collocates to: able, difficult, doctors, problems, treat, used

Distinguish

(1) stand out; tell apart; tell the difference between
(2) perform well and receive recognition

Word Used in Sentence(s)

*(1) "Without feelings of respect, what is there to **distinguish** men from beasts?"*

—Confucius, Chinese teacher, editor, politician, and philosopher (551–479 BCE)

*(1) "Every man's life ends the same way. It is only the details of how he lived and how he died that **distinguish** one man from another."*

—Ernest Hemingway, American writer (1899–1961)

*(1) "Learn to **distinguish** the difference between errors of knowledge and breaches of morality."*

—Ayn Rand, Russian-American novelist, philosopher, playwright, and screenwriter (1905–1982)

Dream

(1) thoughts or emotions passing through the mind; to have an image; vision

Word Used in Sentence(s)

*(1) "Do not dwell in the past, do not **dream** of the future, concentrate the mind on the present moment."*

—Buddha, Indian spiritual teacher from the Indian subcontinent, on whose teachings Buddhism was founded (circa 563 BC–483 BC)

*(1) "There are those who look at things the way they are, and ask why...I **dream** of things that never were, and ask why not?"*

—John F. Kennedy, 35th U.S. President (1917–1963)

*(1) "This is No Place to **Dream** Small"*

—Ad headline for NY state in *Wall Street Journal*, December 12, 2012.

*(1) "**Dream** as if you'll live forever, live as if you'll die today."*

—James Dean, American motion picture actor (1931–1955)

Enhance

(1) add to; grow; improve; increase; make better; make more desirable

Word Used in Sentence(s)

*(1) "For Good Eggs, a San Francisco-based tech start-up aiming to **enhance** local food systems, a process of self-examination forms the very basis of the company's culture."*

—Hann, Christopher. "The Masters," *Entrepreneur*, March 2012: pg. 58.

*(1) "It is important to note, however, that on the basis of current research
and specific conditions (ophthalmologic or age), appropriate magnifica-
tion—through the use of low vision devices and large print—can
enhance the reading performance of individuals with low vision."*

—Russell-Minda, Elizabeth. "The Legibility of Typefaces for Readers
with Low Vision: A Research Review," *Journal of Visual Impairment &
Blindness*, Volume 101, Issue 7, July 2007: pg. 402–415, 14p.

Collocates to: ability, learning, performance, quality, students, understanding

Ennoble

(1)   confer dignity; elevate in degree, elegance, or respect

Word Used in Sentence(s)

*(1) "Good actions **ennoble** us, and we are the sons of our deeds."*

—Miguel de Cervantes Saavedra, Spanish writer (1547–1616)

Epitomize

(1)   abbreviate; abridge; represent; review; serve as the image of; synopsize

(2)   make or be an epitome of

Word Used in Sentence(s)

*(1) "But what is the greatest evil? If you are going to **epitomize** evil,
what is it? Is it the bomb? The greatest evil that one has to fight
constantly, every minute of the day until one dies, is the worse part of
oneself."*

—Unknown

Esteem

(1)   admire; appreciate; have great regard; respect; value highly

(2)   consider; hold to be; regard

Word Used in Sentence(s)

*(1) "Dozens of recent experiments show that rewarding self-interest with economic incentives can backfire. When we take a job or buy a car, we are not only trying to get stuff, we are also trying to be a certain kind of person. People desire to be **esteemed** by others and to be seen as ethical and dignified. And they don't want to be taken as suckers."*

—Bowels, Samuel. "When Economic Incentives Backfire," *Harvard Business Review*, March 2009: pg. 22.

Exemplify

(1) characterize; demonstrate; embody; epitomize; personify; represent; serve as an example; show; typify or model of something

Word Used in Sentence(s)

*(1) "It is easier to **exemplify** values than teach them."*

—Theodore Hesburgh, American priest of the Congregation of Holy Cross, President Emeritus of the University of Notre Dame (1917–)

*(1) "There is only one way in which one can endure man's inhumanity to man and that is to try, in one's own life, to **exemplify** man's humanity to man."*

—Alan Paton, South African writer and educator (1903–1988)

Collocates to: activities, character, leadership, spirit, values, ways

Experiment

(1) research; test; trial; try something new to gain experience
(2) make or conduct an experiment

Word Used in Sentence(s)

*(1) Leaders are not afraid to **experiment**, take risks, and learn from their mistakes.*

Finesse

(1) ability; assurance; dexterity; discretion; flair; grace; poise; refinement; sensitivity; skill; skillful maneuvering; smooth; subtlety; tact; use of subtle charm

Word Used in Sentence(s)

(1) "Experience is what allows us to repeat our mistakes, only with more finesse!"

—Unknown

(1) Be prepared to finesse what we can do; we need to make some hard decisions.

Forge

(1) come up with a concept, explanation, idea, theory, or principle; contrive; create

(2) beat; make out of components

(3) move ahead or act with sudden increase in motion or speed

Word Used in Sentence(s)

(1) "People are more inclined to be drawn in if their leader has a compelling vision. Great leaders help people get in touch with their own aspirations and then will help them forge those aspirations into a personal vision."

—John Kotter, former professor at the Harvard Business School and acclaimed author (1947–)

(1) "The President's offer is very much in keeping with history of insisting that negotiation consists of the other side giving him everything he wants. That approach has given him the reputation as the modern president least able to forge a consensus."

—Strassel, Kimberley. "This Unserious White House," *Wall Street Journal*, November 30, 2012: pg. A13.

(1) "We forge the chains we wear in life."

—Charles Dickens, English writer and social critic (1812–1870)

(1) "Bad men cannot make good citizens. It is when a people forget God that tyrants forge their chains. A vitiated state of morals, a corrupted public conscience, is incompatible with freedom. No free government, or the blessings of liberty, can be preserved to any people but by a firm adherence to justice, moderation, temperance, frugality, and virtue; and by a frequent recurrence to fundamental principles."

—Patrick Henry, American lawyer, patriot, and orator, symbol of the American struggle for liberty (1736–1799)

Gentrify

(1) improve; raise to a higher statue; rebuild; renew; uplift

Word Used in Sentence(s)

*(1) "'If you go down there now, it's a totally different neighborhood,' says William A. 'Billy' Mitchell, Jr., the real estate mogul who co-chaired the Summerhill development project in the early '90s. He and other civic-minded developers who tried to pull Summerhill up by its bootstraps point to all those new homes, many now filled with affluent whites delighted to **gentrify** another new in-town neighborhood."*

—Turner, Melissa. "Unrealized Dream: Summerhill's Olympic Rebirth Started with Visions of a Mixed-income Community," *Atlanta Journal Constitution*, January 14, 2001.

Hypothesize

(1) educated guess of some outcome

Word Used in Sentence(s)

*(1) "In the last five years, though, an expanding number of computer scientists have embraced developmental psychology's proposal that infants possess basic abilities, including gaze tracking, for engaging with others in order to learn. Social interactions, combined with sensory experiences gained as a child explores the world, set off a learning explosion, researchers **hypothesize**."*

—Bower, Bruce. "Meet the Growbots," *Science News*, Volume 179, Issue 3, January 29, 2011: pg. 18, 4 p.

*(1) "I **hypothesize** that the Katrina event has made people think pretty seriously about infrastructure and its vulnerability."*

—Stuart Elway, American business executive

Collocates to: led, may, might, reasonable, researchers, therefore, we

Judge

(1) adjudge; adjudicate; arbitrate; decide; decree; determine; form an opinion; govern; infer; referee; rule on something; umpire

Word Used in Sentence(s)

*(1) "You can easily **judge** the character of a man by how he treats those who can do nothing for him."*

—James D. Miles, American associate professor of Psychology at Purdue University

*(1) "We are not afraid to entrust the American people with unpleasant facts, foreign ideas, alien philosophies, and competitive values. For a nation that is afraid to let its people **judge** the truth and falsehood in an open market is a nation that is afraid of its people."*

—John Fitzgerald Kennedy, 35th U.S. President (1917–1963)

*(1) " 'While weight remains a taboo conversation topic in the workplace, it's hard to overlook. A heavy executive is **judged** to be less capable because of assumptions about how weight affects health and stamina,' says Berry Posner, a professor at Santa Clara University's Leavey School of Business."*

—Kwoh, Leslie. "Marketing," *Wall Street Journal*, January 16, 2013: pg. B1.

Learn

(1) acquire knowledge through study and experience; add to one's store of facts; ascertain; become informed; check; detect; discover; find out; gain by exposure, experience, or example; imply

Word Used in Sentence(s)

*(1) "Who dares to teach must never cease to **learn**."*

—John Cotton Dana, American librarian and museum director (1856–1929)

*(1) "Live as if you were to die tomorrow. **Learn** as if you were to live forever."*

—Unknown

Listen

(1) attend; hark; hear; hearken; lend an ear; list; make an effort to hear and understand something; pay attention; respond to advice, request or command

Word Used in Sentence(s)

*(1) If you **listen** to your customers, you will become a marketing expert.*

*(1) "Leaders who take organizational conversation seriously know when to stop talking and start **listening**. Few behaviors enhance conversational intimacy as much as attending to what people say...Duke Energy's president and VEO, James Rogers, instituted a series of what he called 'listening sessions' when he was the CEO of Cinergy which later merged with Duke."*

—Groysberg, Boris and Michael Slind. "Leadership Is a Conversation," *Harvard Business Review*, June 2012: pg. 79.

*(1) To **listen** is a communication skill and is very different from hearing, which is not a communication skill.*

Litigate

(1) engage in legal proceedings; try in court

Word Used in Sentence(s)

*(1) "You can't legislate or **litigate** good, healthy behavior, but we must be willing to educate people at an early age about the effects of unhealthy living."*

—Zach Wamp, former U.S. Representative for Tennessee's 3rd Congressional district (1957–)

*(1) "They rushed to move it forward, uh, and then a lawsuit was filed, and we spent many months **litigating**, rather than trying to come up with legislation and move forward on that front."*

—Tom Udall, senior U.S. Senator from New Mexico (1948–)

Monitor

(1) check the quality or content; keep track systematically with a view to collecting information; observe or record; watch attentively

Word Used in Sentence(s)

*(1) "As soon as the boss decides he wants his workers to do something, he has two problems: making them do it and **monitoring** what they do."*

—Robert Krulwich, American radio and television journalist

*(1) "To reach that level of maturity, companies need to focus on (1) raising accountability for risk management to the board and executive levels; (2) embedding an enterprise approach to risk assessment and **monitoring**; optimizing risk function by breaking down silos and coordinating risk-related infrastructure, people, practices, and technology across the enterprise..."*

—Herrington, Michael, Ernst & Young. Interaction to *HBR*, September 2012: pg. 18.

Motivate

(1)   cause; egg on; encourage; incentivize; induce; inspire; prompt; provide with a motive; provoke; stimulate; trigger

Word Used in Sentence(s)

*(1) There is more to **motivating** employees than compensation.*

*(1) "Offering ownership opportunities is still a great way to lure and **motivate** top-notch employees."*

—Caggiano, Christopher. "The Right Way to Pay," *Inc.*, Volume 24, Issue 12, November 2002: pg. 84.

Collocates to: ability, action, behavior, employee, factor, inspire, learn, students, teachers, ways

Perambulate

(1)   inspect by traversing; ramble; stroll; walk through, over, and around to do a complete and thorough inspection

Word Used in Sentence(s)

*(1)Today's managers think they invented management by walking around, but 16th century managers **perambulated** 400 years earlier.*

Permeate

(1)   penetrate; seep or spread through

Word Used in Sentence(s)

*(1) "Three-quarters of about 10 million students at four-year colleges and universities in the U.S. take at least one internship before graduating, according to the College Employment Research Institute. Interns **permeate** most every corner of the economy, from Disney World to Capitol Hill, the Fortune 500 to the nonprofit sector, Main Street to Silicon Valley."*

—Italie, Leanne. "New Book Takes Critical Look at Internships," *Domestic News,* April 20, 2011.

Collocates to: air, aspect, culture, entire, every, must, seem, society, space

Perpetuate

(1) carry on; continue; keep up; maintain; make everlasting; preserve; prolong memory or use of; spread

Word Used in Sentence(s)

*(1) "When a government becomes powerful, it is destructive, extravagant, and violent; it is an usurer which takes bread from innocent mouths and deprives honorable men of their substance, for votes with which to **perpetuate** itself."*

—Marcus Tullius Cicero, ancient Roman lawyer, writer, scholar, orator, and statesman (106 BC–43 BC)

*(1) One of the problems with American management isn't the desire to **perpetuate** their positions because the average position expectancy of a CEO is less than 36 months.*

*(1) "No monuments are erected for the righteous; their deeds **perpetuate** their memory."*

—Unknown

Plan

(1) arrange; design; have in mind a project or purpose; intend; prepare; purpose; set up

(2) arrangement of strategic ideas in diagrams, charts, sketches, graphs, tables, maps, and other documents

Word Used in Sentence(s)

*(1) The ability to **plan** and execute the **plan** is a sought-after management skill.*

*(1) Having **planned** the sales meeting and organized all the activities demonstrates superb organization skills.*

*(1) "**Planning** will help you think in terms of laying down a foundation of the particular experiences you need to create a resume to move you into senior management."*

—Wellington, Shelia. *Be Your Own Mentor*, NY: Random House, 2001.

*(1) "One of the four functions of management is **planning**—setting specific performance objectives and identifying the actions needed to achieve them."*

—Schermerhorn, John, Richard Osborn, Mary UHL-Bien, and James Hunt. *Organizational Behavior*, 12th Ed., NY: John Wiley & Sons, Inc., 2012.

*(1) "In order to **plan** your future wisely, it is necessary that you understand and appreciate your past."*

—Jo Coudert, American author (1923–)

Predict

(1)   achieve; acquire; arrive at; attain; come into possession of; find; gain; get; get hold of; take

Word Used in Sentence(s)

*(1) Analysts **predict** the firm would exceed last year's sales figures.*

*(1) Jessie was the only person willing to **predict** we would make our sales projections.*

*(1) "No model or human can perfectly **predict** the future. But the FED models have a more specific problem. Despite all their complexity and sophistication, they have long been plagued by gaps in how they read and project the economy."*

—Hilenrath, Jon. "Fed's Computer Models Pose Problems," *Wall Street Journal*, December 31, 2012: pg. A3.

Prepossess

(1) bias; influence beforehand; prejudice

(2) influence favorable at once

Word Used in Sentence(s)

*(1) Mobile technology is becoming ever more **prepossessing** with each new model's increasing power, incredible capabilities, and stylish looks.*

Quantify

(1) express something in quantifiable terms

(2) numerical expression or explanation

(3) determine or express or explain the quantity of, numerical measure of, or extent of

Word Used in Sentence(s)

*(1) "We should not forget, no matter how we **quantify** it: 'Freedom is not free.' It is a painful lesson, but one from which we have learned in the past and one we should never forget."*

—Unknown

Reason

(1) meaning; purpose; think logically or systematically about

(2) think coherently and logically

(3) draw inference or conclusions from facts or assumptions

(4) argue or talk in a logical way

Word Used in Sentence(s)

*(1) "Once the people begin to **reason**, all is lost."*

—Voltaire, French philosopher and writer (1694–1778)

*(1) "As long as the **reason** of man continues fallible, and he is at liberty to exercise it, different opinions will be formed."*

—James Madison, author of *Federalist Papers*, 4th U.S. President (1751–1836)

Refute

(1)   disprove; prove to be false

Word Used in Sentence(s)

(1) "Silence is one of the hardest arguments to __refute__."

—Josh Billings, American humorist (1818–1885)

Search out

(1)   catch on; discover; get to know something, especially by asking somebody or searching in an appropriate source, or just by chance; get wind;
hear about; learn; note; notice; observe; realize; uncover

Word Used in Sentence(s)

*(1) Leadership involves __searching out__ new opportunities, ways to inno-
vate, change, ideas for growth, and improvement.*

Segue

(1)   continue without break; lead into new areas; proceed without interrup-
tion; smooth change to next topic

Word Used in Sentence(s)

*(1) "Then he quickly __segues__ into the dangers of being too hard on cops
who make an honest mistake. That turns out to be the moral of the story,
the perils of politics intruding on the job."*

—Ted Conover, Book Review of *True Blood*, *New York Times*, April 18,
2004.

Sequester

(1)   isolate a portion from the larger population; keep or set apart
(2)   confiscate; seize; take over

Word Used in Sentence(s)

(1) Juries are sometimes __sequestered__ during the deliberation of a trial.

(1) "Oh to have been able to discharge this monster, whom John now perceived, with tardy clear-sightedness, to have begun betimes the festivities of Christmas! But far from any such ray of consolation visiting the lost, he stood bare of help and helpers, his portmanteau __sequestered__ in one place, his money deserted in another and guarded by a corpse; himself, so sedulous of privacy, the cynosure of all men's eyes about the station; and, as if these were not enough mischances, he was now fallen in ill-blood with the beast to whom his poverty had linked him! In ill-blood, as he reflected dismally, with the witness who perhaps might hang or save him!"

—Robert Lewis Stevenson, Scottish novelist, poet, essayist, travel writer, and author of *Tales and Fantasies* (1850–1894)

Transcend

(1) carry on; conduct; exceed; excel; go beyond; outdo; perform; rise above; surpass

Word Used in Sentence(s)

(1) "An ELECTIVE DESPOTISM was not the government we fought for; but one which should not only be founded on free principles, but in which the powers of government should be so divided and balanced among several bodies of magistracy, as that no one could __transcend__ their legal limits, without being effectually checked and restrained by the others."

—James Madison, American statesman and political theorist, 4th U.S. President, and author of *The Federalist Papers* (1751–1836)

Transform

(1) alter; change the structure; convert from one form to another; make over; transmute; undergo total change

Word Used in Sentence(s)

(1) "Kevin Peters, the new CEO of Office Depot, had conversations with customers and the results gave him three insights into how to __transform__ the business and become more competitive."

—Peters, Kevin. "Office Depot's President on How Mystery Shopping Helped Spark a Turnaround," *Harvard Business Review*, November 2011: pg. 48.

*(1) "Zhongxing Medical **transformed** the medical equipment business by focusing on direct digital radiography in a novel way."*

—Williamson, Peter and Ming Zeng. "Value-for-Money Strategies for Recessionary Times," *Harvard Business Review*, March 2009: pg. 70.

*(1) "In 2003, Apple introduced the iPod with the iTunes store, revolutionizing portable entertaining, creating a new market, and **transforming** the company."*

—Johnson, Mark, Clayton Christensen, and Henning Kagermann. "Reinventing Your Business Model," *Harvard Business Review*, December 2008: pg. 51.

*(1) "In his lifetime, Steve Jobs **transformed** seven industries."*

—Isaacson, Walter. "The Real Leadership Lessons of Steve Jobs," *Harvard Business Review*, April 2012: pg. 94.

Understand

(1)   assume that something is present or is the case; believe to be the case; know and comprehend something; infer from information received; interpret or view in a particular way; perceive the intended meanings of something

Word Used in Sentence(s)

*(1) "Marketing and finance have a famously fractious relationship, with each accusing the other of failing to **understand** how to create value. That tension may seem to be dysfunctional, but when channeled right, it can actually be productive."*

—Reprint F0706D, *Harvard Business Review*, June 2007: pg. 25.

*(1) "**Understanding** the values of the person or team you are developing will enable you to build rapport and create meaningful connections."*

—Hayashi, Shawn Kent. *Conversations for Creating Star Performers*, NY: McGraw Hill, 2012: pg. 41.

*(1) "For the past three years, we have undertaken in-depth case study research on the strategy and leadership of a dozen large global companies...Our goal was to **understand** what makes a company strategically*

agile—able to change its strategies and business models rapidly in response to major shifts in its market space."

—Doz, Yves and Mikko Kosonen. "The New Deal at the Top," *Harvard Business Review*, June 2007: pg. 100.

Validate

(1) confirm; make valid

Word Used in Sentence(s)

*(1) "This is all that is necessary to **validate** the use of images to be made in the sequel."*

—Bertrand Russell, British philosopher, logician, mathematician, historian, social critic, and author of *The Analysis of Mind* (1872–1970)

Venerate

(1) honor as scared or noble; respect deeply; revere
(2) look upon with feelings of deep respect; regard as venerable

Word Used in Sentence(s)

*(1) It is a mystery to me why we prefer to **venerate** people at their death rather than while they are still alive.*

Vent

(1) express oneself directly without holding back; give emotional expression to; relieve oneself of frustration or anger by expressing the feeling outwardly

Word Used in Sentence(s)

*(1) "In recent weeks, Cardinals from around the world have publicly **vented** grievances over the opaque governance of the Roman Curia, the Vatican's scandal-plagued administrative body..."*

—Meichtry, Stacy and John Stroll. "Centuries Old Ritual to Choose Pope Begins," *Wall Street Journal*, March 13, 2013.

Zero in

(1) give full attention to something

(2) aim directly at

Word Used in Sentence(s)

(1) "Steve Jobs' Zen-like ability to focus was accompanied by the related instinct to simplify things by <u>zeroing in</u> on their essence and eliminating the unnecessary components."

—Isaacson, Walter. "The Real Leadership Lessons of Steve Jobs," *Harvard Business Review*, April 2012: pg. 94.

Zero out

(1) eliminate; reduce

Word Used in Sentence(s)

(1) When the Republicans say they want to <u>zero out</u> taxpayer funding for PBS, there is a very good reason to believe the threat.

Zoom through

(1) get through something quickly

Word Used in Sentence(s)

(1) He <u>zoomed through</u> the instructions and went quickly on to the assembly of the robot as though he had done it many times before.

8

100 Top Action Verbs for Schmoozing, Socializing, Shindigs, Getting Sentimental, or Using Your Networking to Work the Room

Accept

(1) admit; agree; believe; consent; say you will

(2) receive with gladness and approval

(3) receive; take something being offered

(4) bow to; endure; put up with; resign yourself to; tolerate

Word Used in Sentence(s)

(1) "We often refuse to __accept__ an idea merely because the tone of voice in which it has been expressed is unsympathetic to us."

—Friedrich Nietzsche, German classical scholar and philosopher (1844–1900)

(1) "__Accept__ your genius and say what you think."

—Ralph Waldo Emerson, American poet, lecturer, and essayist (1803–1882)

(1) "If I __accept__ you as you are, I will make you worse; however, if I treat you as though you are what you are capable of becoming, I will help you become that."

—Johann Wolfgang von Goethe, German playwright, poet, novelist, and dramatist (1749–1832)

*(1) "The leaders who work most effectively, it seems to me, never say 'I.'
And that's not because they have trained themselves not to say 'I.' They
don't think 'I.' They think 'we;' they think 'team.' They understand their
job to be to make the team function. They **accept** responsibility and don't
sidestep it, but 'we' gets the credit.... This is what creates trust, what
enables you to get the task done."*

—Peter F. Drucker, American educator and writer (1909– 2009)

Accommodate

(1)   allow for; assist; be of service; consider; find ways to help; oblige

(2)   adjust; become accustomed; familiarize; get use to; make suitable

(3)   house; lodge; provide accommodations; put up

(4)   adapt; be big enough for; contain; have capacity for; hold; reconcile; seat

(5)   do a favor or a service for someone

Word Used in Sentence(s)

*(1) "We accept and welcome... as conditions to which we must **accommodate** ourselves, great inequality of environment; the concentration of
business, industrial, and commercial, in the hands of a few; and the law
of competition between these, as being not only beneficial, but essential
for the future progress of the race."*

—Andrew Carnegie, American industrialist and philanthropist
(1835–1919)

*(1) "If you accommodate others, you will be **accommodating** yourself."*

—Chinese Proverb

Acquiesce

(1)   accept; agree; assent; comply with passively; concede; concur; consent;
give in; go along with; submit; yield

Word Used in Sentence(s)

*(1) "No man can sit down and withhold his hands from the warfare
against wrong and get peace from his **acquiescence**."*

—Woodrow Wilson, 28th U.S. President (1856–1924)

(1) "Men __acquiesce__ in a thousand things, once righteously and boldly done, to which, if proposed to them in advance, they might find endless objections."

—Robert Dale Owen, American politician (1801–1877)

Collocates to: choice, compelled, council, demands, forced, must, quietly, refused

Adopt

(1) accept; agree to; approve; assume; choose; embrace; endorse; espouse; foster; implement; take in as one's own; take on; take on board; take up

Word Used in Sentence(s)

(1) "__Adopt__ the pace of nature; her secret is patience."

—Ralph Waldo Emerson, American poet, lecturer, and essayist (1803–1882)

(1) "I shall try to correct errors when shown to be errors, and I shall __adopt__ new views so fast as they shall appear to be true views."

—Abraham Lincoln, 16th U.S. President (1809–1865)

(1) "Here is the prime condition of success: Concentrate your energy, thought, and capital exclusively upon the business in which you are engaged. Having begun on one line, resolve to fight it out on that line, to lead in it, __adopt__ every improvement, have the best machinery, and know the most about it."

—Andrew Carnegie, American industrialist and philanthropist (1835–1919)

Agglomerate

(1) accumulate; cluster; gather together; jumbled collection

Word Used in Sentence(s)

(1) "Common property campesino communities fit very uncomfortably in the neoliberal discourse, but in the Mexican context, ejidos and comunidades agrarias are irrevocable, at least in the short and medium term. The reformers, therefore, also created new legal mechanisms for private capital to associate with common property through joint ventures, made it easier to __agglomerate__ land within ejidos, and established new

*mechanisms for associations of individuals within ejidos and comu-
nidades to exploit common properties (Wexler and Bray 1996; Cornelius
and Myhre 1998; World Bank 1995)."*

—Koolster, Dan. "Campesinos and Mexican Forest Policy During the
Twentieth Century," *Latin American Research Review*, Volume 38, Issue
2, 2003: pg. 94.

Anodyne

(1)   capable of showing comfort; eliminating pain

Word Used in Sentence(s)

*(1) "Illusion is an **anodyne**, bred by the gap between wish and reality."*

—Herman Wouk, American author (1915–)

Collocates to: connotations, dominance, imagined, less, making, nothing,
rather

Appertain

(1)   apply; attribute of; be appropriate; be part of; belong; relate to

Word Used in Sentence(s)

*(1) "As Senator Trumbull noted, the 'bill has nothing to do with the
political rights or status of parties. It is confined exclusively to their civil
rights, such rights as should **appertain** to every free man.'"*

—Smith, Douglas. "A Lockean Analysis of Section One of the
Fourteenth Amendment," *Harvard Journal of Law & Public Policy*,
Volume 25, Issue 3, Summer 2002: pg. 1095.

Assemble

(1)   accumulate; amass; bring together; collect in one place; draw together;
gather; get together; join; mass; meet; muster

Word Used in Sentence(s)

*(1) "The next step was to **assemble** the right talent around me."*

—Grossman, Mindy. "HSN's CEO on Fixing the Shopping Networks
Culture," *Harvard Business Review*, December 2011: pg. 44.

*(1) "When you approach a problem, strip yourself of preconceived opinions and prejudice, **assemble** and learn the facts of the situation, make the decision which seems to you to be the most honest, and then stick to it."*

—Chester Bowles, American diplomat and politician (1901–1986)

Assimilate

(1)   absorb; accommodate; incorporate; standardize

Word Used in Sentence(s)

*(1) "True ideas are those that we can **assimilate**, validate, corroborate, and verify. False ideas are those that we cannot."*

—William James, American philosopher and psychologist (1842–1910)

*(1) "Nothing is more revolting than the majority; for it consists of few vigorous predecessors, of knaves who accommodate themselves, of weak people who **assimilate** themselves, and the mass that toddles after them without knowing in the least what it wants."*

—Johann Wolfgang von Goethe, German playwright, poet, novelist, and dramatist (1749–1832)

*(1) "It's important for companies to gather insights from former outsiders who have **assimilated** successfully; managers who have grown up in an organization often don't realize they even have a culture."*

—Watkins, Michael. "Help Newly Hired Executives Adapt Quickly," *Harvard Business Review*, June 2007: pg. 26.

Assist

(1)   abet; aid; back; befriend; collaborate; facilitate; help with; promote; support; sustain

Word Used in Sentence(s)

*(1) "There is no more noble occupation in the world than to **assist** another human being —to help someone succeed."*

—Alan Loy McGinnis, American author and Christian psychotherapist (1933–2005)

Collocates to: design, effort, goals, program, resources

Ballyhoo

(1) advertise; commotion; create a to-do; hullabaloo; kerfuffle; make known; make a racket, ruckus, or uproar; promote

Word Used in Sentence(s)

*(1) "For all the **ballyhoo** about the West's rugged individualism, such alterations required state intervention on an unprecedented scale. The costs of damming and moving water grew prohibitive even for the largest ranchers and growers, particularly as the natural flow of artesian wells ceased."*

—Dawson, Robert and Grey Brechin. "How Paradise Lost," *Mother Jones*, Volume 21, Issue 6, November–December 1996: p38.

Bandy

(1) exchange; give and receive

(2) spread something in an unfavorable context

(3) toss or hit something back and forth

Word Used in Sentence(s)

*(1) "The wise speak only of what they know, Grima son of Galmod. A witless worm have you become. Therefore, be silent, and keep your forked tongue behind your teeth. I have not passed through fire and death to **bandy** crooked words with a serving-man till then."*

—J.R.R. Tolkien, English writer (1892–1973)

*(1) "To judge by the life choices we make, then, there are dozens of reasons for women to be pro-abortion. Yet not since the heady early days of the abortion rights movement in the late 1960s have we heard its leadership **bandy** around the phrase that summarizes the right we want and have come to expect: 'abortion on demand.'"*

—Hax, Carolyn. "No Birth, No Pangs," *Washington Post*, March 21, 1993.

Bump the shark

(1) push back against an aggressive person; stand up against an intrusive, aggressive, or assertive verbal assault

(2) fight back against a bully

Word Used in Sentence(s)

*(1) The last thing the thug expected from a gray-haired woman with a walker was someone who was ready to **bump the shark**.*

Cachinnate

(1)   laugh convulsively or hard; laugh loudly or immoderately

Word Used in Sentence(s)

*(1) You could hear him **cachinnate** all the way down the hall, and because the others in the room were not laughing at the crude joke, it made his behavior even more odd.*

Captivate

(1)   enchant; enthrall; fascinate; infatuate; intense romantic attraction

Word Used in Sentence(s)

*(1) "All kinds of beauty do not inspire love; there is a kind that only pleases the sight but does not **captivate** the affections."*

—Miguel de Cervantes Saavedra, Spanish writer (1547-1616)

Champion

(1)   advocate; back; campaign for; crusade for; excel; fight for; stand up for; support; to be a winner; uphold

Word Used in Sentence(s)

*(1) Sharon was the **champion** for the new compensation plan.*

*(1) "We cannot be both the world's leading **champion** of peace and the world's leading supplier of the weapons of war."*

—Jimmy Carter, 39th U.S. President (1924–)

*(1) "**Champion** the right to be yourself; dare to be different and to set your own pattern; live your own life and follow your own star."*

—Wilfred Peterson, American author (1900–1995)

Choose

(1)   decide; elect; indicate; pick; point out; prefer; select; take; want; wish

Word Used in Sentence(s)

*(1) "Leaders are people who use influence to create change; they have followers because other people see value of their ideas or suggestions and **choose** to go along or align with them."*

—Schermerhorn, John, Richard Osborn, Mary UHL-Bien, and James Hunt. *Organizational Behavior*, 12th Edition, NY: John Wiley & Sons, Inc., 2012, pg. 4.

*(1) "Every act of will is an act of self-limitation. To desire action is to desire limitation. In that sense, every act is an act of self-sacrifice. When you **choose** anything, you reject everything else."*

—G. K. Chesterton, English-born Gabonese critic, essayist, novelist, and poet (1874–1936)

*(1) "Every human has four endowments—self awareness, conscience, independent will, and creative imagination. These give us the ultimate human freedom... The power to **choose**, to respond, to change."*

—Stephen R. Covey, American writer of business books (1932–2012)

Coalesce

(1)   combine; come together as one; grow together; join; unite

Word Used in Sentence(s)

*(1) People with different views and beliefs will sometimes **coalesce** around civic causes.*

*(1) "After a certain high level of technical skill is achieved, science and art tend to **coalesce** in esthetics, plasticity, and form. The greatest scientists are always artists as well."*

—Albert Einstein, American theoretical physicist (1879–1955)

*(1) Bob was able to **coalesce** more than 100 diverse stakeholders into an effective, efficient company asset.*

Collaborate

(1)   act as a team; join forces; team up; work in partnership; work with others
to achieve common goals

Word Used in Sentence(s)

*(1) A professional career counselor will **collaborate** with a client rather
than see him or her as a customer.*

*(1) "The way to create job benchmarks is by inviting the key stakehold-
ers and the team of subject matter experts to **collaborate** on defining the
position."*

—Hayashi, Shawn Kent. *Conversations for Creating Star Performers*,
NY: McGraw-Hill, 2012: pg. 19.

*(1) "EMCF's ability to **collaborate** with industry peers created substan-
tial benefits for society and set an example for others—notably the
Obama administration, which found the pilot and inspiration for its
Social Innovation Fund...."*

—Tierney, Thomas. "Collaborating for the Common Good," *Harvard
Business Review*, July–August 2011: pg. 38.

*(1) "A traditional project management approach would not work for the
proposed project. Success depended on bridging dramatically different
national, organizational, and occupational cultures to **collaborate** in
fluid groupings that emerged and dissolved in response to needs that
were identified as the work progressed."*

—Edmondson, Amy C. "Teamwork on the Fly," *Harvard Business
Review*, April 2012: pg. 74.

*(1) In today's global economy, many businesses must practice co-
opitition which is **collaboration** with not only intradepartmental groups
but also vendors, suppliers, stakeholders, NGOs, and, in some cases,
competitors.*

Communicate

(1)   be in touch; be in verbal contact; call; connect; converse; convey; correspond; e-mail; impart; interconnect; publish; reveal; share; speak; talk;
text; transmit information, thoughts, or feelings; join; wire; write

Word Used in Sentence(s)

*(1) "Great companies have three sets of stakeholders: customers, employees, and shareholders—in order of importance...the board should **communicate** that formula to the shareholders so they understand the greater good that the company represents."*

—Horst, Gary. "Business Advisor, CEOs Need a NEW Set of Beliefs," *HBR Blog,* September 21, 2012: pg. 22.

*(1) "Ninety percent of leadership is the ability to **communicate** something people want."*

—Dianne Feinstein, American senator (1933–)

*(1) "Start with good people, lay out the rules, **communicate** with your employees, motivate them, and reward them. If you do all those things effectively, you can't miss."*

—Lee Iacocca, American, business executive (1924–)

*(1) "Mayor Bill Akers of Seaside Heights, NJ now removed from the whirlwind of Hurricane Sandy's ferocity, and with the benefit of hindsight, the major says he has his regrets. He could, he says, have stopped by one of the shelters to speak to residents personally. He would have **communicated** information sooner."*

—Goldberg, Dan. "Responses to Sandy: From Great to Galling," Middlesex Edition, *Star Ledger,* November 11, 2012: pg. 1.

Collocates to: ability, able, effectively, information, language, ways

Comport

(1) act; agree; behave in a certain way that is proper

Word Used in Sentence(s)

*(1) It is harder for young people today to **comport** themselves with dignity and grace when they have so few role models to follow.*

Condone

(1) forgive; overlook; permit to happen

Word Used in Sentence(s)

*(1) Many people argue that too many public schools **condone** a policy of pushing students through the system.*

Conduct

(1) carry on; control; direct; guide; head; lead; manage; operate; steer; supervise

Word Used in Sentence(s)

*(1) The tests were **conducted** last week.*

*(1) Hank will manage the team **conducting** the prelaunch tests.*

Confabulate

(1) chat, converse, or talk informally

Word Used in Sentence(s)

*(1) "I shall not ask Jean Jacques Rousseau 'If birds **confabulate** or no.'"*

—William Cowper, English poet (1731–1800)

Conflate

(1) blend; coalesce; combine or mix two different elements; commingle; flux

Word Used in Sentence(s)

*(1) "The centerpiece of this pleasantly miscellaneous show is a large cast-aluminum relief and six smaller two-sided ones in cast bronze and silver, which put grids of the numbers zero through nine through elaborate variations in texture, legibility, and suggestion. Among the artist's first cast-metal objects in some years, they exemplify his trenchant recycling of motifs and clarify his tendency to **conflate** aspects of printing, painting, and sculpture (and collage)."*

—Editors. "The Listings," *New York Times*, Section C, Column 0, May 27, 2011: pg. 18.

Collocates to: confuse, process, public, religion, tends, tendency, two, words

Conform

(1) comply; follow actions of others; go along with

Word Used in Sentence(s)

*(1) "This is the very devilish thing about foreign affairs: They are foreign
and will not always **conform** to our whim."*

—James Reston, Scottish journalist (1909–1995)

*(1) "A man's faults all **conform** to his type of mind. Observe his faults
and you may know his virtues."*

—Chinese Proverb

Congregate

(1) assemble; come together; felicitate; gather

Word Used in Sentence(s)

*(1) The freedom to assemble is a constitutional right of people, with a
common cause, to publicly **congregate** to peacefully proclaim their
position.*

Connect

(1) associate; attach; combine; fasten; interrelate; join; link; relate; tie; unite

Word Used in Sentence(s)

*(1) "Self-discipline is an act of cultivation. It requires you to **connect**
today's actions to tomorrow's results. There's a season for sowing, a season for reaping. Self-discipline helps you know which is which."*

—Gary Ryan Blair, American motivational speaker and author

*(1) "We cannot live only for ourselves. A thousand fibers **connect** us with
our fellow men; and among those fibers, as sympathetic threads, our
actions run as causes, and they come back to us as effects."*

—Herman Melville, American short-story writer, novelist, and poet
(1819–1891)

*(1) "Creativity is just **connecting** things. When you ask creative people how they did something, they feel a little guilty because they didn't really do it, they just saw something. It seemed obvious to them after a while. That's because they were able to **connect** experiences they've had and synthesize new things."*

—Steve Jobs, American entrepreneur and co-founder, chairman, and CEO of Apple Inc. (1955–2011)

*(1) "Learn fast, fail fast, correct fast, and **connect** fast."*

—Linda Chandler, American businesswoman, executive, and entrepreneur

Consolidate

(1)   bring together; merge; strengthen; unite

Word Used in Sentence(s)

*(1) We **consolidated** the two shipments and saved hundreds of dollars.*

*(1) One approach the diocese has taken to cut costs is to **consolidate** the five parish schools into one.*

Consort

(1)   accompany; associate; group with; partner

Word Used in Sentence(s)

*(1) "I could tell he liked me, but I'd always been suspicious of fresh guys (what does he want from me? Oh, no, not that.) And I didn't have much respect for guys who would **consort** with people like me (Alvy says that). I think I was afraid I might snag a loser, and I wasn't ready for a winner. Sid suggested we get together after the wedding, but my brother said no, he had to hurry back to San Diego."*

—Yamauchi, Wakako. "Annie Hall," *Hyphen Magazine*, Issue 22, Winter 2010: pg. 56.

Convoke

(1) assemble; call together; convene; summon to a meeting

Word Used in Sentence(s)

(1) "Environmental activists involved in the Chimalapas area claimed the government was also considering decreeing the area a reserva de la biosfera. This idea was rejected by both chimas and environmental activists because they considered biosphere reserves to be areas preserved only on paper, declared 'protected' but without taking local human populations into account. In response, Miguel Angel Garcia and Luis Bustamante, an environmental activist and founding member of several NGOs and networks based in Mexico City, helped __convoke__ a meeting in the capital in October 1991, attended by environmental NGOs and a delegation of Zoques from the Chimalapas."

—Umlas, Elizabeth. "Environmental Networking in Mexico: The Comite Nacional para la Defensa de los Chimalapas," *Latin American Research Review*, Volume 33, Issue 3, 1998: pg. 161.

Coordinate

(1) bring together; combine; direct; harmonize; manage; match up; organize; synchronize; work together

Word Used in Sentence(s)

(1) I want to see marketing and sales __coordinate__ their efforts much better.

(1) "Of all the things I have done, the most vital is __coordinating__ the talents of those who work for us and pointing them towards a certain goal."

—Walt Disney, American film producer, director, screenwriter, voice actor, animator, entrepreneur, entertainer, and international icon (1901–1965)

(1) "My experience in government is that when things are noncontroversial and beautifully __coordinated__, there is not much going on."

—John F. Kennedy, 35th U.S. President (1917–1963)

*(1) "For Hayek, market institutions are epistemic devices—means whereby information that is scattered about society and known in its totality by no one can be used by all by being embodied in prices. It is from this conception of the role of markets that Hayek derives his most powerful argument for the impossibility of successful central planning. Even if the planners are wholly disinterested, they will be unable to collect centrally the information—often ephemeral and local, and sometimes embodied in traditional skills and entrepreneurial perceptions—that they would need to allocate resources and **coordinate** activities effectively. Hayek's insight here is truly profound. He grasps that the problem that central-planning institutions cannot solve is not (as his mentor, Ludwig von Mises, supposed) merely a problem of calculation but rather a problem of knowledge. Because the planner cannot know relative costs and scarcities, the planned economy will in fact be chaotic and vastly wasteful. This is the real explanation for the poverty of all socialist and command economies. Their poverty does not flow from the cultural traditions."*

—Grey, John. "The Road From Serfdom," *The National Review*, Volume 44, Issue 8, April 27, 1992: p32–37, 6p.

Collocates to: activates, agencies, aid, efforts, federal, help, international, response

Coruscate

(1) brilliant in style; flashy; showy; sparkle

Word Used in Sentence(s)

*(1) "A welling, rising, towering rage roared straight up out of the core of Cynthia Maidstone, filling her with a cold, crackling energy so intense she felt that she could point her fingers and chill lightening would **coruscate** from their tips."*

—Unknown

*(1) The knight's highly polished armor seemed to **coruscate** in the light of the burning castle.*

Cowboy up

(1) accept life as it happens; act like a man in all situations; take responsibility for one's actions

(2) accept punishment

Cultivate

(1) civilize; develop; domesticate; educate; encourage; foster; help; nurture; promote; refine; school; support; tame

(2) till; to tend to; work on

Word Used in Sentence(s)

*(1), (2) One must learn to **cultivate** personal contacts in order to build a successful personal network.*

*(1), (2) "So how does a business leader go about **cultivating** a winning culture?... Interviews with academics and entrepreneurs yield some universal themes."*

—Hann, Christopher. "The Masters," *Entrepreneur*, March 2012: pg. 56.

*(1), (2) "How do tactically strong leaders learn to develop a strategic mind set? By **cultivating** three skills: level shifting, pattern recognition, and mental stimulation."*

—Watson, Michael. "How Managers Become Leaders," *Harvard Business Review*, June 2012: pg. 68.

*(1) "Who provides the opportunity to **cultivate** patience? Not our friends. Our enemies give us the most crucial chances to grow."*

—Tenzin Gyatso, the 14th Dalai Lama (1935–)

*(1) "One is wise to **cultivate** the tree that bears fruit in our soul."*

—Henry David Thoreau, American essayist, poet, and philosopher (1817–1862)

Decompress

(1) lay back; regain equilibrium; relax; to be relieved of stress; unwind

Word Used in Sentence(s)

*(1) "Allow yourself time to **decompress** and process what has happened."*

—Unknown

Collocates to: necessary, need, place, time

Deescalate

(1) abate; downsize; dwindle; ease; knockdown; lessen; lower; reduce; to decrease in intensity, magnitude; to diminish in size, intensity, or extent

Word Used in Sentence(s)

*(1) A leader would move to **deescalate** the crisis rather than test fate.*

*(1) "The wives of domestic violence, for their part, are very, very feisty. Once an argument is started, they don't back down. They greet negative statements with negative responses—what psychologists call negative reciprocity. Like their husbands, they don't **deescalate** an argument if one gets started."*

—Editors. "Inside the Heart of Marital Violence," *Psychology Today*, Volume 26, Issue 6, November 1993: pg. 48, 10 p.

Collocates to: anger, crisis, criticism, help, potential, situation, tension, trying

Disseminate

(1) broadcast; circulate; distribute; propagate; publish; scatter; spread

Word Used in Sentence(s)

*(1) "Propaganda has a bad name, but its root meaning is simply to **disseminate** through a medium, and all writing therefore is propaganda for something. It's a seeding of the self in the consciousness of others."*

—Elizabeth Drew, American political journalist and author (1935–)

*(1) "The actions performed by great souls to spread, promote, and **disseminate** knowledge to every strata of society is a great service to mankind."*

—Sam Veda, American yoga wear designer (1945–)

Emanate

(1) arise; come fourth; derive; emit; give off; impart; issue; ooze; radiate; spring or originate from a source; start; stem

Word Used in Sentence(s)

*(1) The sounds **emanating** from the board meeting were not comforting.*

*(1) "Every effort for progress, for enlightenment, for science, for religious, political, and economic liberty, **emanates** from the minority and not from the mass."*

—Emma Goldman, Lithuanian-born American international anarchist (1869–1940)

*(1) "Speech **emanating** from a pure heart and mind of learned men and scholars are naturally pure just like water of a river."*

—Yajur Veda, one of the four canonical texts of Hinduism, the *Vedas*. By some, it is estimated to have been composed between 1000 and 600 BCE.

<u>Collocates to:</u> from, light, rays, seem, sound

Embark

(1) begin something; board; get on; get started; go ahead

(2) put or take passengers aboard a ship or airplane

(3) begin a journey

Word Used in Sentence(s)

*(1) "One company that has **embarked** on an ambitious program based upon the results of a skills-gap analysis is the division of the United Kingdom's Health Services that serves London."*

—Hancock, Bryan and Dianna Ellsworth. "Redesigning Knowledge Work," *Harvard Business Review*, January–February 2013: pg. 62.

Embellish

(1) adorn; aggrandize; elaborate

(2) adorn with gimcrack, gimmick, or gimmickry; decorate or improve by adding detail or ornamentation

(3) improve an account or report of an event by adding factious, imaginary, or audacious details to improve or heighten the acceptance of; touch up

Word Used in Sentence(s)

*(1) "Each of the arts whose office is to refine, purify, adorn, **embellish**, and grace life is under the patronage of a muse, no god being found worthy to preside over them."*

—Ralph Waldo Emerson, American poet, lecturer, and essayist (1803–1882)

Emblazon

(1) celebrate; display; extol; glorify; spread the fame of

(2) decorate or adorn

(3) decorate with bright colors; display brilliantly

Word Used in Sentence(s)

*(1) "In Virginia, an aviation company is working on an idea to **emblazon** company logos on head guards that are then placed on the upper edge of the doorway on regional airplanes. These bumper-like devices keep people from bumping their heads when they board."*

—Negroni, Christine. "Cashing in Before Taking Off," *New York Times*, February 27, 2012: pg. 8.

Embrace

(1) adopt; incorporate; involve; make use of something; support; take on; take up; welcome something

(2) cling to; enfold; hold; hug

Word Used in Sentence(s)

*(1) "Large companies, taking a page from start-up strategy, are **embracing** open innovation and less hierarchical management and are integrating entrepreneurial behaviors with their existing capabilities."*

—Anthony, Scott D. "The New Corporate Garage," *Harvard Business Review*, September 2012: pg. 46.

*(1) "For some firms, history can be instrumental in transforming cultures that are no longer useful. Cultural change, we know, can be extremely difficult for people to **embrace**."*

—Seaman, John T., and George D. Smith. "Your Company's History as a Leadership Tool," *Harvard Business Review*, December 2012: pg. 47.

Emote

(1)   exaggerated expression or show of emotions

(2)   act in an exaggerated or theatrical manner

Word Used in Sentence(s)

*(1)   "'Judge Kagen is not going to **emote** all over you,' says Viveca Novak, who was working for* Time *magazine when she met Kagan through a women's book club in Washington around 1995. 'She is a very grounded person.'"*

—Gerhart, Ann and Philip Rucker. "Her Work Is Her Life Is Her Work," *Washington Post*, June 10, 2010.

Enable

(1)   aid; allow; assist; empower; facilitate; make possible; permit; render capable or able for some task; qualify; support

Word Used in Sentence(s)

*(1)   "The 1648 settlement at Westphalia, though setbacks were many and vicious, **enabled** procedures fostering what eventually would be 'the international community,' a term that curled many a lip in the midst of the twentieth-century world wars."*

—Hill, Charles. "Notable & Quotable," *Wall Street Journal*, December 1, 2012: pg. A13.

*(1)   "Still, creating a system that **enables** employees to achieve great things—as a group—often comes down to the work of a single leader."*

—Hann, Christopher. "The Masters," *Entrepreneur*, March 2012: pg. 58.

*(1)   "Moral courage **enables** people to stand up for a principle rather than stand on the sidelines."*

—Kanter, Rosabeth. "Courage in the C-Suite," *Harvard Business Review*, December 2011: pg. 38.

*(1) "Employees are motivated by jobs that challenge and **enable** them to grow and learn, and they are demoralized by those that seem to be monotonous or lead to a dead end."*

—Nohria, Nitin, Boris Groysberg, and Linda-Eling Lee. "Employee Motivation a Powerful New Tool: Honing Your Competitive Edge," *Harvard Business Review*, July–August 2008, pg. 81.

Encourage

(1) advance; assist something to occur; boost; further; give hope, confidence, or courage; motivate to take a course of action

Word Used in Sentence(s)

*(1) "Our duty is to **encourage** everyone in his struggle to live up to his own highest idea, and strive at the same time to make the ideal as near as possible to the truth."*

—Swami Vivekananda, Indian spiritual leader of the Hindu religion (1863–1902)

*(1) "Leaders must **encourage** their organizations to dance to forms of music yet to be heard."*

—Warren G. Bennis, American scholar, organizational consultant, and author (1925–)

*(1) "Our analysis, to our knowledge, the first of its kind, found that firms that indiscriminately **encourage** all their customers to buy more by cross selling are making a costly mistake. A significant subset of cross-buyers are highly unprofitable."*

—Shah, Denish and V. Kumar. "The Dark Side of Cross-Selling," *Harvard Business Review*, December 2012: pg. 21.

*(1) "Big business can do more to support smaller enterprises in their supply and distribution chains. To **encourage** small- and medium-size businesses on the basis of their productivity rather than their experience or size would help establish the idea that everyone has a stake in the capitalist system."*

—de Rothschild, Lynn Forester and Adam Posen. "How Capitalism Can Repair its Bruised Image," *Wall Street Journal*, January 2, 2013: pg. A17.

Collocates to: designed, development, efforts, growth, investment, polices, students, teachers

Energize

(1) active; arouse; brace; excite; pump up; stimulate; to put forth energy; vigorous

Word Used in Sentence(s)

*(1) "The world of the 1990s and beyond will not belong to 'managers' or those who can make the numbers dance. The world will belong to passionate, driven leaders—people who not only have enormous amounts of energy but who can **energize** those whom they lead."*

—Jack Welch, American chemical engineer, business executive, and author

*(1) "We look at the dance to impart the sensation of living in an affirmation of life, to **energize** the spectator into keener awareness of the vigor, the mystery, the humor, the variety, and the wonder of life. This is the function of the American dance."*

—Martha Graham, American dancer, teacher, and choreographer (1894–1991)

Engage

(1) charter; engross; involve; occupy; participate; pledge; tie up; to bind by a promise

(2) employ; hire; mesh; to arrange for the services of

(3) reserve; to arrange for the use of

(4) involve; to draw into

(5) to attract and hold; to employ and keep busy; to occupy

(6) to mesh together

Word Used in Sentence(s)

*(1) "Those who are too smart to **engage** in politics are punished by being governed by those who are dumber."*

—Plato, Classical Greek philosopher and mathematician (427–327 BC)

*(1) "In motivating people, you've got to **engage** their minds and their hearts. I motivate people, I hope, by example—and perhaps by excitement, by having productive ideas to make others feel involved."*

—Rupert Murdoch, Australian-American media mogul (1931–)

*(1) "Not to **engage** in the pursuit of ideas is to live like ants instead of like men."*

—Mortimer Adler, American philosopher, educator, and editor (1902–2001)

*(1) "Hike to the top floor of Thayer Hall, and you will find Lieutenant Colonel Greg Dardis **engaging** small groups of firsties in discussions of classical leadership, dissecting such leading-edge thinkers as Morgan McCall and Peter Senge."*

—Hammons, Keith. "Grassroots Leadership: U.S. Military Academy," *Fast Company's Greatest Hits, Ten Years of the Most Innovative Ideas in Business*, NY: Penguin, 2006: pg. 173.

Collocates to: activities, behavior, conversation, dialogue, likely, students

Engender

(1) begat; bring about or into being; cause; create; give rise to; originate; produce

Word Used in Sentence(s)

*(1) Good will **engenders** good will.*

*(1) "Consultation helps **engender** the support decisions needed to be successfully implemented."*

—Donald Rumsfeld, American politician and businessman (1932–)

*(1) "For Mark Leslie, CEO of Veritas Software, it all came down to trust. 'I believe if you want to be trusted, you have to trust'…But the value of **engendering** trust is greater than the cost of being betrayed sometimes."*

—Christopher Hann. "The Masters," *Entrepreneur*, March 2012: pg. 56.

Enlist

(1) conscript; count on; engage; enroll; enter; join; join up; procure; recruit; register; sign up; solicit; volunteer

Word Used in Sentence(s)

*(1) "A person who doubts himself is like a man who would **enlist** in the ranks of his enemies and bear arms against himself. He makes his failure certain by himself being the first person to be convinced of it."*

—Ambrose Bierce, American writer, journalist, and editor (1842–1914)

*(1) Leaders **enlist** followers by appealing to a common vision, hopes, and dreams.*

<u>Collocates to:</u> aid, help, military, support, trying, volunteers

Entreat

(1)   ask; beg; beseech; implore; plead; pray; request earnestly or emotionally

Word Used in Sentence(s)

*(1) "I rather would **entreat** thy company, To see the wonders of the world abroad, Than, living dully sluggardized at home, Wear out thy youth with shapeless idleness."*

—William Shakespeare, English poet and playwright (1564–1615)

Espouse

(1)   adopt; advocate; back; champion; promote; support; take up

(2)   take as a wife

Word Used in Sentence(s)

*(1) The governor **espoused** a program of tax cuts.*

*(1) Be careful how many causes you **espouse** because you may have trouble remembering which side of an argument you are supposed to be on.*

Evoke

(1)   call forth or summon; to bring to mind a memory or feeling, especially from the past; to provoke a particular reaction or feeling

Word Used in Sentence(s)

*(1) "Every revolutionary idea seems to **evoke** three stages of reaction. They may be summed up by the phrases: 1. It's completely impossible. 2. It's possible, but it's not worth doing. 3. I said it was a good idea all along."*

—Arthur C. Clarke, English writer (1917–)

*(1) "Merchandisers, by embedding subliminal trigger devices in media, are able to **evoke** a strong emotional relationship between, say, a product perceived in an advertisement weeks before and the strongest of all emotional stimuli—love (sex) and death."*

—Unknown

Extend

(1) cover; encompass; make bigger; open or stretch out into additional space; outrange; spread; spread out

(2) continue something for a time longer than normal; go on; run on; stretch longer than expected

Word Used in Sentence(s)

*(1) "Christopher E. Kubasik, 51, Lockheed's president and chief operating officer, has been named to succeed Robert J. Stevens, 60, as chief executive. Kubasik is part of a new crop of contracting executives who have been groomed within their companies and are being tasked with overseeing a transition that has required layoffs, buyouts, and corporate restructuring. 'When I look at future challenges, I recognize they will certainly **extend** beyond my mandatory retirement age,' Stevens told reporters Thursday morning."*

—Censer, Marjorie. "Lockheed Latest Contractor to Announce New Leadership," *Washington Post*, A section, April 27, 2012: pg. A10.

Extricate

(1) extract; disconnect; disengage; disentangle; free; free from difficulty; get out; remove

Word Used in Sentence(s)

*(1) "Sometimes accidents happen in life from which we have need of a little madness to **extricate** ourselves successfully."*

—François de la Rochefoucauld, French classical author (1613–1680)

*(1) "You know from past experiences that whenever you have been driven to the wall, or thought you were, you have **extricated** yourself in a way which you never would have dreamed possible had you not been put to the test. The trouble is that in your everyday life, you don't go deep enough to tap the divine mind within you."*

—Orson Welles, American motion-picture actor, director, producer, and writer (1915–1985)

Facilitate

(1) aid; assist; ease; help

Word Used in Sentence(s)

*(1) The ability to **facilitate** and manage meetings requires important leadership skills.*

*(1) "The essential job of government is to **facilitate**, not frustrate, job development."*

—Andrew Cuomo, American, 56th and current governor of New York (1957–)

*(1) "Every human being must find his own way to cope with severe loss, and the only job of a true friend is to **facilitate** whatever method he chooses."*

—Caleb Carr, American novelist and military historian (1955–)

*(1) "Boardroom discussions often center on just two questions: How can we sustain innovation? And do we have a plan for developing future leaders who can **facilitate** this goal?"*

—Cohn, Jeffery, Jon Katzenbach, and Gus Vlak. "Finding and Grooming Breakthrough Innovators," *Harvard Business Review*, December 2008: pg. 64.

(1) "To be a leader, one has to make a difference and __facilitate__ positive change."

—DuBrin, Andrew. *Leadership Research Findings, Practice, and Skills*, Boston: Houghton Mifflin Company, 1998: pg.2.

Collocates to: communications, design, development, learning, order, process

Fashion

(1) accommodate; adapt; direct; to give shape or form to; train or influence the state or character

Word Used in Sentence(s)

(1) "At company headquarters, Clint Smith co-founder and CEO of Emma e-mail Marketing, __fashioned__ an open floor plan expressly to inspire a spirit of collaboration among the more than 100 employees."

—Hann, Christopher. "The Masters," *Entrepreneur*, March 2012: pg. 56.

Fast track

(1) bypass others; move in a rapid pace; speed up

Finagle

(1) get, arrange, or maneuver by cleverness or persuasion; manage by guile

Word Used in Sentence(s)

(1) "In the 1960s and early 1970s, many in the counterculture absolutely loathed computers and everything about them. They were seen as part of the Defense Department's War Machine, and also associated with deper- sonalization of a mass society. But boomer math nerds, who figured out how to __finagle__ computer time, didn't care. There was also a geographic exception to those political objections. In Northern California—home of the chip industry and lots of defense work—the idea arose that comput- ers could empower people."

—Levy, Steven. "Power to the People: Computers Once Filled Entire Rooms. Now They Fit in Our Pockets. How a Generation Formed Our Tech Landscape," *Newsweek*, Volume 150, Issue 13, September 2007: pg. 46.

Flaunt

(1) boast; brandish; display ostentatiously; exhibit; flourish; parade; show off; vaunt

Word Used in Sentence(s)

*(1) "They **flaunt** their conjugal felicity in one's face, as if it were the most fascinating of sins."*

—Oscar Wilde, Irish poet, novelist, dramatist, and critic (1854–1900)

*(1) "Wealth is an inborn attitude of mind, like poverty. The pauper who has made his pile may **flaunt** his spoils, but cannot wear them plausibly."*

—Jean Cocteau, French poet, novelist, and actor (1889–1963)

Fleer

(1) deride; jeer; laugh imprudently; mock; ridicule; scorn derisively; sneer

Flirt punch

(1) to touch someone of the opposite sex in a mocking or semi-firm gesture

Focus

(1) center of attention; concentration; direct one's attention to something; effort; focal point; hub; spotlight

Word Used in Sentence(s)

*(1) "In product development, a popular tool is the quick-and-dirty proto-type. Because simple prototypes make the abstract concrete, they can guide innovators' conversations and **focus** their attention, helping them to move forward."*

—Leonardi, Paul. "Early Prototypes Can Hurt a Team's Creativity," Innovations, *Harvard Business Review*, December 2011: pg. 28.

*(1) "Examples of business leaders who rise to the heights of corporate power only to be brought down by their egos include Dennis Kozlowski, former CEO of TYCO, and Carly Fiorina, former head of Hewlett-Packard. As leaders of corporate empires, they **focused** on what flattered instead of what mattered."*

—Forbes, Steve and John Prevas. *Power, Ambition, Glory*, NY: Crown Business Press, 2009: pg.7.

*(1) "Companies that want to make better use of the data they gather should **focus** on two things: training workers to increase their data literacy and efficiently incorporate information into decision making, and giving those workers the right tools."*

—Shah, Shvetank, Andrew Horne, and Jamie Capella. "Good Data Won't Guarantee Good Decisions," *Harvard Business Review*, April 2012: pg. 24.

*(1) "Concentrate all your thoughts upon the work at hand. The sun's rays do not burn until brought to a **focus**."*

—Alexander Graham Bell, American inventor and educator (1847–1922)

Collocates to: attention, groups, issues, main, on, primary

Follow

(1) abide by; adhere; comply; conform; continue in the direction of another; do as someone else has done; emulate; keep in mind; model; obey; observe; pattern; pursue

(2) sign up as one who receives tweet digital messages

Word Used in Sentence(s)

*(1) "You cannot be a leader, and ask other people to **follow** you, unless you know how to follow, too."*

—Sam Rayburn, American politician and lawyer (1882–1961)

Forbear

(1) abstain; hold back from something; refrain; tolerate

Word Used in Sentence(s)

(1) "Follow then the shining ones, the wise, the awakened, the loving, for they know how to work and __forbear__."

—The Buddha, a spiritual teacher from the Indian subcontinent on whose teachings Buddhism was founded

(1) "The wise man... if he would live at peace with others, he will bear and __forbear__."

—Samuel Smiles, Scottish author (1812–1904)

Forego

(1) do without; forebear; to do or go before something in time or position

Word Used in Sentence(s)

(1) "To __forego__ even ambition when the end is gained—who can say this is not greatness?"

—William Makepeace Thackeray, English author and novelist (1811–1863)

(1) "Next to knowing when to seize an opportunity, the most important thing in life is to know when to __forego__ an advantage."

—Benjamin Disraeli, British prime minister and novelist (1804–1881)

(1) "The people who are regarded as moral luminaries are those who __forego__ ordinary pleasures themselves and find compensation in interfering with the pleasures of others."

—Bertrand Russell, English logician and philosopher (1872–1970)

Forsake

(1) abandon; cast off; desert; disown; ditch; leave; quit; reject; relinquish; renounce

Word Used in Sentence(s)

(1) "__Forsake__ not God till you find a better master."

—Scottish Proverb

*(1) "There is not a more repulsive spectacle than on old man who will not **forsake** the world, which has already forsaken him."*

—T.S. Eliot, American-born English editor, playwright, poet, and critic (1888–1965)

Forswear

(1) abandon; abjure; deny; disavow; disclaim; disown; gainsay; reject; renounce; to give up

Word Used in Sentence(s)

*(1) "Did my heart love till now? **Forswear** it, sight, for I never saw true beauty till this night."*

—William Shakespeare, English poet and playwright (1564–1516)

Gallivant

(1) be without an itinerary or agenda; constantly travel to different places; go where the mood takes; play the beau; roam about for pleasure without any definite plan; wait upon the ladies; wander widely

Word Used in Sentence(s)

*(1) "The marketing exec has been cooped up in the house for the last eight months, taking care of her infant son, Jake. But diapers and baby bottles are about to become history, for 10 days anyway, while Candler and a girlfriend **gallivant** around in Norway, as guests of CBS."*

—Hillolympics, Alma. "Lillehammer: Your Guide to the Games," *Atlanta Journal Constitution*, Section H, May 13, 1994.

Gel

(1) come to a useful or firm form; to work out

Word Used in Sentence(s)

*(1) If this international merger doesn't **gel**, the local folks will be left out in the cold.*

Habituate

(1) accustom; adjust; familiarize; get someone accustomed to something; orient; orientate; take to

Word Used in Sentence(s)

*(1) The veteran team members worked hard **habituating** the rookies to a new environment.*

*(1) In most cases, new workers are left alone to **habituate** the best they can to the corporate culture.*

Influence

(1) authority; clout; drag; effect; induce; leverage; manipulate; prestige; pull; sway; talk into; weight; win over

(2) affect; change; have a bearing on; have an effect on; inspire; shape

Word Used in Sentence(s)

*(1) The HR consultant's report will be **influencing** a large number of people.*

*(1) The CEO was **influenced** in a positive way by her work ethic.*

*(1) The most important person you have to **influence** is your direct supervisor.*

*(1) Leaders and managers are much more effective and productive when they apply **influence** rather than force to accomplish tasks and objectives.*

Institute

(1) be first; found; get established; inaugurate; introduce; organize; originate; set some origination or activity in motion; set up; start

Word Used in Sentence(s)

*(1) "There is nothing more difficult to carry out, nor more doubtful of success, nor more dangerous to handle, than to **institute** a new order of things."*

—Niccolo Machiavelli, Italian writer and statesman (1469–1527)

*(1) "Whenever any form of government becomes destructive of these ends (life, liberty, and the pursuit of happiness), it is the right of the people to alter or abolish it, and to **institute** new government..."*

—Thomas Jefferson, 3rd U.S. President (1762–1826)

Integrate

(1) amalgamate; assimilate; combine two; concatenate; fit in; incorporate; join in; make part of; mix; open up; participate; put together; take part; unify

Word Used in Sentence(s)

*(1) "What we should be doing in the EU as a whole is more economic **integration** in the single market, rather than less."*

—Nick Clegg, British liberal democratic political leader (1961–)

(1) "Who owns the NY Post*? 20th Century Fox. Talk about vertical **integration**."*

—Joe Pantoliano, American film and TV actor (1951–)

*(1) "The idea is that we do not have to choose between growth now and cutting deficits later. We can simply put in place an **integrated** policy that does both."*

—Greenhouse, Steve. "Our Economic Pickle," *New York Times*, January 13, 2013: pg. 5.

Interject

(1) butt in; cut in; exclaim; interpose; interrupt; introduce; put or set into between another or other things; speak; throw in

Word Used in Sentence(s)

*(1) "As a privileged survivor of the First World War, I hope I may be allowed to **interject** here a deeply felt tribute to those who were not fortunate enough to succeed, but who shared the signal honor of trying to be the last to salvage peace."*

—Rene Cassin, French jurist, law professor, and judge (1887–1976)

Intermesh

(1)   come or bring together; engage

Word Used in Sentence(s)

*(1) "Educators need to consider global learning in terms of the conditions necessary for it to emerge, the requisite attributes and processes that **intermesh** with the content during global-learning activities, and finally the characteristics and responsibilities of the world citizen in relation to the attributes and processes developed through global learning."*

—Editors. "Developing Global Awareness and Responsible World Citizenship with Global Learning," *Roeper Review*, Volume 30, Issue 1, Jan–Mar 2008: pg. 11–23, 13p.

Intersperse

(1)   combine; comingle; disburse; distribute; intermingle; interpose; pepper; scatter here and there; spread; sprinkle

Word Used in Sentence(s)

*(1) "A collection of anecdotes and maxims is the greatest of treasures for the man of the world, for he knows how to **intersperse** conversation with the former in fit places, and to recollect the latter on proper occasions."*

—Johann Wolfgang von Goethe, German playwright, poet, novelist, and dramatist (1749–1832)

Intervene

(1)   come between points of time, issues, people's ideas, or events; get involved, so as to alter or change an action through force, influence, or power; interfere; interpose; to occur between two things

Word Used in Sentence(s)

*(1) "One man has built his career around trying to help people track their conversational interactions, understand the hidden dynamics in them, and learn how to **intervene** effectively."*

—Kliener, Art. "Building the Skills of Insight," *Strategy + Business*, http://www.strategy-business.com/article/00154?gko=d4421&cid =TL20130117&utm_campaign=TL20130117, accessed January 17, 2013.

Jockey

(1) contend; jostle; maneuver in order to gain an advantage; manipulate; position oneself for better position; skillfully change positions

Word Used in Sentence(s)

*(1) "Steve Jobs took his top 100 people on an annual retreat for the purpose of strategic planning. The main activity was the list of ten things Apple should do. There was a lot of **jockeying** to get one's favorite item on that list."*

—Isaacson, Walter. "The Real Leadership Lessons of Steve Jobs," *Harvard Business Review*, April 2012, pg. 95.

Join forces

(1) combine resources or efforts with another

Word Used in Sentence(s)

*(1) In the value chain model, producers, vendors, suppliers, key customers, NGOs, key stakeholders, and even some competitors with similar interests **join forces** in a coopitive venture.*

Jump Onboard

(1) bustle; decide to join; energetically move on something; full of activity; hustle; join in enthusiastically; obey or decide quickly; rise suddenly or quickly

Word Used in Sentence(s)

*(1) "Aspiring entrepreneurs are increasingly **jumping on board** with sites like Kickstarter, IndieGoGo, Peerbackers, and ChipIn."*

—Moran, Gwen. "Mob Money," *Entrepreneur*, March 2012: pg. 84.

*(1) Job seekers should give serious consideration to the move before **jumping onboard** startups if they have never been in that kind of business environment.*

Jump through Hoops

(1) accommodate without question; exert oneself in a frantic way; obey; serve

Word Used in Sentence(s)

*(1) Alice **jumped through hoops** to please her manager.*

*(1) I had to **jump through hoops** to get you this opportunity.*

Keep on Keeping on

(1) doing one's best; keep trying; maintain; persist

Word Used in Sentence(s)

*(1) In these trying economic times, sometimes all we can do is keep driving, keep moving forward, **keep on keeping on**.*

Leverage

(1) control; force; influence; power; pull; weight

Word Used in Sentence(s)

*(1) "We must develop knowledge optimization initiatives to **leverage** our key learnings."*

—Scott Adams, American cartoonist (1957–)

Manipulate

(1) alter or present data as to mislead; control or influence cleverly or unscrupulously; exploit; handle or control with dexterity; manage or control artfully; maneuver; play

Word Used in Sentence(s)

> *(1) "Blessed is he who has learned to admire but not envy, to follow but not imitate, to praise but not flatter, and to lead but not **manipulate**."*

—William Arthur Ward, American dedicated scholar, author, editor, pastor, and teacher (1921–1994)

Marvel

(1) be amazed or astonished; be bowled over; be in awe; be filled with wonder; to see an awesome sight or an amazing thing; to experience a phenomenon; to wonder

Word Used in Sentence(s)

> *(1) "The **marvel** of all history is the patience with which men and women submit to burdens unnecessarily laid upon them by their governments."*

—Unknown

Mentor

(1) give assistance in career or business matters; provide advice or guidance

Collocates to: assigned, became, coach, facility, former, friend, long time, mentee, relationship, role, served, spiritual, student, teacher

Mobilize

(1) activate; assemble; call up; drum up support for; gather people and resources for something; generate support for something; marshal; muster; organize; rally

Word Used in Sentence(s)

> *(1) I plan to **mobilize** the entire staff for the fund drive.*

> *(1) "Big companies face the challenge of how to **mobilize** vast forces such as employees and new market strategies."*

—Bussey, John. "What Price Salvation," *Wall Street Journal*, November 30, 2012: pg. B1.

(1) "It is a new world of management where managers aren't the only leaders and where part of every manager's success is based on how well he or she __mobilizes__ leadership contributions from others."

—Schermerhorn, John, Richard Osborn, Mary UHL-Bien, and James Hunt. *Organizational Behavior*, 12th Ed., NY: John Wiley & Sons, Inc., 2012: pg. 4.

Mollify

(1)   appease; calm; pacify; placate; soften; soothe

Word Used in Sentence(s)

(1) "Sentimentalists… adopt whatever merit is in good repute, and almost make it hateful with their praise. The warmer their expressions, the colder we feel…. Cure the drunkard, heal the insane, __mollify__ the homicide, civilize the Pawnee, but what lessons can be devised for the debauchee of sentiment?"

—Ralph Waldo Emerson, American essayist, lecturer, and poet (1803–1882)

Mollycoddle

(1)   baby; cater to; cosset; fuss over; humor; indulge; mamma's boy; overprotect; paper; spoil

Word Used in Sentence(s)

(1) It doesn't necessarily help nor harm a person to __mollycoddle__ them; it is the over doing that is the problem.

Necessitate

(1)   call for; compel; demand; dictate; impose; make necessary; need; to obligate

Word Used in Sentence(s)

(1) "Success always __necessitates__ a degree of ruthlessness. Given the choice of friendship or success, I'd probably choose success."

—Sting (Gordon Matthew Thomas Sumner), English musician, actor, and songwriter (1951–)

Network

(1) building personal relationships for mutual benefit; connecting with people with similar interests; exchange cards; interpersonal contacts; make friends; meeting people; reciprocal connections; schmooze

Word Used in Sentence(s)

*(1) "Research shows that today's most sought-after early-career professionals are constantly **networking** and thinking about their next career step."*

—Hamari, Monika. "Why Top Young Managers Are in a Nonstop Job Hunt," *Harvard Business Review*, July–August 2012: pg. 28.

*(1) **Networking** through either one's strong or weak network remains the most effective tool for the job search.*

*(1) "**Networking** is an important strategy for career management, including becoming an influential person. The ability to establish a network and call on support when needed helps a manager or professional exert influence."*

—DuBrin, Andrew. *Leadership, Research Findings, Practice, and Skills*, Boston: Houghton Mifflin Company, 1998: pg. 201.

*(1) "For three decades, most of Doerr's best investments were just around the corner from Sand Hill Road, where he could be in close contact with management and leverage his deep **network** of tech which, Doerr always has acknowledged, is his greatest strength as a Venture Capitalist."*

—Editors. "Cleanup Crew," *Fortune*, Volume 156, Issue 11, November 2007: pg. 82.

Orchestrate

(1) combine and adapt in order to obtain a particular outcome

(2) to arrange or organize surreptitiously so as to achieve a desired effect

Word Used in Sentence(s)

*(1), (2) "U.S. intelligence officials say Zadran helped the Haqqanis **orchestrate** attacks on troops in Kabul and southeastern Afghanistan."*

—Gannon, Kathy, Adam Goldman, and Lolita C. Baldor. "Top U.S. Delegation to Enlist Pakistan's Help," *International News*, November 11, 2011.

*(1) Our goal is to **orchestrate** a partnership with a Chinese manufacturing firm.*

*(1) "Digital convergence has created new opportunities for hitherto separate markets and feed the growing desire among customers for integrated solutions and services. This calls for the development of integrated—or at least commonly **orchestrated**—strategies and actions across business units."*

—Doz, Yves and Mikko Kosonen. "The New Deal at the Top," *Harvard Business Review*, June 2007: pg. 100.

Collocates to: ability, arrange, attacks, campaign, help, trying

Organize

(1) arrange systematically; categorize; make arrangements, plans, or preparations for; order; put in order; sort out; systematize

(2) control; coordinate; fix; manage; take charge

Word Used in Sentence(s)

*(1) "Do you know what amazes me more than anything else? The impotence of force to **organize** anything."*

—Napoleon Bonaparte, French general, politician, and emperor (1769–1821)

*(1) "It is essential that there should be organization of labor. This is an era of organization. Capital organizes and therefore labor must **organize**."*

—Theodore Roosevelt, 26th U.S. President (1858–1919)

*(1) "**Organizing** is one of the four main functions of management—creating work structures and systems, and arranging resources to accomplish goals and objectives."*

—Schermerhorn, John, Richard Osborn, Mary UHL-Bien, and James Hunt. *Organizational Behavior*, 12th Ed., NY: John Wiley & Sons, Inc., 2012, pg. 4.

Partner

(1) ally; common cause; confederate; join; team; work or perform together

Word Used in Sentence(s)

*(1) "Courage makes change possible...Verizon's leaders saw growth limits in traditional telecom, so they invested billions in fiber optics to speed up landlines and **partnered** with Google to deploy Android smartphones, requiring substantial changes in the firm's practices."*

—Kanter, Rosabeth. "Courage in the C-Suite," *Harvard Business Review*, December 2011: pg. 38.

<u>**Collocates to:**</u> <u>business, firm, former, law, longtime, managing, partner, senior, sexual, trading</u>

Query

(1)   ask; ask a query; doubt; interrogate; inquire; question; quiz

Word Used in Sentence(s)

*(1) "To the **query**, 'What is a friend?' his reply was 'A single soul dwelling in two bodies.'"*

—Aristotle, Greek philosopher and polymath (381 BC–321 BC)

Ratchet up

(1)   gradually increase effort or intensity; pressure; turn up the heat

Word Used in Sentence(s)

*(1) There is little doubt that professional athletes **ratchet up** the level of their efforts during the playoffs.*

Reconcile

(1)   make or show to be compatible; restore friendly relations

(2)   make friendly again; win over

(3)   acquiescent to

Word Used in Sentence(s)

*(1) "Habit will **reconcile** us to everything but change."*

—Charles Caleb Colton, English sportsman and writer (1780–1832)

*(1) "To **reconcile** the official U.S. and Canadian bilateral current-
account statistics, the official statistics are first restated to a common
basis—that is, they are adjusted for definitional and methodological
differences—and then statistical adjustments are applied to reach the
reconciled values."*

—Berman, Barbara, Edward Dozier, and Denis Caron. "Reconciliation
of the United States-Canadian Current Account, 2010 and 2011," *The
Free Library*, January 1, 2013.

Rein in

(1) get control of; increase authority over

Word Used in Sentence(s)

*(1) "...This 'new economy' era saw a tremendous misallocation of
resources as firms built paper empires, not sustainable value. Now corporate America has become far too cautious when it comes to growth. A
misguided shift in compensation design is causing this. In the name of
reining in corporate risk-taking, boards have disconnected CEO pay
from the enhancement of equity value across all industries...."*

—Ubben, Jeff. "How to Revive Animal Sprits in CEOs," *Wall Street
Journal*, November 30, 2012: pg. A15.

Relate

(1) apply to someone or something; associate; attach; be relevant to; concern; connect; convey; correlate; get on; give an account to; have a bearing on; have a relationship to; involve; join; link; logical or casual
connection; share

Word Used in Sentence(s)

*(1) "Indra Nooya, Chairman and CEO of Pepsico, has been called a
deeply caring person who can **relate** to people from the boardroom to the
front line."*

—Editors. "Role Models," *Entrepreneur*, March 2012: pg. 63.

Revivify

(1) put new attitude, life, or vigor into a cause; revive

Scrutinize

(1) analyze; dissect; examine very carefully; inspect; pore over; search; study

Word Used in Sentence(s)

*(1) "The blow had struck home, and Danglars was entirely vanquished; with a trembling hand he took the two letters from the count, who held them carelessly between finger and thumb, and proceeded to **scrutinize** the signatures, with a minuteness that the count might have regarded as insulting, had it not suited his present purpose to mislead the banker."*

—Alexandre Dumas, French writer (1802–1870), excerpt from *The Count of Monte Cristo*

Select

(1) choose; pick; vote

(2) choose one in preference over another; pick out one based on some quality of excellence

(3) limit to certain groups based on some standard

Word Used in Sentence(s)

*(1) "In every survey we conducted, honesty was **selected** more often than any other leadership characteristic; it consistently emerged as the single most important ingredient in the leader-constituent relationship."*

—Kouzes, James and Barry Posner. *The Leadership Challenge*, 4th edition, San Francisco, CA: Jossey-Bass, 1999: pg. 17.

Strengthen

(1) bolster; buttress; make stronger

(2) increase the strength of

Word Used in Sentence(s)

*(1) "The research shows that in almost every case, a bigger opportunity lies in improving your performance in the industry you're in, by fixing your strategy and **strengthening** the capabilities that create value for*

customers and separate you from your competitors. This conclusion was reached after analyzing shareholder returns for 6,138 companies in 65 industries worldwide from 2001 to 2011."

—Hirsh, Evan and Kasturi Rangan. "The Grass Isn't Greener," *Harvard Business Review,* January–February 2013: pg. 23.

Stroke

(1) brush or touch lightly; brush repeatedly with brushing motions; treat gingerly or carefully

Word Used in Sentence(s)

*(1) He is the type of person that you need to **stroke** in order to get anything done.*

Support

(1) aid; encourage, help, or comfort

(2) carry or bear the weight for; to keep from falling, slipping, or dropping

(3) give approval; uphold

Word Used in Sentence(s)

*(1) A manager's job is to directly **support** the work efforts of others by providing them with the resources, training, and backing they need.*

Supply the lack

(1) provide or supply what is missing or needed

Sustain

(1) bare; brook; carry on; continue; encounter; endure; hold, maintain, or keep in position; keep up; prolong; prop up; put up with; stand; suffer; tolerate; uphold; weather

Word Used in Sentence(s)

> *(1) "Boardroom discussions often center on just two questions: How can we **sustain** innovation? And do we have a plan for developing future leaders who can facilitate this goal?"*

—Cohn, Jeffery, Jon Katzenbach, and Gus Vlak. "Finding and Grooming Breakthrough Innovators," *Harvard Business Review*, December 2008: pg. 64.

Synchronize

(1) in unison; make agree in time; to cause to take place at the same time

Word Used in Sentence(s)

> *(1) "ConnecTV Ad Sync allows brands to **synchronize** a companion experience with their TV spots, delivering the ability for viewers to instantly buy what they see, get promotional offers, enter contests, find the nearest store, receive marketing alerts, watch related product videos, schedule viewing reminders, and more."*

—Gyulai, Mike. "ConnecTV Launches National and Local Ad Network That Synchronizes with Television Ads," Press release, Beck Media & Marketing, January 4, 2013, http://pdf.reuters.com/htmlnews/8knews.asp?i=43059c3bf0e37541&u=urn:newsml:reuters. Accessed April 20, 2013.

Tout

(1) to boast in an extravagant manner; to praise or recommend highly

Word Used in Sentence(s)

> *(1) Advertisements for children's action toys will often **tout** features that can't be replicated by the child in his home.*

Unify

(1) blend; bring together; federate; merge; solidify; tie; unite

Word Used in Sentence(s)

*(1) The unforeseen problems and difficulties **unified** the project management team like nothing else could.*

*(1) **Unifying** a demoralized and self-interested staff is a very difficult management task.*

Uplift

(1) elevate; hold up; lift; raise up

(2) raise to higher moral, social, or cultural level

Word Used in Sentence(s)

*(1) "The key is to keep company only with people who **uplift** you, whose presence calls forth your best."*

—Epictetus, Greek sage and stoic philosopher (55 AD–135 AD)

*(1) "And it might have been for this reason only, that, when I again **uplifted** my eyes to the house itself, from its image in the pool, there grew in my mind a strange fancy—a fancy so ridiculous, indeed, that I but mention it to show the vivid force of the sensations which oppressed me."*

—Edgar Allen Poe, American author, poet, editor, and literary critic (1809–1849), excerpt from *The Fall of the House of Usher*

Verify

(1) check; prove; validate

(2) confirm or substantiate; prove to be true by demonstration, evidence, or testimony

(3) check or confirm the accuracy of

Word Used in Sentence(s)

*(1) "'I merely want, Mr. Jaggers,' said I, 'to assure myself that what I have been told, is true. I have no hope of its being untrue, but at least I may **verify** it.'"*

—Charles Dickens, English writer and social critic (1812–1870), excerpt from *Great Expectations*

Vie

(1)   compete for something; contend; contest, fight; oppose; rival; strive; struggle

Word Used in Sentence(s)

*(1) "Hannibal was a leader caught in a conflict between two ancient superpowers for control of the western Mediterranean. Carthage and Roam were **vying** for power when Hannibal seized the initiative and turned the ancient world upside down."*

—Forbes, Steve and John Prevas. *Power, Ambition, Glory*, NY: Crown Business Press, 2009: pg. 7.

*(1) "Facebook and Google are **vying** to become the primary gateway to the Internet. Google has long served as a destination to find websites and information; Facebook, to share gossip and photos with friends. But those distinctions are increasingly blurring, and billions in advertising dollars are at stake."*

—Rusli, Evelyn and Amir Efrati. "Facebook on Collision Course with Google," *Wall Street Journal*, January 16, 2013: pg. A1.

Vitalize

(1)   materials or assets; provide resources
(2)   give vigor and animation to; make vital; provide life to

Word Used in Sentence(s)

*(1) "'I'll tell you where you are wrong, or, rather, what weakens your judgments,' he said. 'You lack biology. It has no place in your scheme of things. Oh, I mean the real interpretative biology, from the ground up, from the laboratory and the test-tube and the **vitalized** inorganic, right on up to the widest aesthetic and sociological generalizations.'"*

—Jack London, American author, journalist, and social activist (1876–1916), excerpt from *Martin Eden*

Voyage

(1) go somewhere; take a trip or journey; travel

Word Used in Sentence(s)

(1) "The NASA Mars rover spacecraft __voyaged__ 352 million miles to reach Mars this past August, but the next step will be measured in fractions of an inch. The rovers' drill can chip about 2 inches into the interior of Mars to extract a small spoonful of powdery rock for analysis in an onboard chemistry kit."

—Hotz, Robert Lee. "Mars Rover Ready to Dig in," *Wall Street Journal*, January 16, 2013: pg. B4.

Wane

(1) become less intense, bright, or strong; to decline in power; dim in importance and posterity; to grow gradually less in extent

(2) to approach the end

Word Used in Sentence(s)

(1) "The fire of the regiment had begun to __wane__ and drip. The robust voice that had come strangely from the thin ranks was growing rapidly weak."

—Stephen Crane, American novelist, short-story writer, poet, and journalist (1871–1900), excerpt from *The Red Badge of Courage*

(1) "So the one went off with one group of scholars, and the other with another. In a little while, the two met at the bottom of the lane, and when they reached the school, they had it all to themselves. Then they sat together, with a slate before them, and Tom gave Becky the pencil and held her hand in his, guiding it, and so created another surprising house. When the interest in art began to __wane__, the two fell to talking."

—Mark Twain, American author and humorist (1832–1910), excerpt from *Tom Sawyer*

Wheedle

(1) cajole; coax; persuade or obtain by coaxing

Word Used in Sentence(s)

(1) "Harpring almost wound up at Duke or Northwestern on a football scholarship because his efforts to __wheedle__ a basketball grant-in-aid out of Tech coach Bobby Cremins were going nowhere."

—Wolff, Alexander. "Thrills and Spills," *Sports Illustrated*, Volume 84, Issue 12, 1996: pg. 36.

(1) "For Cocky had a way with him, and ways and ways. He, who was sheer bladed steel in the imperious flashing of his will, could swash-buckle and bully like any over-seas roisterer, or __wheedle__ as wickedly winningly as the first woman out of Eden or the last woman of that descent. When Cocky, balanced on one leg, the other leg in the air as the foot of it held the scruff of Michael's neck, leaned to Michael's ear and __wheedled__, Michael could only lay down silkily the bristly hair-waves of his neck, and with silly half-idiotic eyes of bliss agree to whatever was Cocky's will or whimsy so delivered."

—Jack London, American author, journalist, and social activist (1876–1916), excerpt from *Michael, Brother of Jerry*

Whittle

(1) carve; cut; fashion; sculpt; shape

Word Used in Sentence(s)

(1) "The 94-word intelligence summary emerged from a daylong email debate between more than two dozen intelligence officials, in which they contested and __whittled__ the available evidence into a bland summary with no reference to al Qaeda...."

—Gorman, Siobhan and Adam Entous. "Bureaucratic Battle Blunted Libya Attack," *Wall Street Journal*, December 4, 2012: pg. A1.

Winnow

(1) separate the desirable from the worthless

Word Used in Sentence(s)

*(1) "Skeptical scrutiny is the means, in both science and religion, by which deep thoughts can be **winnowed** from deep nonsense."*

—Carl Sagan, American astronomer, astrophysicist, cosmologist, and author (1934–1996)

Woolgather

(1) appearing to be lost in one's thoughts; daydreaming

Word Used in Sentence(s)

*(1) "'You won't be hurt I tell you, Jack—do you hear me?' roared Hugh, impressing the assurance upon him by means of a heavy blow on the back. 'He's so dead scared, he's **woolgathering**, I think. Give him a drop of something to drink here. Hand over, one of you.'"*

—Charles Dickens, English writer and social critic (1812–1870), excerpt from *Barnaby Rudge—A Tale of the Riots of Eighty*

Yield

(1) give way to another

(2) to produce or bear

(3) give up to another; to submit, surrender

(4) to give way to physical force

(5) to give up willingly a right, possession, or privilege

Word Used in Sentence(s)

*(1) "Assuming the blubber to be the skin of the whale; then, when this skin, as in the case of a very large sperm whale, will **yield** the bulk of one hundred barrels of oil; and, when it is considered that, in quantity, or rather weight, that oil, in its expressed state, is only three fourths, and not the entire substance of the coat; some idea may hence be had of the enormousness of that animated mass, a mere part of whose mere integument **yields** such a lake of liquid as that."*

—Herman Melville, American novelist, short-story writer, essayist, and poet (1919–1891), excerpt from *Moby Dick*

*(1) "You appear to me, Mr. Darcy, to allow nothing for the influence of friendship and affection. A regard for the requester would often make one readily **yield** to a request, without waiting for arguments to reason one into it. I am not particularly speaking of such a case as you have supposed about Mr. Bingley. We may as well wait, perhaps, till the circumstance occurs before we discuss the discretion of his behavior thereupon. But in general and ordinary cases between friend and friend, where one of them is desired by the other to change a resolution of no very great moment, should you think ill of that person for complying with the desire, without waiting to be argued into it?"*

—Jane Austen, English novelist (1775–1817), excerpt from *Pride and Prejudice*

*(1) "A troublesome crow seated herself on the back of a Sheep. The Sheep, much against his will, carried her backward and forward for a long time, and at last said, 'If you had treated a dog in this way, you would have had your desserts from his sharp teeth.' To this the crow replied, 'I despise the weak and **yield** to the strong. I know whom I may bully and whom I must flatter; and I thus prolong my life to a good old age.'"*

—Aesop, a fabulist or story-teller credited with a number of fables now collectively known as *Aesop's Fables* (620–560 BC), excerpt from *The Crow and the Sheep*

Yield the palm to

(1)   admit defeat to; give up; give way; grant; pay; reward; surrender; yield to another

Word Used in Sentence(s)

*(1) The game of chess, like business and military matters, teaches that there can be times of glories and times when one must **yield the palm** to desperate defeat.*

Additional Sources

American Heritage Publishing Staff, *400 Words You Should Know*, NY: Houghton Mifflin Harcourt Publishing Co., 2010.

Babe, Gregory. "On Creating a Lean Growth Machine: How I Did It," *Harvard Business Review*, July–August 2011.

Bennsinger, Greg. "Poison Pill at Netflix," *Wall Street Journal*, November 6, 2012.

Bertrand, Marc. "The Adult Learner, the K-12 Connection," *Career Convergence Magazine*, December 12, 2012. http://associationdatabase.com/aws/NCDA/pt/sp/career_convergence, accessed December 29, 2012.

Beyer, Thomas, Jr., Ph.D. *501 English Verbs*, Second Edition, NY: Baron's Educational Series, 2007.

Bhide, Amar. "Bootstrap Finance," *The Art of Start Ups*. Boston, MA: HBR Entrepreneurial Press, 1988.

Bly, Robert. *The Words You Should Know to Sound Smart*, Avon, MA: Adams Media, 2009.

Buzzeta, Mary and Makela, J.P. "A Case Study Approach to Ethics in Career Development: Exploring Shades of Gray," *Career Coverage Magazine*, NCDA, 2009, http://associationdatabase.com/aws/NCDA/pt/sd/news_article/29424/_PARENT/layout_details_cc/false, accessed December 29, 2012.

Cook, Marshall J. and Laura Poole. *Effective Coaching*, 2nd Edition, NY: McGraw-Hill, 2011.

Crystal, David. *The Cambridge Encyclopedia of the English Language*, Cambridge: Cambridge University Press, 1995.

Daley, Jason. "New Market Opportunities," *Entrepreneur*, March 2012.

Daly, Suzanne. "A Post-Apartheid Agony: AIDS on the March," *New York Times*, July 23, 1998.

Darmody, Stephen. "The Oil Pollution Act's Criminal Penalties: On a Collision Course with the Law of the Sea," *Boston College Environmental Affairs Law Review*, Volume 21, Issue 1, Fall 1993.

"Dictionary by Hampton," application on iPhone, 2013.

Editors. "Perceptions of Goal-Directed Activities of Optimists and Pessimists: A Personal Projects Analysis," *Journal of Psychology*, Volume 136, Issue 5, September 2002.

Editors. "Power of Russian Parliament's Leader Is Becoming Vexing Issue for Yeltsin, " *New York Times*, November 25, 1992.

Editors. *Roget's II The New Thesaurus,* Boston: Houghton Mifflin, 2003.

Editors. *The America Heritage Dictionary*, Boston: Houghton Mifflin Co., 1980.

Exforsys, Inc. "About Different Coaching and Mentoring Styles," http://www.exforsys.com/career-center/coaching-mentoring/coaching-and-mentoring-styles.html, December 2010, accessed April 20, 2013.

Fenell, Barbara, A. *A History of the English*, Oxford, England: Blackwell Publishers, 2001.

Fink, Bill. "Opening Doors to the Essence of Santa Fe," *Houston Chronicle*, May 15, 2005: pg. 1.

Gallison, Dave, "Recovering Self-Identity Amidst Long-Term Unemployment," National Career Development Association, http://associationdatabase.com/aws/NCDA/pt/sp/career_convergence, accessed December 29, 2012.

Hill, Charles. "Gun Showdown at Work," *Wall Street Journal*, December 1, 2012.

Knowles, Jonathan and Richard Etterson, "Reconcilable Differences," Reprint F0706D, *Harvard Business Review*, June 2007.

Kohan, John. "Hastening the End of the Empire," *Time,* January 28, 1991.

Letters to the editor. Open Forum, *Denver Post*, August 23, 2008.

"List of Action Verbs," www.rfp-templates.com/List-of-Action-Verbs.html, accessed August 2–12, 2008.

Lublin, Joann. "To Climb the Ladder, Try Joining a Group," *Wall Street Journal*, December 26, 2012.

Lucas, Stephen. *The Art of Public Speaking*, 9th Edition, Boston: McGraw-Hill, 1983.

Macroow, Athena. "Vongalis Blog," *Harvard Business Review*, September 2011.

Marano, Hara Estroff. "Inside the Heart of Marital Violence," *Psychology Today*, Volume 26, November 1, 1993.

Marquand, David. "IX: Big Ends or Little Ends," *History Today*, Volume 41, Issue 9, September 1991: pg. 38–41.

McCleary, Carol. *The Alchemy of Murder,* First Edition, New York: Forge, 2010.

Mikotaj, Jan Pisorski. "Social Strategies That Work," *Harvard Business Review*, November, 2011.

Montefiore, Simon Sebag. *Speeches That Changed the World*, London: Quercus Publishing, 2005.

National Career Development Association. *Process of Career Development, Policy, and Procedures Manual*, Broken Arrow, OK, August 2012.

Nigro, Nicholas. "Mentor and Mentoring: Words and Reality," http://www.net-places.com/coaching-mentoring/the-role-of-a-lifetime-a-script-for-mentoring/mentor-and-mentoring-words-and-reality.htm, accessed January 12, 2013.

Noonan, Peggy. "To-Do List: A Sentence, Not 10 Paragraphs," *Wall Street Journal*, June 26, 2009.

Orden, Erica. "How to Train Your Branding," *Wall Street Journal*, December 10, 2012.

Orwell, George. "Politics and the English Language," http://georgeorwell novels.com/essays/notes-for-politics-and-the-english-language/, accessed October 20–24, 2012.

Ready, Douglas and Jay Conger. "Make Your Company and Talent Factory," *Harvard Business Review*, June 2007.

Revell, Janice. "Bye-bye Pension," *Fortune*, Volume 147, Issue 5, March 2003.

Rich, Jason. *Your Career: Coach Yourself to Success*, NY: Learning Express, 2001.

Sabeti, Heerad. "The For-Benefit Enterprise," *Harvard Business Review*, November 2011.

Sawhill, Isabel V. "The Behavioral Aspects of Poverty," *Public Interest*, Issue 153, Fall 2003.

Sisson, A.R. *Sisson's Word and Expression Locator*, West Nyak, NY: Parker Publishing Co., 1979.

Sweeny, Berry. "Mentoring Glossary," International Mentoring Association, http://mentoring-association.org/resources/mentoring-glossary/#Mentor, accessed December 27, 2012.

Thurm, Scott. "Putting the Storm Behind Them," *Wall Street Journal*, November 19, 2012.

White Paper from the Association for Experimental Education, Adventure Therapy, and Adjudicated Youth, 2011, http://www.aee.org/files/en/user/cms/whitepaper-Adventure-Therapy-AEE-2011-v2.1.pdf, accessed January 3, 2013.

Wilfred, Funk, Dr. and Norman Lewis. *30 Days to a More Powerful Vocabulary*, NY: Simon & Shuster, N1942.

WriteExpress Staff Writers, "Action Verbs for Resumes," www.writeexpress.com/action-verbs.html, accessed August 2–12, 2008.

Index

E

F

G